Reprint Publishing

For People Who Go For Originals.

www.reprintpublishing.com

LIFE OF
DANTE ALIGHIERI

THE BARGELLO PORTRAIT OF DANTE
Drawn by Mr. Seymour Kirkup before it was retouched by Marini

LIFE OF
DANTE ALIGHIERI

BY
CHARLES ALLEN DINSMORE

With Illustrations

BOSTON AND NEW YORK
HOUGHTON MIFFLIN COMPANY
MDCCCCXIX

COPYRIGHT, 1919, BY CHARLES A. DINSMORE

ALL RIGHTS RESERVED

TO MY DAUGHTER
RACHEL
"LEI LO VEDERE, E ME L'OPRARE APPAGA"

PREFACE

BEFORE the Great War the growing interest in Dante was notable. James Bryce, in his Lowell Institute lectures, referred to it as "the literary phenomenon of England and America." Groups of eager students of the great Florentine were appearing in the most unexpected places. To meet the demands of this increasing number of Dante lovers the publishers of the present volume suggested to me, some ten years ago, the writing of a popular biography of the poet. I was reluctant to undertake the task, for very meagre information of the events of Dante's life has drifted down the intervening centuries. Fitly to commemorate the six hundredth anniversary of the poet's birth the libraries of Italy were ransacked for all possible data. Little of the first importance has been discovered since, and probably the future will yield few significant facts. "Great geniuses," says Emerson, "have shortest biographies . . . the Genius draws up the ladder after him, when the creative age goes up to heaven, and gives way to a new age, which sees the works and asks in vain for the history." And then who could make the little knowledge we possess "popular"! One is reminded of another publisher's alleged request for a "Life of Christ, short and snappy."

Two considerations, however, had sufficient weight to overcome my reluctance. First, no exhaustive "Life" of Dante has been written on this side of the Atlantic. There have been most excellent translations of his minor works and of the "Comedy," brilliant volumes interpreting the age in which he lived, his power, the meanings of his lyrics and his epic; but no American has attempted a comprehensive biography. Secondly, Dante's true life is not to be learned from any facts which the documents record; it is to be found in his own self-revealing books. The personality there made manifest presents a most interesting psychological problem: What forces changed the gentle dreamer of the "Vita Nuova" into the stern prophet of the "Divina Commedia"? What influences nourished in him an extraordinary delicacy of feeling while his character was developing such rugged strength? By what miracle did he transmute the bitterness of defeat into spiritual victory?

Here is a problem of vast import to every pilgrim and militant soul. Outwardly Dante walked in a way that was all humiliation, disillusionment, disaster; inwardly he trod a path to power, vision, and final peace. In him is disclosed, to a degree unequaled except by a few rare spirits, the secret, which we all yearn to know, of meeting the evils of life victoriously.

In the first section of this study, I have endeavored to outline the general character of the age in which Dante lived, and the city which he loved: in the second, I have stated the facts of his life which are definitely known, together with some traditions; I have also indicated the development of his genius and character at the different stages of his career: in the concluding section I have sought to lift the veil from those processes of thought and will by which he won a victory over himself and his misfortunes, and became Dante, fiercest of haters, gentlest of lovers, as majestic among the warriors of the spirit as he is commanding among the poets.

Fortunately I have been able to submit the proof-sheets of this biography to Professor Oscar Kuhns of Wesleyan and to Professor Charles H. Grandgent of Harvard and to benefit by their suggestions. I could have found no more competent critics. Both have greatly increased the number of Dante lovers by their teaching, and both have enriched by their writings the literature dealing with the poet. The authorities used are sufficiently indicated by the footnotes; the translations, unless otherwise stated, are Professor Norton's.

CHARLES ALLEN DINSMORE

CONTENTS

PART I

The Century and the City

CHAPTER I. THE THIRTEENTH CENTURY

I. Its achievements and ideals — One of the greatest of the centuries — Its unity — Its ideal of holiness — The sacramental conception of the world — Individual of small importance — Preoccupied with death — A brighter side — An awakening world — Sense of beauty — Passion for knowledge — Chivalry — Romantic love   3

II. Conflict between Church and State — Charlemagne's conception of the Empire — Hildebrand's of the Church — Inevitable conflict — Political results of the union between Germany and Italy   11

III. Rise of the Free Cities — Unique importance of cities in Italy and Germany — Value of the city in stimulating genius — Favored by the struggle between Emperors and Popes — Conditions against their natural development   16

IV. Guelfs and Ghibellines — Origin and meaning of the parties   22

V. End of the power of the Ghibellines and of the German Emperor — Introduction of French influence into Italy   24

CHAPTER II. FLORENCE: A STUDY IN DEMOCRACY

Introduction — Establishment of the city — Its early character — Business enterprise and fatal policy — Conflict between nobles and burghers   27

CONTENTS

I. Divided into Guelfs and Ghibellines — 31

II. *Primo Popolo* — Ghibellines humbled — Their return — 32

III. The Guelf party — 37

IV. The Guilds — Their character — Control the city government — 38

V. Ordinances of Justice — Framed against the nobles — 41

VI. Causes of Florentine instability — Dante's statement — Machiavelli's — A conflict between Roman and Teutonic blood — The feudal and commercial ideals — The Commune a federation of political and industrial units. — Florentines deficient in reverence for law and in self-control — Civic immaturity — Influence of a city's walls — Stupendous vitality — The fifth element — 43

VII. Famous cities — Babylon contrasted with Jerusalem — Rome and Athens — Venice and Florence — The stable *vs.* the brilliant cities — 55

PART II

Dante's Life and Works

CHAPTER I. DANTE'S YOUTH: PERIOD OF THE *Vita Nuova*: 1265–1290

I. Ancestry and boyhood — 61

II. Youthful studies — 70

III. Sweet new style — 73

IV. Growth of Dante's passion — 76

V. Date of the *Vita Nuova* — 88

VI. Truth of this self-revelation — 90

VII. Slow development of his genius — 93

CONTENTS

VIII. Character and ability	96
IX. As he appeared to the Florentines	98
Note on the Identity of Beatrice	101

CHAPTER II. PERIOD OF DISCIPLINE: 1290–1313
a. Following False Images of Good: 1290–1300

I. Similarity between the careers of Dante and Milton	110
II. Intellectual awakening	113
III. False images of good	118
IV. Marriage	121
V. Ordinances of justice	123
VI. Political interests and debts	126
VII. The year 1300	129

b. The Path in the Savage Wood: 1300–1313

VIII. Political activities	136
IX. Decree of exile	139
X. Wanderings	141
XI. Literary a. *Il Convivio* — b. *De Vulgari Eloquentia* — c. *De Monarchia*	148
XII. Mind and character — Zest for knowledge — Attitude toward exile — His dominant mood — Originality — Sense of mission — Wrath	163

CHAPTER III. THE CRUCIAL YEAR: 1313

Two previous periods reviewed — Disillusioned — Watching for the good of the world — Interpretation of the first canto of the *Inferno* — The known facts — Definitely outlined the Divine Comedy — Finding of former manuscript — Consolations of study — Fonte

Avellana — Sought the confusion of courts to do his writing — Reasons therefor — Power of concentration — Changed apparatus — Different attitude toward work and discipline — Dante's equipment for his task 171

CHAPTER IV. YEARS OF THE DIVINE COMEDY: 1314-1321

I. Letter to the Italian Cardinals 189
II. Letter to a Florentine friend 192
III. Verona 195
IV. Ravenna — Del Virgilio — *Paradiso* — Letter to Can Grande — *Credo* — *Questio de Aqua et Terra* 202
V. Death and burial 218
VI. The lost cantos 220
VII. Dante's sepulchre 222

PART III

Qualities of Genius and Character

CHAPTER I. MEANING OF THE DIVINE COMEDY

Introduction — Its complexity — Peril of self-conscious effort 229

I. A unique political document — Art in the service of reform — Extraordinary political pamphlet — Use of the supernatural to influence politics — Dante's failure 230

II. Its religious significance — A guide to the way of life — The *Inferno* a vision of sin — The *Purgatorio* shows the way to liberty — The *Paradiso* the supreme achievement of his genius — The Beatific Vision 233

III. Its permanent element — Unearthly beauty — The emotional elevation it produces — It fertilizes the mind — Quickens the sense of an inexorable

CONTENTS

justice — The Divine in the Comedy — Its moral insights — The soul's inferno — The way to liberty — The supreme felicity   237

CHAPTER II. INFLUENCE OF THE COMEDY UPON DANTE

I. Influx of power — Nothing in the earlier works to prepare us for extraordinary display of power — Comes from maturity of mind — Self-surrender — Greater theme — The Catholic system — The times evil — Improved style   244

II. Self-valuation — Sense of mission — An elect man   247

III. Moral effects — Passion for fame absorbed in a greater passion for truth — His increasing sense of God   250

CHAPTER III. THE SECRET OF DANTE

Introduction — Tennyson and Fitzgerald — The divine intensity   253

I. Intellectual mysticism — Fascinated by "the splendor of the true" — Could not be a misanthrope   254

II. Imagination — Vaguest of impressionists — A perilous gift — Influence on literary style   257

III. Extreme sensitiveness — Every truth a passion — Emerson on impressionability — Consistency of mind — Made for suffering — His reserve   259

IV. The supreme need of his nature to love — Ruled by his admirations — Love the centre of his life and philosophy — Scorn incidental — A lover of truth rather than of persons — Hatred of evil — Personal resentment — His philosophy of anger — A studied wrath   260

V. Love of order — His whole nature outraged by the discords of Italy   264

CONTENTS

VI. Energy of his will — He met evil patiently — But triumphantly — The charm of Francis and the energy of Hildebrand — Uncommon egoism   265

VII. His faith: 'a. His conception of God; b. His conception of man; c. His conception of immortality — His reasons for believing   267

VIII. Summary.   273

CHAPTER IV. DEFECTS OF CHARACTER

Ungracious — Women held to be inferior — Liaisons — Self-pity — Intolerant of heresy — A reactionary in politics — Vindictive — Treatment of Guido Cavalcanti — Aristotle's dictum — Fierce hater — His hell filled with virtuous characters — A defense — Magnificent even in his faults   275

CHAPTER V. THE ARTIST

I. Wrote with ease — Love of technique   282, 283

II. Sources of style — Chivalry and Latin   284

III. Predilections — Grace and light   284

IV. Mysticism of beauty — The mysticism of Shelley maturing into that of Plato   287

V. Minute observation and epic imagination   289

VI. Art for art's sake   293

CHAPTER VI. CONCLUSION

Dante's unique greatness and individuality — Paradoxes in character and career — Not conspicuous as a thinker — The satisfactions of his life — Its completeness — Turned tragedy into comedy   294

INDEX   299

ILLUSTRATIONS

THE BARGELLO PORTRAIT OF DANTE *Frontispiece*
Drawn by Mr. Seymour Kirkup before it was retouched by Marini

FARINATA DEGLI UBERTI 36
From the painting by Andrea del Castagno in the Royal National Museum of Florence

MAP OF FLORENCE AT THE END OF THE THIRTEENTH CENTURY 66
From Karl Witte's *Dante-Forschungen* (Heilbronn, 1879)

THE TOMB OF FOLCO PORTINARI 104
From a copyright photograph reproduced in Isidoro del Lungo's *Women of Florence* (New York: Doubleday, Page & Co.)

BONIFACE VIII, BY ARNOLFO DI CAMBIO 132

THE TOMB OF CINO DE' SINIBALDI AT PISTOIA 156
Sculpture by Cellino di Nese

THE TOMB OF DANTE: INTERIOR 222

GUIDO CAVALCANTI 278
From a painting in the collection of Archduke Ferdinand of Tyrol, reproduced in *Jahrbuch der Kunsthistorischen Sammlungen des Allerhöchsten Kaiserhauses*, vol. 18.

DANTE ALIGHIERI

PART I
The Century and the City

DANTE ALIGHIERI

CHAPTER I
THE THIRTEENTH CENTURY

To understand Dante one must have a clear apprehension of the character and temper of the age in which he lived. Genius is frequently born out of due time, and is in revolt against the controlling ideals of the day. Not so with the great Florentine. No poet or thinker ever was more completely moulded by the spiritual forces of his epoch. God matched him with his hour. His nature was "subdued to what it worked in, like the dyer's hand." Homer and Shakespeare did not so perfectly mirror the aspirations, the sorrows, the philosophy of their times. Only by being so thoroughly a medieval man could he be the interpreter of those ten tumultuous centuries. Doubtless he thought that his lot was cast in evil days: on the contrary, his life spanned momentous and crucial years when the energies of one civilization were culminating and those of another were first revealing themselves. To him was given the rare privilege of writing a recessional of one of the noblest periods in human history and of heralding another.

I. ITS ACHIEVEMENTS AND IDEALS

The thirteenth is one of the most notable of all the centuries. The Creative Energy works in history with intermittent power. There are centuries when the tide of life mounts high; there are others when the ebb is noticeable and disheartening. What a flood of spiritual vitality flowed round the world in the sixth century before Christ — Buddha preaching in India, Confucius moulding the forms in which the thought of China would flow for many centuries, Æschylus impressing upon the Athenians the inexorable justice of that Supreme Being whose comforting love the great unknown Prophet was proclaiming to the exiled Jews in Babylon! There was another tidal wave of vitality in the Golden Age of Augustus; another during the Revival of Learning and the Reformation. But among the great centuries the thirteenth is not the least conspicuous. It was big with creative forces of the highest quality in art, poetry, statesmanship, and philosophy. The materials with which men worked were, according to our modern ideas, meagre enough, but the genius of the workers was of the first rank. Recall the illustrious names: Francis of Assisi, sweetest of all the saints; Giotto, painter and architect; Roger Bacon, who preserved a scientific temper in an intolerant and superstitious age; Thomas of Aquino, whose mind, profound, exact, capacious, is not excelled in philosophy. Among the world's rulers Frederick II, Edward I, and Saint Louis are not undistinguished.

It was a century of remarkable achievements. It witnessed the zenith of the Papacy under Innocent III and the establishment of popular government in the Italian cities. Its spiritual emotion expressed itself in the rise of the mendicant orders, the building of some of Europe's most famous cathedrals, and the launching of at least four powerful crusades. Its intellectual energy is seen both in the great literature it produced and in the astonishing expansion of the universities. Learned tradition declares that there were thirty thousand students at Oxford in 1300, while twenty thousand are credited to Paris and fifteen thousand to Bologna. Probably these numbers are greatly exaggerated, but eager youths came to these educational centres in multitudes. The century is also memorable for the balance of its interests. Some epochs are famous for their artistic energy, others for the prevailing scientific spirit, others for important political and social movements inaugurated, but in the thirteenth the tide was high on every shore of human endeavor.

During this period there was a mental unity which Europe had not known before and has failed to attain since. There was one universally recognized Church, one accepted philosophy, one language familiar to all learned men; in short, a European mind, an international consciousness.

It was a time also of amazing spiritual ambitions — ambitions quite foreign to our age. There is truth in Browning's contention that, in the final analysis, a man's ideals are the measure of his worth:

> "All I could never be,
> All man ignored in me,
> That I was worth to God."

This applies also to nations and epochs of history. The loftiest and most generally recognized ideal of the twentieth century is the brotherhood of man. We emphasize the second commandment to the neglect of the first. It seems to us more comprehensible and practical, even if more difficult to obey. But a different ideal dominated the thirteenth century. Elect minds, believing that they could know God, thirsted for a supernatural union with him, in which they should realize ineffable satisfactions and receive in their characters the imprint of the divine nature. To-day we try to be kindly, just, decent: they were eager to enjoy a superhuman holiness, a constant communion with the Highest, the raptures of the redeemed. They fell as far short of attaining their ideals as we do of attaining ours; but the difference between the controlling aspiration of that day and of our own is worthy of notice.

The mental attitude of our own age is so antipodal in almost every respect to the science and philosophy of Dante's world, that we can understand the forces which influenced him only by divesting ourselves of our habitual mode of thought. Every trained and competent mind to-day works under the transforming influence of some theory of evolution. We habitually view nature and her activities and man and his experiences as in process of becoming. Our era has transformed the science of language, literature, philosophy, and of the human mind into their history. We follow the unfoldings of thought and institutions, rather than seek to trace the structure and laws of what we believe to be immobile and finished. What the evolutionary conception is to our century the sacramental was to the thirteenth. To that generation the things which are seen are but a thin veil hiding the unseen Reality. To them material things are not objects of exact knowledge and God a vague phantom of faith. Quite the contrary, God is the object of real and immediate apprehension and nature is his tenuous garment. Tennyson was uttering a conviction of the nineteenth century when he wrote —

> "We have but faith; we cannot know;
> For knowledge is of things we see."

The medieval man would have scorned such an inversion of truth. He believed himself to have by spiritual intuition direct commerce with the Unseen; that substantial word "knowledge" he would not have surrendered to the scientist. It is God who can be known with certainty, but nature is cloudy stuff. Therefore he would have thought himself trifling with truth and wasting time to be much absorbed in studying habits of insects and the ways of birds! Nature was too inconsequential to engage his interest for long. Only man and his destiny were deemed worthy of serious contemplation, and theology the one science worth while.

As the seen was regarded as the door into the Unseen, symbolism would naturally prevail both in literature and art, and allegory would be the favorite device of writers. This sacramental world, static and complete, could be known and accurately analyzed. Moreover, it was very small as man then conceived it, and he moved about with a confidence which is strange to us. Heaven was just above the stars, and hell underneath the earth. Revelation of the way of life was clear, truth was definite, man had sinned, an atonement had been made, the judge was at the door. Why be tolerant! Rather be vigorous and teach positively to love righteousness and hate iniquity. To clear the world of false guides was to do God's service. To exterminate the enemies of the Most High was a duty. The temper still lingered which had led so fine a spirit as Saint Bernard to declare of the crusaders: "They are the ministers of God to inflict his vengeance. For them to give and receive death is not a sin, but a glorious deed. The Son of God delights to receive the blood of his enemies; he is glorified in the death of pagans."

It was an age when authority was more regarded than individual freedom. God did not make known his will through the fickle and ill-mannered multitude, but through properly constituted channels. Submission and obedience were cardinal virtues. Men being in profound ignorance of nature neglected it; being as profoundly ignorant of their own past, they held it in highest veneration. Especially did they reverence classical antiquity. Through the mists of the years they saw giants walking, and listened to the ancient oracles with unskeptical ears. Men's minds were critical of the processes of reasoning, but not of the premises on which they built the superstructures. Hence their elaborate systems have fallen because of inadequate foundations.

The individual was of small importance and was merged in the mass. The emphasis was on the strength and glory of institutions and not on personal rights. Who knows the names of cathedral-builders? Yet the architects and toilers were not greatly concerned, for the Virgin and the saints knew. They were very near while their temples were builded, and the sense of supernatural benediction was better than earthly fame. Death and the life hereafter occupied a far more commanding place in the thought of the medieval man than they do to-day. The typical twentieth-century man arranges his affairs to meet the inevitable end and prepares his soul for the great change, then he dismisses the thought of death from his mind as far as possible. Immortality may be a blessed hope, but it is not a preoccupation, for he realizes how vague is his knowledge and how inadequate his conception of a future state. He believes in bringing in as much of the Kingdom of God upon the earth as is possible, and that if he fights well his earthly battle he can leave the final issue with God.

This was not so with the representative man of the thirteenth century. Death threw its shadows over all his life; his chief thought was to prepare himself to pass triumphantly through the dark gates. The offices of the Church were designed to carry him safely through the supreme experience and to unite the prayers of the living and the redeemed in helping him out of the fires of purgatorial pains into the realm of blessedness. Man's true home was the mansion above the stars; why spend much thought on the condition of the hostelries in which he rested but a night, or in improving the road that led thither? The salvation of the soul, in the sense of getting it into heaven, assessed the value of all knowledge and of every effort.

But there was a brighter side. The fact is the prophets of that day were wrong in their pronouncements upon the times. The final judgment was not impending. Only the old order was vanishing, giving place to the new. Instead of late autumn with the winter of doom fast approaching, it was early spring. The world was awakening from a long sleep, there was tonic in the air, and everywhere the gathering of forces for a glorious outburst of joy and power. A multitude of aroused and ardent minds were turning away from the dead conventions of the past and looking at life and nature with their own eyes. Moreover, they were having an ever-increasing courage to report what they saw and felt. There was a mighty passion for beauty, first in dress, then in public architecture, next in song and in painting. The troubadours sang their conventional lyrics of love in Provence, in northern Italy, in Sicily, then came the *dolce stil nuovo* in Tuscany. Artists found in Cimabue "a morning star" and in Giotto "a rising sun."

Equally powerful and more widely spread was the passion for learning. Men in the last half of the century had the glowing confidence of youth in their ability to penetrate all mystery and sweep the circle of all knowledge. The mind had not yet learned its limitations, and was unwavering in its assurance that, either by its own rational processes or by revelation, it could know, analyze, and classify everything in heaven and on earth. In this faith the schoolmen patiently elaborated their complex and vast systems of thought. Chivalry as an institution lost its fascination in the failure of the crusades, but its cardinal virtues of honor, loyalty, and courage still threw their spell over the minds of ingenuous youth. Romantic love had deserted the ranks of knights and troubadours to become the studied art and the holy ideal of the poets, and at length found its highest expression in the exaltation of the Virgin.

Into such an atmosphere and into such a system of thought the impressionable soul of Dante was born.

If the medieval scheme of things shaped Dante's thought and influenced his temper, the political activities of his century determined the courses of his fortune, stung his spirit into intensest vigor, and gave rugged strength to his character.

II. CONFLICT BETWEEN CHURCH AND STATE

As the relationship of the Church to the Holy Roman Empire was a subject of capital importance to Dante, and as the conflict between them exerted a powerful influence upon his career, we shall review the main points of the ancient debate. When in the fourth century Constantine the Great made Christianity the religion of the Roman Empire, he considered himself to be the head of the Church as truly as the sovereign of the State. Likewise in the year 800 A.D. on Christmas Day, when Charles the Great, King of the Franks, was crowned Roman Emperor, he believed himself to be the successor of Constantine, and as such supreme ruler of both Church and State.

In theory, he was but continuing the succession of the Cæsars, and reclothing Rome with its former glory. In fact, he was asserting a political ideal which was to drain Germany of its strength, intrude foreign dominion into distracted Italy, and flit like a ghost, both for inspiration and for alarm, over the battle-fields and through the cabinets of Europe for a thousand years, until exposed and discredited, it was formally abandoned by Francis II in 1806. With so powerful a monarch as Charles claiming temporal lordship of the world, the Roman Empire was a practical force, but after him there rose no sovereign of equal ability, and the Holy Roman Empire became in reality only the political union of Germany and Italy with sovereignty in the hands of the German Emperor. The imperial throne of Germany, being elective, was open in point of law from the tenth to the nineteenth century to any orthodox Christian. In fact, however, competition was confined to the few noble houses capable of contending for a prize so dazzling. The crown remained in the Saxon House of Otto until 1024, then it passed into the Franconian line until 1125, it was held by the Hohenstaufens for a century or more, was possessed by the house of Luxemburg for three reigns, and in the fifteenth century passed to the House of Hapsburg. The interpretation of their divine authority put forth by the emperors is comprehensible and impressive. Even as Israel was the chosen people of God to give religion to the world, so the Romans were his foreordained instruments to dispense the knowledge of the law and to maintain justice. The German Emperors, being the consecrated successors of the Roman Emperors, ruled in the name of God; and their empire was the visible Kingdom of God on earth. In spiritual affairs the Pope

THE THIRTEENTH CENTURY 13

was supreme, but in all temporal concerns he was a subject of the Empire.

So long as the imperial sceptre was held by men of commanding ability and the papal throne was occupied by priests of unworldly ambitions, or of only ordinary efficiency, this theory of government would pass without serious challenge. But in the later part of the eleventh century the conditions were reversed. In 1073 there came to the papal throne one who in many respects was the ablest man who ever sat upon it. The grim and militant figure of Hildebrand arrests the attention of every student of the Middle Ages. He was one of those rarely gifted men whose coming always marks an epoch in human affairs: single of purpose, and chaste in thought, more subtle and sagacious than any trained counselor of kings, having a will as imperious as the will of an Eastern despot, loving righteousness and hating iniquity with intense passion, withal a transcendent idealist smitten with so lofty a vision of the Kingdom of God that to achieve it, he subordinated every personal interest and pursued it with a zeal unflagging and inexhaustible.

To his reality-loving mind the Kingdom of God, whose glory prophets had foreseen, for which saints had prayed, and the Redeemer had died, was not represented by an empire divided by factions, powerless to maintain order, shifty in its policies, corrupt in its practices, the easy prize of ambitious warriors. The unity of the Kingdom, he was persuaded, was represented in but one institution, the Church, a divine creation, eternal in its nature, ecumenical in its scope, established by the word of Christ, attested by innumerable miracles, declarative of God's purposes and judgments, and commanding the total subordination of all temporal concerns to spiritual authority. The Pope as its head was the supreme sovereign of the world. To vindicate these divine rights and to establish these awful prerogatives, he gave himself with passionate and unremitting energy.

There could not be two temporal lords of the world, and a prolonged war between the Church and the Empire for supremacy was inevitable. The immediate occasion of controversy was over the right of investiture. Every bishop of the Empire, because he held lands from the crown, was more than a clergyman, he was a civil officer with prescribed duties to the throne. He was a feudal subject of the Emperor and owed to the sovereign homage for the lands he held. To the Emperor he must take the oath of allegiance and from the Emperor he received the insignia of his office. Hildebrand as head of the Church asserted that all its officials must be subject to him alone, and forbade any bishop to receive investiture from the hands of any layman, whether king, noble, or common man. Evidently a contest was impending that would fill every court of Europe with intrigue, and send the sword of war and the gloom of superstitious terror into every hamlet of Germany and Italy. The strife was waged with varying success. It brought Henry IV, fasting and barefooted, to stand for three days in the snows of Canossa, and drove Hildebrand himself into exile. The papal power culminated in Innocent III, who could plausibly affirm that the Church is to the State what the sun is to the moon. Under Frederick Barbarossa, and his still more brilliant grandson Frederick II, the power of the Empire once more became formidable. But by the defeat of the Hohenstaufen at Benevento in 1266, a year after Dante's birth, the power of the Teuton over the Italian was finally broken, and the victory of the Church was so complete that in 1300, the year Dante chose as the date of his wonderful journey, Boniface VIII, arrayed in the crown, sceptre, and sword of temporal dominion, could announce himself, to the pilgrims who flocked to Rome, to be "Cæsar and Emperor," successor to Augustus as well as to Saint Peter.

This partnership of Germany and Italy, growing out of the fascinating and illusory dreams of the Holy Roman Empire, an empire which merited Voltaire's jibe that it was neither holy, nor Roman, nor empire, affected the world for good or ill in many ways. It drained Germany of her strength in endless struggles abroad, and profoundly influenced the political structure of the nation. In the absence of the Emperors, the ecclesiastics and the nobility seized both land and power, limiting the authority of the throne. While in France and England absolute sovereignty was being gathered into the hands of the King and centralized states were forming, in Germany the feudal lords grew strong at the expense of the nation, local jealousies and ambitions divided the German people, and the forces which in other lands worked for political unity, here were hindered. Italy suffered in like manner. The presence of a foreign invader, whose rights were so plausible and yet questionable, could not be other than divisive and preventive of national integration. Therefore while one after another of the great European people have come to national self-consciousness and formed their institutions according to their genius, Germany and Italy have been the last to achieve political unity. Italy won nationality in that sublime struggle of which Mazzini was the prophet, Garibaldi the most brilliant soldier, and Cavour the far-seeing statesman; and Germany, by the genius of Bismarck, subordinated petty states to an imperial throne and introduced into the Europe of the nineteenth century a belated state structured according to the medieval pattern.

There were two results of this political union between Germany and Italy which claim our interest because of their direct influence on the character and career of Dante. One was the rise of the free cities, and the other the development of the Guelfs and Ghibellines.

III. RISE OF THE FREE CITIES

Until the beginning of the nineteenth century both Germany and Italy have been notably richer in cities of venerable traditions, and of commercial and literary importance, than either France or England. The history of Italy, expecially, has been the story of famous towns. One is amazed, as his mind sweeps over the peninsula, at the number of municipalities which have profoundly influenced the course of the world's thought and activities. England, indeed, had her London and France her Paris; but authority centred in a strong monarch was not conducive to the development of numerous centres of self-assertive and vigorous life. The very lack of national unity in Germany, and the racial and political diversity of Italy, tended to nurture independence, and afforded rare opportunities for the growth of powerful municipalities.

Goethe has observed that "Talent forms itself in solitude: character in the great currents of the world." But assuredly it is in the solitude of the city attic that the flame of genius burns most brightly, and not in the loneliness of the cave. Man's nature is alive only where it has been struck forcibly by something from without. He exists only when he is consciously allied to something external to himself. The city, with its diversified interests, its constant and exacting demands, its immense stimulation, calls forth all the reserves of talent, the energies of the will and the passions of the heart, as the country cannot. A Burns may sing at his plough, and Wordsworth "murmur by the running brooks a music sweeter than their own," but the vast majority of names which history will not let die are associated with the large centres of population. A land rich in cities will also be rich in distinguished men, and renowned for enterprise.

And yet, although cities are the inspiration of culture in its varied forms, no conspicuous city has been organized specifically in the interests of the spirit; they have been founded to meet the exigencies of war and commerce. Even Jerusalem was builded upon Mount Zion for reasons of defense. Italy has been no exception to the general rule. War and commerce were the stern parents of her cities. Being a peninsula extending into the chief sea of the ancient and medieval world, blessed with deep harbors and navigable rivers, lying in the paths of the crusades, and the trade between the East and the West, swept by an incessant storm of war, the history of Italy is of necessity a history of militant and jealous cities.

The incursion of the barbarians into Italy left the ancient cities dismantled and defenseless. Desolate as the country seemed, an auspicious change was taking place. The features, the habits, the constitution of the inhabitants were being altered. A fresh, vigorous race was forming. The Roman stock, worn out by luxury, gave place to a new folk, of mixed blood, inured to privation, and made sturdy by hardship. In the ninth century the people began to rebuild the walls of their cities, and to purchase or manufacture arms. In this they were not prevented by the Emperors. Allured by the greater security of the walled towns, the inhabitants of the rural districts sought them as a place of refuge. Industries began to flourish. As the cities increased in population they grew strong. Security and numbers begat varied industries and with diversified industry came wealth, and with wealth came power and pride. The conditions of the time favored municipal independence. When the Emperors on their way to Rome encamped on the plains of Roncaglio to issue decrees and to secure homage and tribute, the cities sent their representatives — an elected magistrate, a prelate, or a noble — to meet him. Provided the payments of tribute were prompt the Emperors were quite

THE THIRTEENTH CENTURY 19

ready to acknowledge whatever local authority had asserted itself.

During the sixty years of the war of investitures the municipalities gained constant concessions, now from the Pope and now from the Emperor, in return for sympathy and supplies.

For nearly a hundred years the Italian cities had escaped the interference of the Emperors, and consequently had increased in strength and independence of spirit, when Frederick I, called Barbarossa on account of his red beard, encamped with his army on the famous Roncaglio fields and commanded the representatives of the cities to appear before him. Frederick Barbarossa was one of the most commanding figures of the Middle Ages. Stalwart and comely of person, fashioned both in body and in mind for large undertakings, fond of letters and art, he was the embodiment of the finest chivalry of his age. About such a figure tradition clings. Thoroughly imbued with the absolutism of the old Roman law and having a most exalted sense of his prerogative as head of the Holy Roman Empire and lord of the world, he was amazed when he learned that the rights of sovereignty were exercised by the Lombard cities. Between an emperor determined to maintain the dignity of his throne, and municipalities proud of their strength and equally determined to preserve their hard-won independence, a struggle was inevitable. For thirty years war was waged with varying success, until the battle of Legnano was fought in 1176, ending in an utter and humiliating defeat of the Emperor. Six years later a treaty was drawn up between Frederick and the cities, which was the first compact in Europe between a sovereign and his people which traced the line dividing authority from liberty. Self-government was subsequently conceded to the cities. They also might fortify themselves, levy armies, make war, and extend the bounds of their dominion. The rights of the Emperors as overlords were recognized and defined, an imperial judge was appointed in each town to whom important cases might be appealed. This was the first establishment of liberty upon a legal basis which the people of modern Europe won in their long struggle against monarchical tyranny. As the Germans could not well refuse to their allies the same liberties which had been granted to their enemies, freedom of the cities was recognized and established throughout Italy. In 1876, on the seventh centennial anniversary of the battle of Legnano, a great concourse assembled on the spot to celebrate what is generally regarded as the natal day of Italian liberty. Wordsworth in an imperishable sonnet has told us that Liberty has two voices, one of the mountains, and the other of the sea. But in Italy, the voice of Liberty is the hum of the city. The municipal republics, as the foregoing pages have recalled, grew up as buffer states between ambitious Emperors at the north and determined Pontiffs at the south.

Charlemagne's fascinating and dangerous dream of the Kingdom of God made visible in a universal Empire, and Hildebrand's ideal of a Kingdom embodied in a Church, ecumenical, supernatural, and eternal, having sovereignty in all earthly affairs, made a murderous and prolonged duel inevitable.

THE THIRTEENTH CENTURY 21

Political theorists, like Dante, might vainly dream of compromise of a divided sovereignty in which the Emperor would be supreme in temporal affairs, and the Pope lord of things spiritual. It was impossible, even for the most conciliatory minds, to draw a sure line between the temporal and the spiritual, especially when an overwhelming personality represented the one or the other. The two swords representing kingly and priestly power when thrown into the scales could never be made to balance. One was heavier, according to the strength of the hand which grasped it.

Yet out of this conflict, so much to be deplored, grew one undoubted good. The cities, by siding now with the Pope and now with the Emperor, won their freedom, and their abounding vitality gave stimulus and scope for that genius for architecture, painting, sculpture, and letters which is Italy's imperishable glory. But while these free cities of Italy teemed with valorous life, they were like children unrestrained. That reverence for law which was the religion of the classic world was unknown to them. Suspicious of one another they became the easy prey of despots. Left to themselves they might have passed through the successive stages of evolution and attained unity and stability, but the conditions for this natural development were against them. France and Germany stood by to foment strife, and in their midst was the Papacy, claiming the authority of heaven and frequently using the methods of hell to further her own selfish ends, setting city against city, and party against party. Here were all the elements of savage and fiendish strife to embitter a spirit like Dante's.

Another consequence of the strife between the Pontiff and the Emperor, which not only aroused the free cities against each other, but separated the inhabitants of those cities into hostile camps and shaped Dante's fortunes, may now be mentioned.

IV. GUELFS AND GHIBELLINES

The names "Guelfo" and "Ghibellino," which are so conspicuous in Italian history, are of German origin. The descendants of the Emperor Conrad were often called by the name "Waiblingen" from one of their castles in Augsburg. The rival house of Bavaria was often known by the name of many of its princes — "Welf"; "Hie Waiblingen!" and "Hie Welf!" were first used as rallying cries on the battle-field of Weinsberg in 1140, when Conrad fought victoriously against Count Welf. These names were Italianized into "Guelfo" and "Ghibellino" and were used to designate the adherents of the Pope and the followers of the Emperor respectively. It would be impossible as well as unprofitable to follow the separate threads of contention between the two parties through the tangled skeins of Italian politics. From 1167, when the Lombard cities were leagued against Frederick Barbarossa, until long after Dante's death, these names were conspicuous and potent. Viewed in the mass the Ghibellines were the party of imperial authority and international unity; the Guelfs contended for the rights of the Church and the independence of Italy from foreign dominion. The Ghibellines were the Cavaliers, and the Guelfs were the Round Heads of

THE THIRTEENTH CENTURY 23

medieval times. But this general distinction was often obscured by the rivalry of cities, by geographical position, by the fluctuation of politics, and by family feuds. For the most part the nobles adhered to the Emperor and the Ghibelline party, while the strength of the Guelfs was in the rising middle class which has always been the support and defense of the Church. With the growth of commerce and the development of cities, this class became numerous and influential in Italy. Its interests would be in the destruction of feudal privileges, and in increasing the liberty of the people who by instinct were religious, and from policy would champion the Church, which protected Italian independence and restrained the ambition of the Emperor. The Guelf leaders would naturally be found in the families which had risen to prominence through sagacity and industry, and had won eminence through trade rather than upon the field or in the court. The party would have also all the faults of the commercial and industrial class, and a love of money which led Dante to symbolize it by a wolf.

Yet the Ghibellines were cherishing the political ideal of a past era, and were relying upon a waning power. The future was clearly with the Guelfs, whose strength was in the rapidly augmenting power of the common people.

How the strife between the Guelfs and the Ghibellines entered Florence and its effect upon Dante's philosophy and his fortunes will be treated in a subsequent chapter. It is important now to fix our attention upon the event which broke the power of the

Ghibellines in Italy, secured the supremacy of the Guelfs, ended the long battle between the Church and the State in the triumph of the Church, drove out Germany forever from the Italian peninsula, introduced instead the power of France — a power which ceased only with the withdrawal of French troops from Rome, in 1870 — which led to the humiliating captivity of the Popes in Avignon, and ultimately to that degradation and secularization of the Papacy which made the German Reformation possible.

V. BENEVENTO

Frederick II had died in 1250. The wonder of his own generation and the enigma of succeeding ages, he was the last reputed successor of the Cæsars who had "ruled from the sands of the ocean to the shores of the Sicilian Sea." The rights of the Hohenstaufens now passed to Conradin, a child of three years; Manfred, the natural son of Frederick, being made Regent.

The Pope could not endure that a Ghibelline and a heretic should hold the sceptre of Sicily and offered the crown to Charles of Anjou, brother of Louis of France, and the most powerful prince (not reigning sovereign) in Christendom. He was "wise, prudent in counsel, valiant in arms, and harsh, much feared and redoubted of all the kings of the earth." It was in the year, and probably the month, of Dante's birth, that Charles landed in Italy, proceeded to Rome, and in the following January was crowned King of Naples, Sicily and Apulia, and although it was in the depth of winter, set out to win his kingdom. At Benevento on February 26,

1266, he encountered Manfred and his army. After a desperate engagement, Manfred was defeated. With his fall the power of the Hohenstaufens in Italy passed away, and the noble dream of Charles the Great came to an end.

The passing of German influence from Italy, and the introduction of the power of France marks the end of the old era and the beginning of the new. In the long and fiercely contested battle between the Emperor and the Pope, the supreme pontiff has won. The spiritual sword is now above the temporal. The Lord of the world is the successor of Saint Peter. Although the name and some of the pretensions of the Holy Roman Empire persist into the beginning of the nineteenth century, it is never again to be a formidable power in Europe.

While it is often arbitrary to set definite bounds to historical epochs, yet it is convenient and profitable for Dante students to remember that in 1266, the year after the poet's birth, at the battle of Benevento, Germany was compelled to unclasp her hand and release Italian territory from her grasp, the Ghibellines were broken, French influence became powerful and the Pope with the Guelf party, which supported him, felt that they held the mastery by divine intervention and authority.

But their triumph was short-lived. Boniface soon was engaged in a life-and-death struggle with Philip, King of France, and in the end Boniface was driven for refuge to his own town of Anagni, smitten with blows, and made a prisoner. His career has been described in an apt epigram, "He entered like a fox, reigned like a lion, and died like a dog." Thus Anagni offsets the memory of Canossa.

This contest of Philip with Boniface led to searching investigations of the relation of the Church to the State and prepared the ground for Dante's famous treatise on the Rights of Monarchy.

CHAPTER II
FLORENCE: A STUDY IN DEMOCRACY

THE Romans were the road-builders of antiquity. As the Empire extended its borders, these world conquerors constructed highways from the Eternal City to the extreme limits of their dominions. One of these roads, passing northward from Rome to Lombardy, crossed the Arno at the head of its navigable waters. The river was not then, as now, an insignificant rivulet in summer, becoming a torrent during the season of the early and late rains. At that time thick timber covered the hills of the water-shed and the spongy soil of the woodlands maintained the river at a higher and more constant level than it has to-day, making the stream navigable by the ordinary boats of the period. The spot where the Roman highway crossed the river would be a natural place for a commercial settlement to spring up. The first settlers were from the neighboring Etruscan city of Fiesole; their number was swelled later by Roman colonists, and the hamlet was called Florentia, Italianized into Fiorenza. The Italians connect this name with Fiore, a lily. Hence a lily became the emblem of the city. Her cathedral built in after years was named Santa Maria del Fiore, and her standard coin was called a florin from the lily stamped upon it. Florence was by its origin and location destined to be a commercial city, and he who would understand her history must bear constantly in mind this mercantile spirit, the power of the trading classes, and their unalterable determination to manage the affairs of the city in the interest of commerce and industry. The primitive town was destroyed by Sulla in 82 B.C. and the site again built upon under Cæsar about 49 B.C. For a time the community greatly flourished and then, in sympathy with the declining Empire, languished. During the terrible centuries which followed the fall of Rome, Florence was repeatedly captured and plundered by the barbarians as they ravaged Italy. After Charlemagne took upon himself the temporal sovereignty of Christendom, Tuscany was governed by German Margraves, most of whom were of Frankish blood. The presence of these foreign lords with their feudal traditions is one of the factors to be noted in Florentine history. From them came many of the noble families of Tuscany, whose northern origin is betrayed in their names. The Commune of Florence came into existence in 1115 with the death of the Countess Matilda, and during her reign Dante's great-great-grandfather, Cacciaguida, was born. In his conversations with Dante in paradise the old crusader gives us a charming glimpse of the simple manners and sturdy virtues of those times. The description has no other historic value than a presentation of "the good old days" as the poet saw them through the haze of his imagination. The city abode in "peace, sober and modest. She had not necklace nor coronal, nor dames with ornamented shoes, nor girdle which was more to be looked at than the person." [1] Men of noble families were content to be

[1] *Paradiso*, xv, 99 ff.

FLORENCE: A STUDY IN DEMOCRACY 29

clad in garments of plain dressed skin, and their dames, clothed in homespun, came from their mirrors with unpainted faces. Citizened by such people, Florence was "so glorious and so just that the lily was never set reversed upon the staff, nor made vermilion by division."

This rude simplicity could not long endure. Cacciaguida was scarcely in his grave before a new Florence began to manifest itself. The city originally founded, not for military defense, but for purposes of wealth and greater comfort of living, now developed a conspicuous talent for business enterprise. The manufacture of silk soon became an extensive industry. The making of paper, furs, and carved ivory gave employment to many, and the craft of the goldsmith became notable. The people organized themselves into guilds, a vigorous trade was opened with neighboring cities, banking houses were established to facilitate the ever-enlarging volume of business, becoming famous for their wealth and the extent of their transactions. In 1252 the florin was coined, and when a Florentine invented bills of credit, he dealt to brigandage its severest blow. A traveler henceforth could carry the power of wealth with him, and yet have his silver and gold in places of safety.

With the growth of industries, and the development of commerce, the common people of Florence became increasingly conscious of their power. The rule of the knight and the iron baron was passing and the day of the trader and banker was dawning. A conflict between the old feudal order and the new industrial classes was inevitable. In the twelfth century the citizens began a well-planned campaign against the nobles and their strongholds. The names of two hundred and five castles, which existed in the country around Florence about the year 1200, have been preserved, and, undoubtedly, there were many more. One after another these fell before a determined and aggressive people. But the valor of the Florentines was superior to their political wisdom, for they adopted the fatuous policy of compelling the humbled aristocrats to become members of the Commune, and spend part of the year within the city.

These arrogant chieftains were a perpetual source of civil strife, for they made their homes formidable forts, building them side by side and rearing over them lofty towers from which projectiles might be shot, and for further protection formed themselves into Societies of the Towers. To meet this aggressive spirit on the part of the nobles the burgher class grouped themselves into the Greater and the Lesser Guilds. The presence within the narrow limits of a walled city of entrenched feudal lords confronting a resourceful, prosperous, and growing burgher class presages future conflicts.

To limit as far as possible the confusion arising from these factions, Florence, imitating other Italian cities, established in 1207 the office of "Podestà." This official must be a foreign nobleman and abstain from all social intercourse with citizens. As a compensation for his social loneliness he lived in great state and was clothed with almost dictatorial powers.

FLORENCE: A STUDY IN DEMOCRACY 31

I. GUELFS AND GHIBELLINES

But before the nobles joined inevitable issue with the commoners they indulged in a deadly feud among themselves. Until 1215 Florence had been a Guelf city, but in that year a quarrel between two patrician families divided the inhabitants into two opposing factions, which, according to the predilections of their leaders and the temper of the members, took the names of Guelf and Ghibelline, and thus, the ancient chronicler asserts, those accursed names first became potent political factors in the life of the city. Villani quaintly tells the story:[1] "In the year of Christ 1215, M. Gherardo Orlandi being Podestà in Florence, one M. Buondelmonte dei Buondelmonti, a noble citizen of Florence, had promised to take to wife a maiden of the house of Amidei, honorable and noble citizens; and afterwards as the said M. Buondelmonte, who was very charming and a good horseman, was riding through the city, a lady of the house of Donati called to him, reproaching him as to the lady to whom he was betrothed, that she was not beautiful or worthy of him, and saying, 'I have kept this my daughter for you'; whom she showed to him, and she was most beautiful; and immediately by the inspiration of the devil he was so taken with her, that he was betrothed and wedded to her, for which thing the kinsfolk of the first betrothed lady, being assembled together, and grieving over the shame which M. Buondelmonte had done them, were filled with accursed indignation, whereby the city of Florence was

[1] *Chronicle of Villani*, Book v, § 38. Selfe and Wicksteed's trans.

destroyed and divided." M. Buondelmonte was slain at the foot of the statue of Mars and the citizens took sides with one party and the other to the grievous disaster of the city.

It will be noticed that the leaders of this feud were all noble families and Ghibelline by instinct, tradition, and interest. The Buondelmonti and the families allied with them, in order to avenge themselves, sided with the middle classes and became leaders of the Guelf party in Florence, while the aristocrats were headed by the Uberti. The hostility of the clan was thus added to class prejudice, giving to the civil wars that ensued during the next fifty years a peculiar bitterness and intensity.

II. PRIMO POPOLO

In the first trial of strength the Guelfs were defeated, the influential persons among them were banished, and their property confiscated. In less than two years the people wearied of the despotic exactions of the Ghibelline nobles, and for the first time showed their real strength. The 20th of October, 1250, is notable in Florentine annals. On the morning of that day the people crowded into the square in front of the Church of the Minor Friars at Santa Croce, remaining under arms all day lest they be dispersed by the Uberti and the nobles. The Ghibellines, seeing that the popular discontent was fast becoming organized revolution, withdrew to their strongholds and were "in great fear." With a genius for political organization that evokes astonishment, the untrained people, ere the day closed, had reorganized the political constitution of the Commonwealth, and drawn up a document which was the admiration and the aspiration of later days. The Podestà was deposed, and in his stead was appointed a Captain of the People, who was to be the military leader of the citizens, and to be clothed with the judicial functions of the Podestà. All the able-bodied citizens were divided into twenty companies, and were bound to appear under their ward captains whenever summoned by their officers. The highest legislative authority was conferred upon twelve Signori or Ancients of the People, two being chosen from each ward. These twelve magistrates were to eat together, sleep in the public palace, and could never go out unless they were together. Their term of office was to be two months. This constitution was afterwards modified somewhat by restoring the Podestà so that he might watch the Captain of the People, while the Signoria was to be in constant assembly to supervise both. Although there was much that was good in this constitution, it is a sad commentary on the condition of the public mind, and explains the instability and constant friction of municipal affairs. The constitution was organized suspicion of human nature, and indicates a lamentable lack of confidence in the public spirit and the disinterested virtue of officials.

Yet the popular purpose is easily understood. What the citizens feared was tyranny, which they had so often experienced through power being centralized in one man or in one class. This was to be prevented by a system of checks and balances, setting one officer over against another to watch him, and dividing authority between coördinating bodies. The growth of despotic power was further guarded against by limiting the terms of office to ridiculously short periods. This would indeed hinder the acquisition of arbitrary power, but it would also insure incompetent officials and a shifty government. The people in their exultation over their greater importance acted with singular moderation. Instead of demolishing the fortresses of the nobles, it was decreed merely that for future safety no palace should have a tower over one hundred and eighty feet in height. The banner of the Commune was changed; the white lily on a red field being replaced by the red lily on a white field. Fighting under this standard, the democracy humbled Pisa, and forced Pistoia and Volterra into subjection. Within the walls of Florence the triumphant people laid the foundations of the Palazzo del Podestà, and showed their determination to preserve the strength and unity of the republic by recalling the exiled Guelfs, and compelling a reconciliation between them and the Ghibelline nobles. Under this Primo Popolo the city had ten years of internal prosperity, and almost uninterrupted victory in war.

Then came the terrible end. The Ghibelline nobility, led by the Uberti, conspired against this revolutionary and portentous constitution. In 1258 a well-laid plot to crush the democratic government was discovered, and the people, summoned by the tocsin, thronged into the Piazza del Popolo. The palace of the Uberti was stormed, and the leading conspirators were beheaded. Then the fury of the populace vented itself on the homes of the Uberti; the walls of their strongholds were leveled to the ground, the spot was cursed, and when nearly half a century later the Palace of the Commonwealth — now the Palazzo Vecchio — was planned, it was determined, even at the cost of convenience and symmetry, to set the building obliquely that it might not encroach upon ground that had been polluted by so many conspiracies against the Commonwealth. The land has never been built upon and to-day is the great square of Florence. The defeated Ghibellines betook themselves to Siena, and against this city Florence declared war. At the instigation of Farinata degli Uberti, King Manfred sent to the aid of the exiles eight hundred horsemen. Florence equipped an army of thirty thousand foot and three hundred horse, which, centring around the sacred Carroccio, marched against the exiles and their allies. At Montaperti a battle was fought on the 4th of September, 1260. That day, says Dante, the Arbia flowed red, and although the battle occurred five years before his birth the memory of its carnage was a household tale in his early years. The Florentines were utterly defeated and left twenty-five hundred dead upon the field, and more than fifteen hundred of their best troops were taken prisoners. The Guelf leaders lost no time in leaving Florence, and the Ghibellines returned in triumph. But most of them found their homes in ruins, and the Uberti looked upon the leveled foundations of their palace. A desolated Florence had little value in their eyes, and in bitterness of soul they were ready to give their consent in the council of Ghibelline chiefs to the razing of the city. All but Farinata degli Uberti, the "high-minded," Dante calls him. When the proposal was made he arose in hot indignation declaring that he would turn his sword against his allies rather than see Florence destroyed. The weight of his influence saved the city, and although Dante's stern sense of justice made him place Farinata in the burning graves of the heretics, yet he is painted as an heroic figure, holding "hell in great scorn," challenging our admiration by his lofty fortitude.

With the coming of the Ghibellines the popular constitution was abolished, and for five years the old aristocrats ruled Florence despotically. Then their authority came to an end forever. When Charles of Anjou defeated Manfred at Benevento in February, 1266, the broken power of the Empire made Ghibelline supremacy in Florence impossible. Two years after Dante's birth, on Saturday of Easter week, 1267, the Ghibellines left the city never to return. "And it may be noted," says Villani, "concerning the banishment of the Ghibellines, that it was on the same day, Easter Day of the Resurrection, whereon they had committed the murder of M. Buondelmonte de' Bondelmonti, whence the factions in Florence broke out, and the city was laid waste; and it seemed like a judgment from God, for never afterward did they return to their estate." [1] The conflict between Guelf and Ghibelline lasted in Florence precisely fifty-two years.

[1] *Op. cit.*, Book VII, § 15.

FARINATA DEGLI UBERTI
From the painting by Andrea del Castagno.

III. THE GUELF PARTY

To secure the results of this triumph and to perpetuate Guelf influence a unique political organization sprang into existence, known as the "Guelf Party." At the battle of Benevento, fighting under the banner of King Charles, were some four hundred Guelf refugees from Florence, men of gentle lineage and proved in war. Pope Clement had given them his own arms for their standard and seal — a vermilion eagle clutching a green serpent, on a white field. When these knights entered Florence as victors they became the nucleus of the Guelf Party — an independent element in the State, a republic within a republic, a political club to enjoy political patronage and to maintain political power, not unlike the Jacobin Club of Paris, or Tammany Hall in New York.

The leaders, having seized the property of the exiled Ghibellines, by the command of Pope Urban gave one part to the Commonwealth, the second to the Guelfs who had suffered losses, and the third to be held by the Guelf Party. Later all confiscated goods were returned by the party, forming a fund to be used for party purposes. When the Cardinal, whom Dante afterwards placed in hell in the same glowing circle with Farinata, heard thereof, he remarked: "Since the Guelfs of Florence had funded a reserve, the Ghibellines will never return thither." The party was closely organized, had a common palace, a secret committee, and a syndic to prosecute the Ghibellines. The arms of the Parte Guelfa are still to be seen on the battlements of the Palazzo Vecchio.

The victorious Guelf nobility behaved arrogantly toward the merchants and tradesmen, asserting the rights of their class, and demanding what they contended to be their due, which was very much more than the commonalty was ready to give. The consequent discontent of the people manifested itself in a second democratic uprising in 1282. A new constitution was drawn up and imposed, centring governmental power in the hands of the upper middle class, the guild being the political unit. As the guilds were the most permanent and fundamental element in the political history of Florence, it will be well to pause a moment to consider their character and influence.

IV. THE GUILDS OF FLORENCE

Community of interest, the advantage of coöperation, and the common need of protection, early joined together men of like employment. In the days when the traders found their chief foes in the nobility the guilds had military features, and their members were trained for self-defense. As the burgher class increased in power the guilds flourished. They had their secrets, their oaths of initiation, their common funds, and officers to supervise production, fix prices, and prevent underselling. The greater guilds were the Guild of Judges and Notaries, the Guild of Calimala, or Dressers of Foreign Cloth, Guilds of Silk, of Wool, of Money Changers, of Doctors and Druggists, of Skinners and Furriers. There is abundant documentary evidence to prove that the greater guilds were miniature republics within the State. They had their consuls who administered their laws, represented the guild, carried its banner, and when in emergency its members assembled under arms, acted as military commanders. There was a treasurer, who had charge of the revenues of the association, and an accountant, who investigated the actions of outgoing magistrates of the order. All the officials of the guilds were sworn adherents of the Guelf Party, and their consuls, who represented the councils of the Captains and the Podestà, were pledged to protect the guild and advocate laws in its favor. To the credit of these organizations be it said that they enacted and enforced some most wholesome laws against themselves. The product of their industries must bear the label of the guild, every defect must be recorded, defective work rigorously punished, and measures must be carefully examined and absolutely correct. Severe penalties were inflicted on those who sent forth counterfeit goods, or goods of bad quality. All accounts were strictly examined by experts, especially appointed tribunals settled all disputes affecting the trade, and members were summarily punished who carried their controversies to the ordinary courts. The guilds also sent their representatives all over the civilized world, who extended trade, guarded the rights of members in foreign countries, and protected them from reprisals in a day when no international law existed.

Villani informs us that in 1308 there were two hundred factories and warehouses belonging to the Guilds of Wool in Florence and immediate vicinity, employing upward of thirty thousand operatives, wherein were manufactured from seventy to eighty thousand pieces of woolen cloth.[1] In the year 1358, in the Guild of Judges and Notaries there were nearly one hundred judges and five hundred notaries. The city's health was watched over in 1300 by sixty physicians, and there were about one hundred shops of the apothecaries. These strongly organized and powerful guilds, being self-governing, exerted a steadying influence during these troublous days of the Commune. They were also training schools of able men skilled in affairs and capable of performing distinguished services for the State. The lesser guilds were the small merchants of cloth, the shoemakers, the butchers, the stocking weavers, the carpenters and masons, and the smiths and iron workers. They numbered fourteen in all, but not until later did they come to political prominence.

This new constitution made the guilds the basis of the city government. At the head of the administration were placed six priors, representative of the six greater guilds, whose duty it was to "supervise the treasury, deal justice to all, and to protect the weak and powerless against the great and strong." The Podestà retained the highest judicial power, and the military command devolved upon the Captain of the People. The priors were limited in action by a council of one hundred good men of the people without whose deliberation no great thing could be done. For the Captain of the People there was a special council of eighty members called the "Council of the Captain and Capitudine" — the latter composed of the consuls of the guilds. Below these was a general council of the popo-

[1] Staley: *The Guilds of Florence*, p. 163.

FLORENCE: A STUDY IN DEMOCRACY 41

lani. The Podestà consulted with a council of ninety members, and the General Council of the Commune.

This combination of liberty, responsibility, and opportunity awoke all the latent energies of the Florentine people. It produced a class of merchants renowned throughout Europe for diplomacy, shrewdness, and ability for handling large affairs. The independence and closely articulated organization of these units explain how Florence could prosper so astonishingly even in the midst of the enormous confusion of her political life.

The large freedom which Florence enjoyed explains also her conspicuous culture and her supremacy in art and literature. Liberty awakened the genius of the people and the energy of their aroused minds flowed in every channel of greatness. While in other countries during the Middle Ages art and literature were the concern of patricians, the galaxy of immortals who shed their lustre upon Florence were the children of the middle class, or of the populace.

V. ORDINANCES OF JUSTICE

The natural inclination of those in power to exercise despotic authority, and the steady purpose of the people to break down the privileged classes and to render citizen opinion and citizen law supreme, resulted in 1293 in the further enlargement of the constitution in the popular interests. The leader was one Giano della Bella, by birth a nobleman, but strongly in sympathy with the people. By his influence an entirely new code, entitled the "Ordinances of Justice," intended to suppress the violence of the nobles, was enacted. A new office was created having the title of "Gonfaloniere della Giustizia" who was to be president of the Board of Priors. The banner of the people — a white field with a red cross — was entrusted to his keeping, and a thousand soldiers were placed under his command. By these Ordinances of Justice all noblemen were to be excluded from participation in the government. A noble killing a man of the people was to be beheaded, his home destroyed, and his goods confiscated. Two witnesses or public report were sufficient to convict a nobleman, and no nobleman was allowed to carry arms unless he made a deposit of five hundred lire. Any man of the people showing hostility to the Republic, or breaking its laws, could be proclaimed by the magistrates a noble, and thus be excluded from participation in the government. These ordinances with their supplementary provisions, added at different times between 1293 and 1306, comprise one hundred and fifteen chapters; consequently only the merest outline is given above.

The democratic movement, however, was not confined to Florence. In all the republics of Tuscany, and throughout the greater part of Lombardy, the turbulent nobility were excluded from the magistracies. Dante was in his twenty-eighth year when this astonishing assertion of popular privileges — we cannot call them rights — took place.

Having touched thus at length the rise of the upper middle class — for the "mob" has not as yet been granted governmental privileges — the final expulsion

FLORENCE: A STUDY IN DEMOCRACY 43

of the Ghibellines, and the exclusion of the Guelf nobles from power, we shall leave the description of the pernicious feuds between the Blacks and the Whites until a future chapter, when they can be treated more directly in reference to Dante's political fortunes. Florence being thoroughly mercantile and Guelf, her future civic quarrels have little political significance. Henceforth the heroic struggles for Church and State, for inherited privileges or popular government, degenerate into something like a Corsican vendetta.

VI. CAUSES OF FLORENTINE INSTABILITY

As the factions of his native city drove Dante into exile, and profoundly influenced both his thought and character, it is essential to inquire into the causes which made the Florentines so extraordinarily unstable and capricious. Both Dante and Villani attribute much importance to the mixed character of the population of Florence. The original stock was a cross between the first sturdy Roman settlers and the contentious refugees from Fiesole. This mongrel strain was made still further conspicuous and hurtful by the infusion of more alien blood. "The citizenship," says Dante, "is now mixed with Campi and with Certaldo and with Fighine." "The intermingling of persons," he continues, "was ever the beginning of harm to a city, as food which is loaded on is to the body."[1] But as the places named were small towns in the near neighborhood of Florence, the presence of settlers from them, especially as they were substantially of the same blood as

[1] *Paradiso*, xvi, 49 and 68 ff.

the common people of Florence, does not seem menacing to us who draw immigrants from all quarters of the globe. A more evident cause of irritation was what Dante considered the fatal policy of compelling the nobility to abandon their fortresses and take up their abode in the city. The presence of these proud and quarrelsome nobles within the walls undoubtedly constituted a large element of discord.

Machiavelli's diagnosis is somewhat different. In his "History of Florence" he declares that what kept the city in dissension was the "natural enmities, which occur between the popular classes and the nobility, arising from the desire of the latter to command, and the disinclination of the former to obey." "And from this diversity of purpose," he says, "all the other evils which disturb republics derive their origin. This kept Rome disunited; and this, if it be allowable to compare small things with great, held Florence in disunion; although it produced in each city a different result; for animosities were only beginning when the people and nobility of Rome contended, while ours were brought to a conclusion by the contentions of our citizens. A new law settled the disputes of Rome; those of Florence were only terminated by death and banishment of many of her best people. Those of Rome increased her military virtue, while that of Florence was quite extinguished by her divisions. The quarrels of Rome established different ranks of society, those of Florence abolished the distinctions which had previously existed. This diversity of effects must have been occasioned by the different purposes which the two peoples had

FLORENCE: A STUDY IN DEMOCRACY 45

in view. While the people of Rome endeavored to associate with the nobility in the supreme honors, those of Florence strove to exclude the nobility from all participation in them: as the desire of the Roman people was more reasonable, no particular offense was given to the nobility; they therefore consented to it without recourse to arms; so that, after some disputes concerning particular points, both parties agreed to the enactment of a law which, while it satisfied the people, preserved the nobility in the enjoyment of their dignity.

"On the other hand, the demands of the people of Florence being insolent and unjust, the nobility became desperate, prepared for their defense with the utmost energy, and thus bloodshed and the exile of citizens followed. The laws which were afterward made did not provide for the common good, but were framed wholly in favor of their conquerors. This too must be observed, that from the acquisition of power made by the people of Rome, their minds were very much improved; for all the offices of state being attainable as well by the people as the nobility, the peculiar excellencies of the latter exercised a most beneficial influence upon the former; and as the city increased in virtue she attained a more exalted greatness. But in Florence, the people being conquerors, the nobility were deprived of all participation in the government; and, in order to regain a portion of it, it became necessary for them not only to seem like the people, but to be like them in behavior, mind, and mode of living. Hence arose those changes in armorial bearings, and in the titles of families, which the nobility adopted, in order that they might seem to be of the people; military virtue and generosity of feeling became extinguished in them; the people not possessing these qualities, they could not appreciate them, and Florence became by degrees more and more depressed and humiliated." [1]

This shrewd and competent observer fails to note, however, that the nobles of ancient Rome were of the same stock as the citizens, making the adjustment of differences a far more easy problem than in Florence, where aristocracy and commonalty were of antagonistic race and traditions. In Florence it was the inevitable and bitter conflict of two civilizations; the warrior feudal order clinging to its ancient privileges, and the rising commercial and industrial order determined to achieve opportunities and power. Yet if the burghers and magistrates of Florence had possessed more of the old Roman sense of justice, and of the authority of the law, the outcome of the conflict would have been a constitution embodying the rights and duties of each class, rather than a miscalled "Ordinances of Justice" which sought to discredit and crush the natural social and military leaders of the people.

To the antagonism of Roman and Teutonic blood, the mistaken policy of compelling the nobles to take residence in the city, the inevitable conflict between a decadent feudal aristocracy and the growing industrial classes, we may add two other causes which undoubtedly were influential. The conditions enumerated may account for many personal quarrels and for

[1] *History of Florence*, Book III, c. I.

FLORENCE: A STUDY IN DEMOCRACY 47

thoroughgoing revolutions, they do not explain that chronic instability of civic affairs which Dante declared with bitterness did not permit what was spun in October to reach until November.[1] One cause of agitation Florence had in common with all the free cities of Italy. The Medieval Commune was a confederation of closely organized units, it was an assemblage of small associations rather than a state; there were republics within the republic. The nobles came together in the Societies of the Towers, the burghers formed their guilds. Upon the complete victory of the latter, and the passing of the control of the State into the hands of the greater guilds, the humbler callings founded the minor guilds. Between the greater and the lesser arts there was not only the difference in temper between men trained in extensive commercial enterprises and artisans habituated to narrow horizons and more irksome toil; there was a radical difference of interest. The greater guilds with their world-embracing trades flourished in proportion as they made the city commercial rather than aristocratic. They favored wars of conquest, which enabled them to introduce their goods into conquered cities. But Florentine merchants, while princely in entertainment and lavish in their expenditures on state occasions, were proud of the frugal simplicity of their daily lives.

The minor arts, however, lost custom by the expulsion of the extravagant nobles, while foreign war levied heavily upon their numbers and resources, without increasing their markets. This difference in tem-

[1] *Purgatorio*, VI, 143

per and interest between the greater and the lesser arts, each having its political representatives, its captains and armed men, was fruitful of constant debate and conflict.

Beside these industrial units there were political ones as well. The Parte Guelfa, with its officers, its invested funds, its vast political power, did not always harmonize its interests with those of the Commune, while outside the walls were the exiles, mostly Ghibellines, ever intriguing for reinstatement. A confederacy of such differentiated units could not have stability. Therefore the course of Florentine history was the passing of power from the nobles to the greater guilds, from the greater guilds to the lesser, then the alliance between the nobles and the mob, and then the tyrant.

This system of representation by groups was not without distinct advantages, for it coördinated legislation with representation. To-day we send to the Legislature or to Congress men who represent our localities. We are taxed as employers, mulcted as inheritors, helped as workingmen, but we are represented in none of these capacities. Our legislation is aimed at groups and classes, but the men who legislate are chosen, not as representatives of the persons affected, but of certain stretches of territory.

The medieval statesmen proceeded on a different principle. Edward I, King of England from 1272 to 1307, in an edict, enjoined his people to send to Parliament, not anybody who could win their support, but a member of the classes most likely to be affected by legislation. This principle prevailed also in Florence.

Men were represented in the capacities for which they were taxed.

There was yet another cause lying deeper than the loose structure of the Commune. A free people to maintain a stable government must have reverence for the law, respect for the rights of others, and individual self-control. The Florentines had none of these. They had little reverence for statutory law. Loyalty they had in abundance, but it was to persons and a visible party rather than to an abstraction called the honor of the State.

In primitive society, loyalty is the sovereign virtue. The clansman will die for his chief or his tribe. In the days of chivalry this virtue was refined by the willing service and honor which the knight rendered to his lady. But the tribe, the captain, the lady are personal and concrete objects, easily apprehended and making strong appeal to the imagination and the heart. To be equally devoted to an abstract ideal, or to a form of words embodied in a constitution, demands a more mature intelligence, and comes with a more advanced civilization.

In Florence there were the adherents of Pope and Emperor, there were retainers willing to give their property and lives in the service of their feudal lords, there were merchants and tradesmen who sacrificed all for their class, but the Florentines as a whole had not reached that civic maturity which would compel them to keep a contract even to personal detriment, and maintain a constitution to the impairment of individual and party interests. "A new law," says Machiavelli, "would settle the disputes of Rome; those of Florence were only terminated by the death and banishment of her best people." A law-abiding spirit is a nobler virtue than personal loyalty, and indicates greater civic maturity. The Florentines of Dante's time were clansmen and not citizens. Personal friendship counted more than constitutional obligations.

"The entire history of the Commune," says Villari, "demonstrates a constant tendency to harmonize all these distinct and often jarring elements — political, social, and legislative — but this problem it never succeeds in solving, and ends by relapsing into despotism. A true conception of social unity was wanting; the idea of a true distribution of authority was unknown, either in real life or in theory; accordingly whoever happened to have a share in the executive authority, also assumed, as necessarily connected with it, a share not only in judicial, but likewise in administrative and legislative functions. Wherefore it seemed that the only way to preserve liberty was to parcel out the government among an infinity of hands, and to contrive that parties, associations, cliques, families, and quarters of towns should each and severally serve as checks on all the others. In this process of division and subdivision all the elements constituting modern society were prepared, but the State in its true sense was never discovered. Without ballast to steady her, the ship of the Commune, driven hither and thither in a ceaseless storm and buffeted by winds from all quarters, could neither find anchorage nor keep a steady course. No clear and certain conception was ever reached of that law which, by limiting and defining the amount of liberty guaranteed to each individual, secures freedom to all." [1]

The failure to distinguish between the executive, legislative, and judicial functions of the State, to which Villari wisely draws attention, indicates how slowly the modern idea of liberty under law emerged. It was not until the fourteenth century that the distinction between the executive and legislative functions of government was made. And the greater distinction, which is the noblest feature of our American Constitution, the complete separation of the judicial from the legislative and executive departments of State, is a discovery of the eighteenth century. "There is no liberty," said Montesquieu, "if the judicial power be not separated from the legislative and executive." This insight of the French philosopher profoundly influenced the founders of our Republic, and saved us from many of the mistakes of the medieval experiments in democracy. But the Florentines not only failed in legal definitions of liberty, and in its constitutional guarantees; they failed to have an adequate conception of its true nature and hence to sufficiently respect it. Among us liberty is considered to be a natural right. It belongs to every man. The State exists to protect the individual in his freedom. Liberty, being sacred, must be held inviolate. As it is the right of all, its protection, even at personal cost, is the duty of all. Such a noble and compelling ideal was scarcely known in medieval Italy. It

[1] *The First Two Centuries of Florentine History*, translated by Linda Villari, p. 428.

is true that in the statute of 1289, by which the complete abolition of serfdom was accomplished, the sentiment is expressed that "liberty is a natural and therefore an inalienable right." But this sentiment had not crystallized into a principle which citizens would enforce at cost to themselves. Florentine constitutions, therefore, were not formulations of principles guarding the rights of all; they were rather written agreements between allied interests, usually with the purpose of discrediting and crippling antagonists. Such agreements called forth no reverence, developed no spirit of obedience, and established no lasting peace. The city was full of loyal men, but was sadly wanting in coöperative men. Citizens would associate and sacrifice for the clique, the family, the class; but only the few maintained that conception of a state which compelled them to hold sacred the rights of others, and sacrifice class interests to the common weal.

To the political and constitutional faults of the Florentines may we not add the influence of a walled city on its inhabitants as a contributory cause to a violent factional spirit? In our day, when access to the open country is easy, and the love of nature is promoted in a thousand ways, when travel, and clubs, and interests are world-wide, it is easy to realize the insignificance of the individual, and to be tolerant of the faults of others. How different the training of a group of people who are instinct with vigorous life, crowded between narrow walls, meeting continually, acting and reacting upon one another, the majority seldom traveling beyond the limits of their province! Such people would grow self-conscious and intense, and would be given to magnifying trivial personal affairs into matters of grave importance. They would mistake the cackle of their burg for the murmur of the world. May it not be that much of the contentiousness of the medieval folk was due to the frictions incident to life within a walled city? Nevertheless, divisions and struggles have their compensations. If not too exhausting, they quicken the mental and moral qualities of a people to great activity. They save from self-indulgent sloth, they train the citizens to self-sacrifice, devotion, steadfast loyalty to a common cause. The glory of Florence was synchronous with her militant and fevered life. All her immortal works were done during those periods when the tide of battle flowed frequently through her streets. Her world-famous citizens, from Dante to Savonarola, were born and trained during her periods of storm and stress. When quietness and order settled upon the city after the expulsion of the Medici, then the people had peace, but it was the peace of spiritual and intellectual death.

The Florence of Dante's time had a vitality so stupendous that it was able to flourish in spite of the devastation of this perpetual strife. At the Jubilee of 1300 Florence sent to Rome a splendidly equipped embassy, representing every era of her history. More than this, she contrived to have distinguished Florentines the representatives of Germany, Byzantium, France, England, and other European states. Boniface, astonished at the magnificence and bounty of the Florentines, exclaimed: "What sort of a city is this

Florence?" A cardinal evasively remarked: "Your Holiness, Florence is a good city." "Nonsense," replied the Pope: "she is by far the greatest of all cities! She feeds, clothes, and governs us all! Indeed she appears to rule the whole world! She and her people are, in truth, the fifth element of the universe!" [1]

Machiavelli, in the introduction to his "History of Florence," calls attention to the extraordinary virtues of a city that could grow great in the presence of so much evil. "In Florence," he says, "at first the nobles were divided against each other, then the people against the nobles, and lastly the people against the populace; and it oftentimes happened that when one of these parties got the upper hand, it split into two. And from these divisions there resulted so many deaths, so many banishments, so many destructions of families, as never before befell in any other city of which we have record. Verily, in my opinion, nothing manifests more clearly the power of our city than the result of these divisions, which would have been able to destroy every great and most potent city. Nevertheless, ours seemed thereby to grow even greater; such was the virtue of those citizens, and the power of their genius and disposition to make themselves and their country great, that those who remained free from these evils could exalt her with their virtue more than the malignity of those accidents, which had diminished them, had been able to cast her down. And without doubt, if only Florence, after her liberation

---

[1] *Bibl. Laurenziana, Osserv. Fior.* vi, 21; also, Staley: *The Guilds of Florence*, p. 562.

FLORENCE: A STUDY IN DEMOCRACY 55

from the Empire, had had the felicity of adopting a form of government which would have kept her united, I know not what republic, whether modern or ancient, would have surpassed her — with such great virtue in war and in peace would she have been filled." [1]

VII. FAMOUS CITIES

A mind eager to note curious phenomena will be interested to observe the contrasted character of the world's famous cities at the different epochs of history. In ancient times there was great Babylon, seat of an ordered and powerful government, capable of initiating large movements and ruling vast populations, yet bequeathing to posterity the result of group activities rather than the memory of great individuals. To the southwest lay Jerusalem, never a political power of the first magnitude, too factious and turbulent to become a powerful state, yet whose very excess of energy flamed forth in poets and prophets of imperishable influence. She challenges the attention of the world by the character and genius of her distinguished men rather than by her massed efficiency.

In the classic epoch there were likewise two contrasted and illustrious cities: Rome, the seat of disciplined power, fountain of law and justice, mistress of the world, because her citizens were possessed of those civic virtues which subordinated individual passion to the good of the common weal; and Athens, whose fierce democracy, too impatient of restraint to preserve the liberty she loved, was as prolific of brilliant

[1] Quoted by E. G. Gardner: *Florence*, p. 35.

geniuses as a fire of sparks, and whose poets, philosophers, and sculptors have subdued a vaster multitude by their personal ascendancy than Rome ever conquered by her short sword, and have won the loyalty of more centuries than the countries annexed by the imperial city.

In the Middle Ages the counterpart of Rome was Venice, whose inhabitants, trained to obedience and team-work by the stern discipline of the sea, maintained a strong, autocratic government for many centuries; while Florence, on the other hand, spiritually was not "the most famous daughter of Rome," as Dante stated, but of Athens. Fitful, capricious, strong in centrifugal forces, her far-shining lustre is the splendor of her great names in art and letters. From her limited population she produced four geniuses of the first order, — Dante, Leonardo da Vinci, Michael Angelo, and Machiavelli. Galileo also was of Florentine stock. Beyond this glowing circle of superlative minds one may discern a multitude in whom is the "true sparkling of the Holy Ghost."

If one wishes to trace the comparison to our own day and land, we have Boston, — "the past at least is secure," — cradle of liberty, renowned for her great men of statecraft and literature, individualistic, unconventional, incessantly agitating in the interests of the ideal; in contrast there is a great city to the west whose material greatness has somewhat dwarfed and conventionalized the individuality of her sons.

Beautiful for situation were Jerusalem, Athens, and Florence as compared with Babylon, Rome, and Ven-

FLORENCE: A STUDY IN DEMOCRACY

ice. In the former, liberty is justified of her children; in the latter, authority achieves stability and power for the State. The deduction to be drawn is that a democracy, whether in Florence or in America, lacking a strong central government and the habit of obedience to properly constituted authority, may have a few brilliant centuries, but awaits either disintegration or the despot.

PART II
Dante's Life and Works

CHAPTER I

PERIOD OF YOUTH : 1265-1290

I. ANCESTRY AND BOYHOOD

THE higher forms of human excellence in Dante's judgment are not to be explained by the law of heredity. This God wills that we may know that we come from him alone. The poet was not without family pride, but he considered his lofty genius to be a direct gift from heaven. A notable passage in the "Paradiso"[1] gives his own knowledge of his ancestors and his opinion of them. In the planet Mars, standing before the cross in which the constellated warriors flash forth Christ, he beheld a resplendent star run from the right arm of the cross down to the foot. "Nor from the ribbon did the gem depart, but through the radiant strip it ran along and seemed like fire behind alabaster." "O blood of mine," the light exclaimed, "O overflowing grace of God! To whom as to thee was ever the gate of heaven twice opened?" After the bow of his ardent affection had so far relaxed that his speech descended towards the poet's understanding, Dante learned that this "living topaz" was his great-great-grandfather, made both Christian and Cacciaguida in the ancient baptistry of Florence. The splendor goes on to affirm that he was born in that section of Florence known as the Gate of Saint Peter, about the year 1090. One of his brothers was named Eliseo, which has led to the sur-

[1] *Paradiso*, xv.

mise that he belonged to the ancient house of the Elisei, who boasted Roman descent. His wife, Alighiera degli Alighieri, came to him from the valley of the Po, and from her, through her son Alighiero, Dante derived his name Alighieri. Cacciaguida further declares that he was among those who followed the Emperor Conrad III in the second crusade, and was made a belted knight for gallant deeds. About the year 1147 he had fallen by the hand of the infidel, and had come from "martyrdom to this peace." Dante's pride in this knightly strain in his blood is seen in the prominent place assigned this crusader ancestor in Paradise. The poet presents him as a great artist among the singers of heaven, associating intimately with Judas Maccabeus, Godfrey of Bouillon, and Robert Guiscard. A document quite recently brought to light contains the name of Cacciaguida, son of Adamo, and is dated April 28, 1131. Mr. Paget Toynbee[1] considers that this document pushes our knowledge of the poet's ancestry one generation farther back. Cacciaguida's son, as we have mentioned above, was named Alighiero. Evidently there was a family tradition of the haughty temper of this ancestor, for the old knight declares that for over a hundred years [2] Alighiero has been expiating the sin of pride in Purgatory. His name appears, with that of his brother Preitenitto, in a document dated December 9, 1189, while another document shows him to have been alive on August 14, 1201.[3]

---

[1] Paget Toynbee: *Dante Alighieri*, p. 40.   [2] *Paradiso*, xv, 92.
[3] This document shows Dante to have been guilty of a slight inaccuracy, for by Easter, 1300, Alighiero had been in Purgatory not quite ninety-nine years.

PERIOD OF YOUTH

The patronymic Alighieri may be of Teutonic origin. If so, it helps to explain some qualities of Dante's genius which are characteristic of the North. The scholars who hold to this Northern origin derive the first part of the name from "*alt*" meaning "old," and the termination from "*geirr*," or "*gar*," signifying "spear." This derivation, if correct, gives the loftiest of Italian poets a surname curiously like that borne by the greatest of English bards. Others find the root of the word to be "*aliger*," meaning the "wing-bearer." Of Alighiero's son, Dante's grandfather, we know nothing except that he bore the name Bellincione. Of the poet's father, also named Alighiero, we have happily more information, though our knowledge is all too meagre. He was a notary. At the foot of three documents still extant his name appears (Alagerius ymperiali auctoritate iudex atque notarius); one document being dated 1239 and the other 1256. Forese Donati's taunting line —

"Well know I thou wast Alighieri's son" [1]

would indicate that Dante's father was a man not greatly esteemed. A recently discovered document [2] dated 1283 states that "Dante del gia Alighieri del popolo di S. Martino del Vescovo, come herede del padre, vende." This proves that the father died before the son had attained his nineteenth year. It is recorded that the notary was twice married. The name of the first wife was Bella, and the second Lapa. Both of these names appear in a document dated May 16, 1332, while

[1] Sonnet, LIV, 1. [2] Toynbee: *Dante Alighieri*, p. 38 n.

Lapa was still alive. Dante was the only child of the first wife, and a son, Francesco, and a daughter, Tana, were the children of Lapa. There appears also to have been another daughter who married one Leon Poggi, but her name has not come down to us. Her son Andrea Poggi was an intimate friend of Boccaccio, who testifies to his straightforward and honest character. He much resembled Dante in both face and stature, walking as though he were slightly hump-backed, as Dante himself is said to have done. From him Boccaccio says he obtained much information respecting the poet's ways and habits.

The family could not have been prominent else it would have been exiled from Florence with the leading Guelfs after the battle of Montaperti in 1260. If the father did go out with his party, he must have returned before 1267, the year in which the Guelf nobles were restored to their native city. To the relative obscurity of his family Dante owed the good fortune to be born in Florence, "that most beautiful and famous daughter of Rome," which he so passionately loved, but which seemed to him an ungrateful mother. Regarding his own mother, there is a conjecture that she was the daughter of Durante di Scolaio degli Abati. If so, it was by the contraction of the name of this maternal grandfather, Durante, "the enduring one," that the poet received a name so descriptive of fortitude amid bitter experiences. Whether the unknown mother was, like the mothers of so many distinguished men, conspicuous for unusual qualities of mind and heart and will, may never be ascertained. As she died in

PERIOD OF YOUTH

Dante's childhood he seems to have cherished no recollections of her. The only reference to her in the "Divina Commedia" is contained in the exclamation of Virgil: "Blessed be she who bore thee!" [1] Boccaccio gives us a bit of gossip regarding the mother's prophetic dream. "This gentle lady seemed in her dream to be beneath a lofty laurel tree, in a green meadow, beside a clear spring, and there she felt herself delivered of a son. And he, partaking merely of the berries that fell from the laurel and of the waters of the clear spring, seemed almost immediately to become a shepherd that strove with all his power to secure some leaves of the tree whose fruit had nourished him. And as he strove she thought he fell, and when he rose again she perceived that he was no longer a man but a peacock; whereat so great a wonder seized her that her sleep broke. Not long after it befell that the due time for her labor arrived, and she brought forth a son whom she and his father by common consent named Dante; and rightly so, for as will be seen as we proceed, the issue corresponded exactly to the name." [2]

It was in the year 1265 in Florence that Dante first felt the Tuscan air. Whatever else was unpropitious to him Dante always maintained that the heavens were benignant at his natal hour. According to the astrology of the day the sun was in the constellation of the Gemini and to this happy adjustment of the heavens the poet ascribed his lofty power. Over this hea-

[1] *Inferno*, VIII, 45.
[2] C. A. Dinsmore: *Aids to the Study of Dante*, pp. 73, 74. The translation of Boccaccio's "Vita di Dante" which I use in this and subsequent pages is by Mr. James Robinson Smith.

ven of the Fixed Stars preside the Cherubim, "who," says Saint Bernard, "draw from the very fountain of Wisdom, the mouth of the Most High, and pour out the streams of knowledge upon all His citizens." These glorious stars, impregnate with great virtue, rained down their mystic fire into the mind of the babe, endowing him with genius and anointing him for his prophetic work of coöperating with the Cherubim in spreading the knowledge of God among men. We are ignorant of the exact day of his birth, but as the sun entered the Gemini on May 18 the poet was born after that date. Witte suggests that Dante evidently felt himself to be under the special protection of Lucia. It was she who in the "Inferno" brought Beatrice to his aid. In the "Purgatorio" she bears him to the gateway of Saint Peter, and in the "Mystical Rose" she occupies a high place opposite to Adam. Moreover, Virgil speaks of Dante to Lucia as "thy faithful one." As there was a Saint Lucia associated with the convent of Saint Clara outside of Florence whose festival was on May 30, Witte is inclined to assign that day as the date of the poet's birth.[1] He was born in the Sesto di Piero Maggiore. Of the immediate neighborhood of the house there is no question. In the document already mentioned, dated 1283, Dante is spoken of as "del popolo di S. Martino del Vescovo." Leonardo Bruni Aretino, most reliable in judgment and careful in statement, in describing a visit which Dante's great-grandson paid to Florence, says:

---

[1] *Dante-Forschungen*, II, 30–31; also Paget Toynbee: *Dante Dictionary*, art. "Lucia."

"The descendants of Messer Cacciaguida called the Aldighieri dwelt at the piazza behind San Martino del Vescovo, against the street that runs to the house of the Sacchetti, and in the other direction stretches the houses of the Donati and the Giuochi. . . . He had a very good house in Florence, next to that of Geri di Messer Bello. . . . And it is not long since this Lionardo (Alighieri) came to Florence with other young men of Verona, well appointed and in good style; and he paid me a visit as a friend of the memory of his great-grandfather, Dante. I showed him Dante's house, and that of his forbears, and I pointed out to him many particulars with which he was not acquainted, because he and his family had been estranged from their fatherland."[1] Tradition places this house just opposite the Piazza San Martino in what is now known as the Via Dante Alighieri, and official sanction sets its seal on the witness of tradition. The building now shown as the birthplace of the poet probably stands on the ground owned by the Alighieri, but the house itself has been thoroughly modernized.

Near by were most of the families with whom his fortunes were intimately associated. Folco Portinari was but a block away. Across the narrow street from them was the stronghold of the Donati. The Cerchi, with whose political fortunes Dante allied himself, were in the immediate neighborhood, while farther off, to the south, was the home of Guido Cavalcanti.

It was the custom in Florence in those days for

[1] Witte: *Essays on Dante*, p. 156 n. Translated by Lawrence and Wicksteed. See also my *Aids to the Study of Dante*, pp. 115–28.

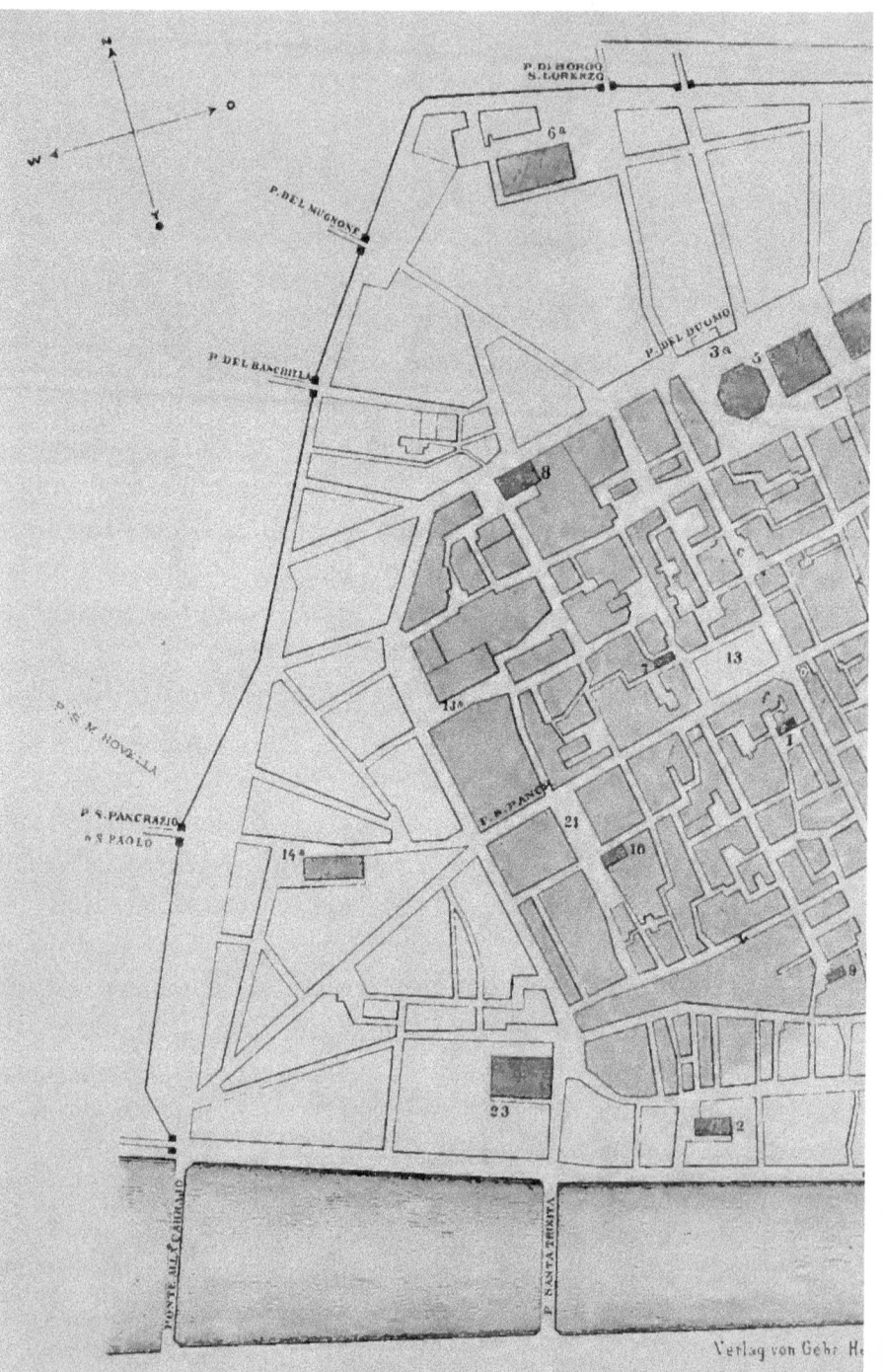

MAP OF FLORENCE AT THE EN
From Karl Witte's *Dante*
a. Houses of the Alighieri.   g. House of the Cerchi.   h. Hou

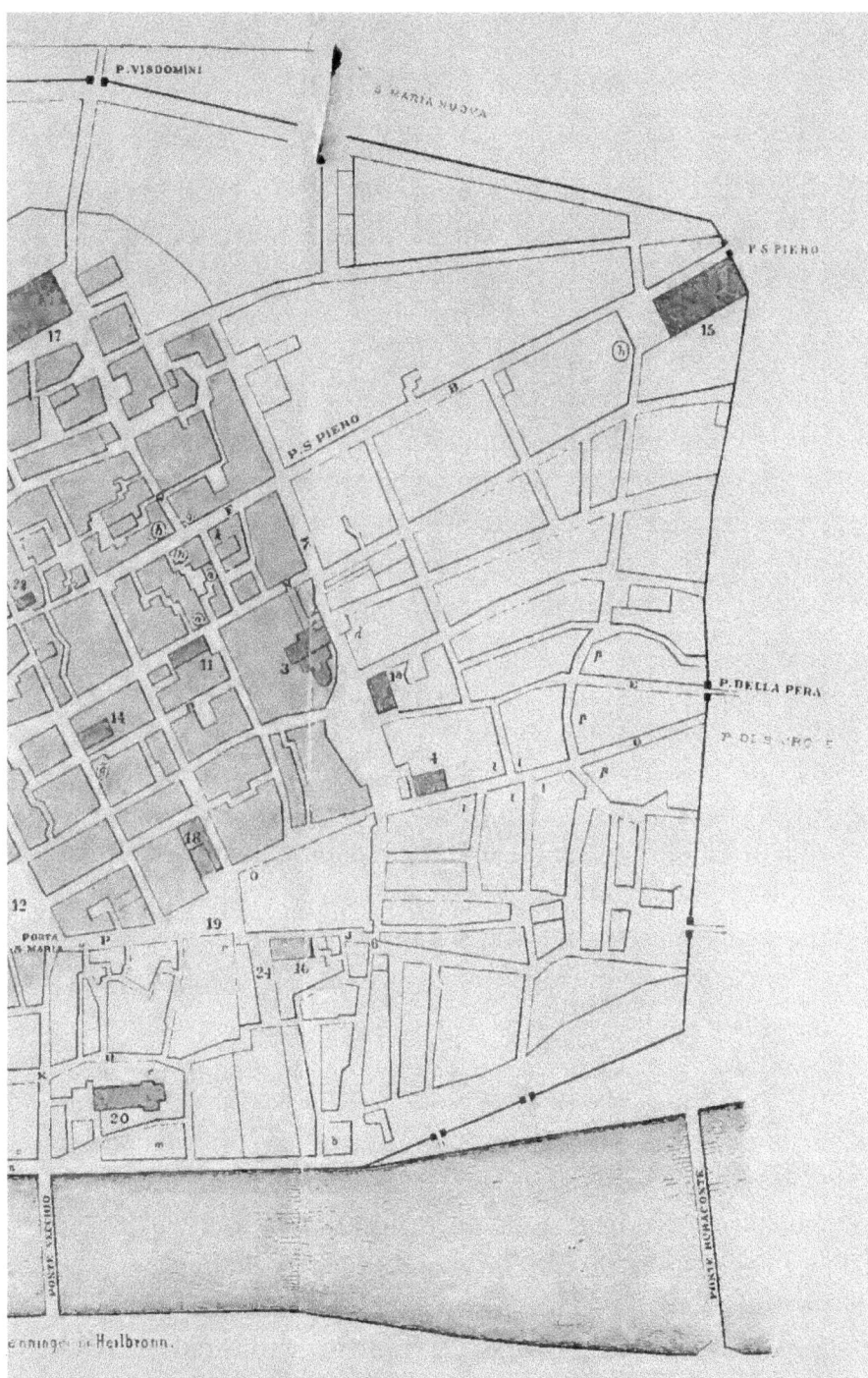

D OF THE THIRTEENTH CENTURY

Forschungen (Heilbronn, 1879)

of the Donati.   i. House of the Elisei.   q. House of the Portinari.

all children born during the year to be immersed on the 24th of June, Saint John the Baptist's Day, in the font of the Baptistry of the city. Here Dante was baptized and "entered into the Faith which makes the soul known to God." It was ever after a spot most dear to him, and, that he might be recalled from bitterness of exile to take the poet's crown at this sacred font, was the continuous and cherished ambition of his life. Dante's childhood years must have been passed under the care of his stepmother, Lapa, and we trust that she did not treat him in a stepmotherly fashion. An incident recorded in the "Vita Nuova" throws a clear, sweet light upon the home life and Dante's fondness for one of his half-sisters. "It fell out that a grievous infirmity came upon me in a certain part of my body, from which I suffered nine days most bitter pains, which brought to me such weakness that I was forced to lie as one who cannot move." By his bedside sat one who was connected with him "in the nearest kinship," and whom he describes as

> "A very pitiful lady, very young,
>   Exceeding rich in human sympathies,
>   Stood by, what time I clamor'd upon death." [1]

This young and gentle lady in all probability was one of Dante's half-sisters, and his admiration of her seems to have been deep and genuine.

The only event of his boyhood which he thought suitable of record was his meeting with Beatrice. Justly celebrated is the passage: "Nine times now since my

[1] *Vita Nuova*, XXIII.

birth, the heaven of light had turned almost to the same point in its own gyration, when the glorious lady of my mind, who was called Beatrice by many who knew not what to call her, first appeared before my eyes. She had already been in this life so long that in its course the starry heaven had moved toward the region of the East one of the twelve parts of a degree; so that at the beginning of her ninth year she appeared to me, and I near the end of my ninth year saw her. She appeared to me clothed in a most noble color, a modest and becoming crimson, and she was girt and adorned in such wise as befitted her very youthful age. At that instant I say truly that the spirit of life, which dwells in the most secret chamber of the heart, began to tremble with such violence that it appeared fearfully in the least pulses, and trembling said these words: 'Ecce deus fortior me, qui veniens dominabitur mihi'" (Behold a god stronger than I, who coming shall rule over me).[1]

However much the magic of memory transfigured this early meeting, Dante has certainly sketched for us his own portrait as a lad, impressionable, vivid, full of the wonder which grows out of a rich imagination.

In this earliest insight into his character he lays claim to a mental quality without which no man achieves greatness; namely, the capacity of conceiving and of being dominated continuously by a strong passion. "I say that from this time forth Love lorded it over my soul, which had been so speedily wedded to him; and he began to exercise over me such control and such

[1] *Vita Nuova*, II. Norton's translation.

lordship, through the power which my imagination gave to him, that it behooved me to do all his pleasure."[1] There are many who feel intensely but lack that toughness of fibre which enables them to hold impressions through the years. The boy's passion is like heated steel, not like burning hemp. Yet powerfully as he can be affected by his emotions he is no reed shaken by the wind. Dante claimed for himself even in that early year the superb self-restraint which was so marked a characteristic of his genius. "And though her image, which stayed constantly with me, gave assurance to Love to hold lordship over me, yet it was of such noble virtue that it never suffered Love to rule me without the faithful counsel of the reason in those matters in which it were useful to hear such counsel."[2]

II. YOUTHFUL STUDIES

During the nine years which elapse before the next recorded meeting with Beatrice, Dante was laying the foundation of that generous culture which distinguished him among his contemporaries. "From his earliest boyhood," says Boccaccio, "having already learned the rudiments of letters, he gave himself and all his time, not to youthful lust and indolence, after the fashion of the nobles of to-day, lolling at ease in the lap of his mother, but to continued study, in his native city, of the liberal arts, so that he became exceedingly expert therein."[3] Lionardo confirms this opinion: "In his boyhood he received a liberal education under

---

[1] *Vita Nuova*, II. Norton's translation. [2] *Ibid*.
[3] Dinsmore: *Aids to the Study of Dante*, p. 75.

teachers of letters, and at once gave evidence of a great natural capacity equal to excellent things." [1] But his studious tastes did not absorb him so exclusively that Beatrice was forgotten. "I, in my boyhood, often went seeking her, and saw her of such noble and praiseworthy deportment, that truly of her might be said that word of the poet Homer, 'She seems not a daughter of mortal man, but of God.'" [2]

At this time there dwelt in Florence a man of notable influence and authority, Brunetto Latini by name, "a great philosopher, and a perfect master in rhetoric, understanding both how to speak well, and how to write well." A contemporary, Villani,[3] accorded him the high praise of being "the beginner and master in refining the Florentines, and in teaching them how to speak well and how to guide and rule our republic according to policy." His literary productions were a "good and useful book called 'The Treasure,' and 'The Little Treasure,' and 'The Key to the Treasure,' and many other books in philosophy, and concerning vices and virtues." Dante's description of the meeting with him in hell is a passage of notable power and beauty.[4] As Latini died in Florence in the year 1294, being then over eighty years of age, he was in the fullness of his fame and vigor when Dante's mind was opening to the worth of learning and the beauties of literature. Their relations must have been intimate, for he declares, on meeting the shade of Latini in hell, "Hour by hour

[1] *Op. cit.*, p. 116.   [2] *Vita Nuova*, II.
[3] *Chronicles of Villani*, translated by Selfe and Wicksteed, p. 312.
[4] *Inferno*, xv.

you taught me how a man makes himself eternal." [1] "Ad ora ad ora" indicates that the influence was transmitted through many and repeated contacts, that it taught the writer the path of eternal honor testifies to its nobility. Youth could pay no finer homage to age. From the conversation we may also infer that Latini cast Dante's horoscope and predicted for him a brilliant future. "If thou follow thy star," he says, "thou shalt not miss the glorious port, if, in the fair life, I discerned aright."

At the close of his eighteenth year the event occurred that kindled the fires of poetry in Dante's soul. His description of the Lady of the Salutation has become classic. "When so many days had passed that nine years were exactly complete since the above described apparition of this most gentle lady, on the last of these days it happened that this wonderful lady appeared to me, clothed in purest white, between two gentle ladies who were of greater age; and, passing along a street, turned her eyes toward that place where I stood very timidly; and by her ineffable courtesy, which is to-day rewarded in the eternal world, saluted me with such virtue that it seemed to me then that I saw all the bounds of bliss. The hour of her most sweet salutation was precisely the ninth of that day; and since it was the first time that her words came to my ears, I took in such sweetness, that, as it were intoxicated, I turned away from the folk; and betaking myself to the solitude of my own chamber, I sat down to think of this most courteous lady." [2]

[1] *Inferno*, xv, 55 ff.   [2] *Vita Nuova*, III.

PERIOD OF YOUTH

III. THE SWEET NEW STYLE

The casual salutation which Beatrice bestowed upon Dante that golden day awoke the slumbering fires of his soul. It is the old story of love awakening genius. Retiring to his chamber the youth wrote a sonnet which he sent to a circle of poets in Florence.

"To every heart which the sweet pain doth move,
    And unto which these words may now be brought
    For true interpretation and kind thought,
Be greeting in our Lord's name, which is Love.
Of those long hours wherein the stars, above,
    Wake and keep watch, the third was almost naught,
    When Love was shown me with such terrors fraught
As may not carelessly be spoken of.
He seemed like one who is full of joy, and had
    My heart within his hand, and on his arm
    My lady, with a mantle round her, slept;
Whom, (having wakened her) anon he made
    To eat that heart; she ate as fearing harm.
    Then he went out; and as he went, he wept." [1]

Poetry was in that day much affected by the young men of talent and culture. The inspiration to song had come into Tuscany by way of Sicily from the troubadours of Provence. The minstrels of southern France had sung of love, feudal and courtly, in language stiff with flattery and insincere compliments. The Italians of central Italy who wore the singing robes were not only more sincere and deep-souled than the Provençals, they were for the most part learned men. They combined philosophy with their passion, and

[1] Rossetti: *Dante and his Circle.*

the songs they sang were more spiritual; celebrating the glory of a metaphysical ideal rather than the charms of a lady of flesh and blood.

It was Guido Guinicelli who uttered the first fresh note whose beauty and originality not only marked him as a lyric poet of rare ability, but attracted other singers who imitated his sweet and graceful rhymes of love. The school of poetry which he inaugurated had two distinguishing characteristics; its ideals were spiritual, and were expressed with a passion and simplicity which were absent from the poets of the old school. In the sweet new style the woman loved is a symbol of truth and beauty, whose gracious spell interprets to the lover the loftiest good and persuades him to seek the pure heights of blessedness. Love is purged of all sensuality; it is holy and spiritual. Poetry thus becomes the utterance of the soul's divinest yearnings, rather than the vehicle through which a love-sick heart pours its plaint.

There was in Florence at this time a group of young gallants who assiduously cultivated the Muse. They formed a cult of Love. Love ethereal, beauteous, divine, was personified in some fair woman, who was the source of grace, and of all sweet, ennobling and heavenly influences. To her the lover paid his court, expressing his idealized passion in a tender and lofty style which breathed the spirit of knightly honor. One of the most conspicuous of this group was Guido Cavalcanti, a scion of one of the most ancient families of Florence, distinguished for personal beauty, renowned for varied and brilliant intellectual gifts, and honored for his impetuous nobility of soul. Although full of courage and courtesy, he was a lover of solitude and was devoted to study. Whatever he did, a chronicler tells us, he could do better than any one else. Withal he was abundantly rich. Many of his poems have come down to us, and are found excellently translated in Rossetti's "Dante and his Circle." The verse of so fine and chivalrous a spirit could not fail to be pure and elevated, while his style is natural, facile, and of poetic charm. Although retaining the loftiness of his ideals, his susceptible and unstable heart made him an inconstant lover.

Next to him in talents and accomplishments was Cino de Sinibaldi da Pistoia, five years Dante's junior, and in later life a writer of sweet sonnets. Prosperity was his portion. Becoming famous for legal as well as literary attainments, he is commemorated in an interesting monument which still stands in the Cathedral of Pistoia. To this group belonged also Lapo Gianni, Dino Frescobaldi, Guido Orlandi, and Cecco Angiolieri. These last two Rossetti well characterizes as the "bore" and the "scamp." With all their high pretensions this group of poets seem to have been very mortal. The best of them found it difficult to

> "breathe in that fine air,
> That pure severity of perfect light."

They frequently fell from the height of the ideal to the common levels of the amorous passion, and were continually chiding each other for inconstancy to the chosen lady. One has but to read their sonnets, odes, and ballads to feel how immeasurably Dante surpasses them all in depths of feeling, felicity of versification, range of talent, height and steadiness of moral passion. In that sphere of exalted sentiment to which they occasionally ascended he held a strong and sustained wing and at times swept up into a higher ether than was possible to their flight.

IV. GROWTH OF DANTE'S PASSION

According to what seems to have been the custom of the time, Dante sent this first sonnet of which we have knowledge to the different members of this group, asking for its interpretation. The sonnet, both in conception and style, so clearly identified Dante with the new school of poetry, that Guido Cavalcanti in his reply answered, "All worth in my opinion, thou hast seen." "And this," says Dante, "was the beginning of a friendship between him and me," a friendship so sympathetic that the poet considered Guido the first of his friends. Dante da Maiano, however, who clung to the old traditions, ill-naturedly scoffed. He felt that one who had such fine visions needed a purgative.

> "To expel this overplus
> Of vapor, which hath made thy speech to err,
> See that thou lave and purge thy stomach soon."

The strength and intensity of his passion, Dante affirms, began to affect his health. He became so frail and feeble that his appearance was grievous to many of his friends. One day in church he was looking so intently at Beatrice that his friends, mistaking the object of his

PERIOD OF YOUTH

gaze, supposed him to be looking at another maiden, and the poet, being comforted at their error, resolved to make the other a screen protecting the real object of his affections, and with this lady he dissembled for months and years. In order to carry out the deception he wrote for this lady of the screen certain trifles in rhyme; only to Beatrice did he feel himself bound by strange, mystical ties. One day he assembled the names of sixty of the most beautiful ladies in Florence and composed an epistle in the form of a "serventese," and it fell out marvelously that the name of the blessed one would not bear to stand but as the ninth in the number among the names of these ladies.

To the young poet's dismay the lady whom he had used for a defense removed to a distant place, and to keep his secret the better Dante wrote a sonnet as though deeply grieved. Knowing that the first lady for whom he had feigned love would not return, in order still to guard his secret the poet chose another, and so zealously did he celebrate the charms of this second gentle lady that many people spoke of it beyond the terms of courtesy. Because of this injurious talk, Beatrice, passing a certain place, denied to Dante her most sweet recognition. The poet pauses a moment in his narrative to declare the virtue which her salutation wrought in him. "I say that, whenever she appeared in any place, in the hope of her marvelous salutation there no longer remained to me an enemy: nay a flame of charity possessed me, which made me pardon every one who had done me wrong." In a dream occurring in the mystic ninth hour of the day, Love, disguised as a youth in the whitest raiment, appeared to him with the command to address his lady directly, telling her of his unswerving fidelity. This Lord of Noblemen uses some words which are extremely interesting as indicative of the type of Dante's genius and as forecasting its development. "I am," he says, "as the centre of a circle to which the parts of the circumference bear an equal relation; but thou art not so." The bent of Dante's mind was decidedly mathematical. Instinctively he conceived of spiritual truth in the symbols of that science. This quality which gave shape to the "Paradiso" and the form and language of geometry to the Beatific Vision here makes a pronounced appearance. On discovering that his love is selfish he thinks of it as out of centre. To have a new intelligence of its meaning, and an inner peace, he must ennoble and rightly centre it. From this period the circle with love as its centre became the symbol of all perfection.

Soon after this experience, attending a wedding feast with a friend, a wonderful premonitory trembling seized him, and looking up he saw among the ladies this most gentle Beatrice. Perceiving his extreme confusion the ladies, including Beatrice, began to mock him. Led by a friend from the room, he exclaimed, "I have held my feet on that part of life beyond which no man can go with intent to return."

Some eminent biographers of the poet attribute his distress to the fact that this feast was connected with the marriage of Beatrice herself to Simone de' Bardi. This conclusion seems unwarranted, for Dante clearly indicates that it was a surprise to him to find Beatrice

PERIOD OF YOUTH

in attendance. Others suggest that this was the poet's first meeting with her after her marriage.

As this was their first meeting since he had pleaded with her to restore to him her sweet salutation, and her reply had been mockery, his extreme confusion and humiliation are not strange. This experience marks a deepening of the poet's sentiment. Heretofore he has been toying with his love, using it as a means of training his poetic gifts. He has been an artist nurturing his passion in the interest of his song. Now he comes more completely under the sway of his lady. Having more genuine emotions, he sloughs off something of artificiality from his verses and compels them to express more naturally his real feelings. The next three sonnets from his pen bear the marks of greater sincerity. Beatrice still withholding her salutation, the youthful poet, having sufficiently disclosed his feelings and condition, resolves to find his beatitude in praising his lady.

This selection of a nobler theme for his verse is so distinctly noted that it serves as the opening of a new section of the "Vita Nuova," and introduces a new quality in his work. The loftier subject proves more difficult, "And thinking much on this," he writes, "I seemed to myself to have undertaken a theme too lofty for me, so that I dared not begin: and then I tarried some days with the desire to speak, and with fear of beginning." [1] More careful and prolonged thought strengthens his powers. Thereafter his pen, instead of following the models of former poets, kept close to the movements of the dictator love. From this greater

[1] *Vita Nuova*, xviii.

faithfulness to nature came "the sweet new style," and Dante's mastery of the graceful rhymes of love. The first fruits appeared in the canzone beginning: "Ladies that have intelligence of Love." In these verses the great poet stands revealed. The 'prentice days are drawing to a close. The shackled imagination is beginning to feel its power of flight. This canzone ever remained a favorite with Dante. The naturalness and grace of its lines seem to have won for it popularity in Florence and to have brought a good measure of fame to its author.

With this canzone, which fitly opens the second section of the "Vita Nuova," the burden of Dante's song changes from an analysis of his own emotions to the praise of Beatrice; the nature of Beatrice becomes exalted in his thought.|Heretofore, his love, though pure, was earthly, now it is spiritualized. The apotheosis of Beatrice commences. He conceives her to be a miracle, a soul whose splendors fare even to heaven; she is one for whom God's chosen pray: those who gaze upon her are ennobled; whosoever speaks with her can never come to ill. The loftier theme kindles the poet's imaginative energies, and unseals the deeper fountains of his spiritual nature. The change in his poetic power is further emphasized by the adoption of a "nuova rima." Soon after he wrote the sweet sonnet, "Love and the gentle heart are the selfsame thing." Later, in what Gaspary calls one of the most fragrant blossoms of Italian lyrical poetry, the will came to him to show how his most gentle lady both awakened and created love and he devised the sonnet beginning:

"Within her eyes my lady beareth love."[1] Not many days after writing this sonnet the death of Beatrice's father called forth two more sonnets upon the sorrow of his lady. Next we read of a grievous infirmity afflicting the young poet, and, upon the ninth day of his illness, his own enfeebled life suggested the reflection, "It must needs be that the most gentle Beatrice will sometime die." Then in his solemn fantasy the sun grew dark, the stars sombre, birds fell dead out of the sky, and there were great earthquakes. He beheld the dead body of his lady whose aspect of humility seemed to say: "Now do I behold the beginning of peace." Afterwards being healed of his infirmity, Dante describes his doleful yet prophetic imaginings in the most perfect poem of his youth. This canzone begins with the words:

"A lady pitiful and young in years."[2]

Sitting one day in a certain place, Dante saw coming toward him the lady of his first friend, Guido Cavalcanti, followed by Beatrice. In the order of their coming the poet conjectured a mystic significance which he communicated in a sonnet to his friend. This was soon followed by one of the most beautiful of Italian sonnets, in which the poet describes the sweet and gracious influence of his lady upon all who knew her. In another sonnet he relates how her virtue wrought in other ladies, and, to complete the description of her influence by celebrating its effects upon himself, Dante began a canzone with the words:

"So long hath love retained me at his hest."

[1] *Vita Nuova*, xxi. [2] *Ibid.*, xxiii.

"I was yet full of the design of this canzone, and had completed this above written stanza thereof, when the Lord of Justice called this most gentle one to glory, under the banner of that holy queen Mary, whose name was ever spoken with greatest reverence by this blessed Beatrice."[1]

The reader naturally expects an outburst of grief that will, at least for a moment, sweep away the iron restraints of Dante's self-control; but instead we are calmly informed that although to treat of her departure would be pleasing, yet there are three reasons why this is impossible. It is no part of the design of the book, his pen is not sufficient to treat thereof, and he could not describe her death without praising himself, which would be blameworthy. Why he could not recount the death of his lady is evident for his purpose has been to reveal his life as it was influenced by love. To treat of her departure would be to do what heretofore he had not done, that is, relate events in the life of Beatrice. The third reason has given rise to much conjecture. What occurred at Beatrice's death of which Dante could not write without self-praise? The most plausible answer seems to be that Beatrice, who had refused Dante her salutation, and, after he had sent her a ballad affirming his fidelity, mocked in the presence of others, now in her last hours expressed interest in him and his future. This supposition is warranted by the solicitude Dante ascribes to her in the "Divina Commedia." In the second canto of the "Inferno,"[2] she declares that her interest in Dante moved her to leave the seats of the

[1] *Vita Nuova*, XXIX.　　　　[2] *Inferno*, II, 52–117.

PERIOD OF YOUTH 83

blessed to summon Virgil to the rescue of her friend. And in the thirtieth canto of the "Purgatorio"[1] is the statement that she visited the portals of the dead for his salvation. If we consider the change of attitude between the mocking Beatrice of the "Vita Nuova" and the solicitous Beatrice of the "Divina Commedia," together with Dante's statement that he could not describe the circumstance of her departure without praise to himself, we are not without justification in assuming that at the time of her death her attitude changed toward him. If Dante is restrained both by modesty and the limitations of his theme from writing of the departure of the blessed one, he can at least affirm her significance to his heart and thought. This he does by showing that she is a nine. She died on the ninth day of the month, in the ninth month of the year, and in the year when the perfect number ten had been completed for the ninth time. That is she died an hour after sunset on the 8th of June, 1290. He also declares that at her birth the nine heavens were in perfect relation. But she was not only accompanied by the mystical blessings of the number nine, she was a nine, that is, a miracle, for her being was rooted in the marvelous Trinity, even as the number nine is three multiplied by itself. The sweet lady of the salutation is now apotheosized into a miracle of God.

With this change in his life, a new section of the "Vita Nuova" appropriately begins it. It is indicated by the solemn words of Jeremy the prophet, "Quo modo sedet sola civitas plena populo! facta est quasi

[1] *Purgatorio*, xxx, 139-41.

vidua domina gentium." To Dante Florence was indeed desolate, despoiled of every dignity. As a vent to his grief the poet wrote a letter to the chief men of the city beginning with the sentence quoted above. That his grief was genuine is seen in the canzone which Cino da Pistoia wrote to him at this time. We quote a few lines from Rossetti's translation: [1]

> "However shouldst thou see the lovely face
> If any desperate death should once be thine?
> From justice so condign
> Withdraw thyself even now; that in the end
> Thy heart may not offend
> Against thy soul, which in the holy place,
> In heaven, still hopes to see her and to be
> Within her arms. Let this hope comfort thee."

Farther on in the poem are lines which indicate that the attractions of Beatrice were remarked by others:

> "Even as she seemed a wonder here below,
> On high she seemeth so, —
> Yea, better known, is there more wondrous yet."

Dante's praises of her had evidently won him honor in Florence:

> "Of thee she entertains the blessed throngs,
> And says to them: 'While yet my body thrave
> On earth, I gat much honor which he gave,
> Commending me in his commended songs.'
> Also she asks alway of God our Lord
> To give thee peace according to His word."

His first sorrow being somewhat spent he composed a most sweet and affecting canzone, addressed to dames

[1] *Early Italian Poets*, Temple Classics, p. 265.

and damosels who have intelligence of love. After this canzone was devised there came to him one who was his friend next to the first, and so near in blood to his lady that none could be nearer — probably her brother — asking for some poem on a lady who was dead. Dante complied both with a sonnet and a canzone.

On the first anniversary of the death of Beatrice, the poet was sketching an angel upon certain tablets, having her in mind.[1] While he was drawing, certain men to whom it was meet to do honor stood by his side, observing for some time before he was aware of them. Dante arose, and saluting them, said, "Another was just now with me, and on that account I was in thought."

This incident throws light upon two accomplishments of Dante, his artistic ability and his unusual power of concentrated attention. "He drew exceeding well," affirms his early biographer, Lionardi Bruni. Cimabue was at the time the admiration of Florence. In the church of Santa Maria Novella was his famous picture of the Virgin and her Child, and the beauty of the angels who were grouped about the central figures had greatly impressed the art-loving people of Florence. The movement toward naturalness in art, inaugurated by the great artist, was so akin to Dante's effort at genuineness in poetry that it would be strange indeed if the young poet did not come under the influence of the older painter. The tradition that he as

---

[1] "You and I would rather see that angel,
 Painted by the tenderness of Dante,
 Would we not? than read a fresh Inferno."
  Browning: "One Word More."

well as Giotto studied under Cimabue may not be without foundation. His complete absorption in his task is the first recorded instance we have of that capacity of mental abstraction so extraordinary that the remembrance of it lingered long in tradition.

After this event the poet was standing filled with distressful thought when, lifting up his eyes, he saw a gentle lady, young and very beautiful, looking at him from a window with a face full of compassion. Her pitying gaze so wrought upon Dante's heart that he addressed to this lady of the window several sonnets. One day at noon, when the new love was beginning to usurp the place of the old, there arose in his mind a strong imagination in which he saw the glorified Beatrice in those crimson garments in which she first appeared to his eyes. This vision recalled him to himself, and the spell of the enchantress was broken.

The identity of the lady of the window has evoked much discussion, Fraticelli and Scartazzini going so far as to conjecture that she was none other than Gemma Donati, who afterwards became Dante's wife. It is a conjecture woven out of airy nothingness. There is far more reason for believing her to be the "pargoletta," the little girl, whom Beatrice scornfully mentioned in her rebuke,[1] an unidentified damsel for whom Dante felt a brief attachment.

In the closing sonnet of the "Vita Nuova" we can almost trace the apotheosis of Beatrice. We see Dante's spiritualizing imagination ascending into the lofty altitudes where the supreme resolve, out of which grew

[1] *Purgatorio*, XXXI, 59.

the "Divina Commedia," is born. Love, he affirms, is imparting a new power to his mind. His lady he beholds clothed in such splendor that in its light the pilgrim soul is amazed, blinded by her incomprehensible glory as the eye by the sun. Into her gentle face has come the splendor and majesty of the Eternal. The mortal is swallowed up of immortality. The spell which she has cast over one worshiping soul is seen expanding until it becomes the type of the revealed light of God. Her beauty is the splendor of all redemptive truth. More than the mediator to Dante's soul of life's higher ideals, she is now the mediator of God to all humanity. No other woman has ever been a symbol at once so divine and comprehensive. No other imagination ever took so bold a flight. It is not strange that Dante laid down his insufficient pen. In the presence of a Beatrice thus elevated and transfigured love sonnets and canzoni were inappropriate and impertinent. Years of study and statelier verse were needed for so high a theme. Out of this apotheosis of Beatrice was born a vision and a life resolve.

"After this sonnet, a wonderful vision appeared to me, in which I saw things which made me resolve to speak no more of this blessed one, until I could more worthily treat of her. And to attain to this, I study to the utmost of my power, as she truly knows. So that, if it shall please Him through whom all things live, that my life be prolonged for some years, I hope to say of her what has never been said of any woman. And then may it please Him who is the Lord of Grace, that my soul may go to behold the glory of its lady, namely, of that blessed Beatrice, who in glory looks upon the face of Him qui est per omnia sæcula benedictus (who is blessed forever)."[1]

V. DATE OF THE "VITA NUOVA"

The date when Dante gathered these poems and his comments into a little volume entitled "La Vita Nuova" can be fixed with reasonable assurance. The commentary is plainly much later than the poems, for meanings which he did not understand when he composed them are seen to be prophetic of what actually occurred. As events are related which took place more than a year after the death of Beatrice, the volume was not completed earlier than 1292. This date agrees with the statement of Boccaccio that "this glorious poet . . . while his tears were yet fresh for the death of his Beatrice, about his twenty-sixth year put together in a little volume, which he called the 'Vita Nuova,' certain small works, as sonnets and canzoni, made by him in rhyme at divers times and of marvelously beautiful writing at the head of each, severally and in order, the occasions which had moved him to make it, and adding at the end the divisions of each poem."[2] In the first treatise of the "Convivio" Dante confesses that the "Vita Nuova" was fervid and impassioned as suited the age at which it was written, for "in that I spoke before entrance upon the prime of manhood." As "prime of manhood" in his thought extended from the twenty-fifth to the forty-fifth years, he can only mean that the range of emotion contained therein pertains to the

[1] *Vita Nuova*, XLIII.   [2] Boccaccio: *Vita di Dante*, § 13.

PERIOD OF YOUTH

period of his youth. Probably somewhere between 1292 and 1295 he collected these poems, wrote his commentary, and dedicated this his first volume with all the pride of a young author to his first friend, Guido Cavalcanti.

Perchance the book did not then take its final form. It may be that there is truth in the interesting surmise of some writers that finishing touches were put upon it much later. In support of this assumption they maintain that the pilgrims mentioned in section XLI as on their way "to see the blessed image which Jesus Christ left to us as a likeness of his beautiful countenance" belonged to the throngs which passed through Florence in the Jubilee year 1300 on their way to behold the Veronica displayed in Saint Peter's.

This surmise has the further advantage of making Dante's wondrous vision of Beatrice, his return to her, and his lofty resolve to say of her what never was said of any woman, coincide with the awakening in the dark wood, which he places in the year 1300. According to this theory Dante wove together his lyrics with their prose explanation soon after the death of his lady. Time passed. He was engrossed in war, study, politics, and the active pursuits of life. In 1300 he awoke to find himself entangled in the political and ecclesiastical confusion of his day. Resolving to find a better way of life, he returned to those ideals and moods associated with the name of Beatrice. He began to plan the "Commedia," and by way of preparation revised the "Vita Nuova," moulding it in such wise as to make it a suitable introduction to his masterpiece.

This conjecture has the advantage of giving unity to Dante's life. It also saves the "wondrous vision" which closes the "Vita Nuova" from being what Scartazzini considered it to be — an inspiration having no lasting effect.

Whatever the date of the final recasting, the poet evidently desired the book to stand as an expression of the ardent and impassioned emotions of his youth.[1]

VI. THE TRUTH OF THIS SELF-REVELATION

Let not the reader conclude that Dante during the period covered by the "Vita Nuova" was merely an introspective idler, sauntering in the land of dreams. Italy was too turbulent and Florence too intense and unstable for that. Yet no echo of the strenuous life around him sounds in this little book. The "Vita Nuova" was not only his "new life," but his true life, and to learn what manner of youth he was we must observe him as he walks in his realm of gold. To what extent is this unique volume the transcript of actual experiences, and to what degree is it the creation of his own imagination?

The incidents recorded are probably true in their general outline, though not necessarily in detail. We may be confident that it was love which first smote the chords of his life and awoke the marvelous music of his genius. We may also feel assured that the event was that salutation of Beatrice which caused him to touch all the bounds of bliss. It is not improbable that an earlier meeting was afterwards recalled and given im-

[1] *Convivio*, I, 1.

portance to complete the allegorical and poetical significance of the whole. Believing as Dante did that the world perceived by the senses is but the medium through which the spiritual or real world communicates itself, he was in the habit of seeing in temporal events and experiences spiritual meaning. He was too truthful to invent facts, though he did not hesitate to employ all the skill of his intellect in forcing facts to fit into his scheme.

As we follow the narrative, the gradual unfolding of the poet's artistic and spiritual capacities are clearly discerned. In the first section of the volume, comprising the first ten poems, no powerful, elemental feelings are in evidence. The prevailing mood is one of delicate tenderness. The "marvelous boy" is indeed awakening to love, but he is more concerned with the artistic felicity of his phrases than with the expression of genuine passion. He is tuning his lyre, and imitating the best conventions of the day. These demand that he choose a lady to be the central figure of his verse. She must be of ideal beauty, serene and untouched by passion. Like other troubadours of love he is to find his happiness in his lady's salutation, and in the contemplation of her arresting charms. While to add zest to passion he may conceal her true name and feign love for another. All this Dante did in punctilious observance of the fashion of the day. The poems of the first section of the "Vita Nuova" differ from the best of those written by other singers of the times only in displaying the author's preëminent ability to apply the rules of his art. To an imaginative youth inexperienced in real sorrow "nothing 's so dainty sweet as lovely melancholy." It is the food with which poets in the larval state feed their genius. In this Dante differed from others not at all. That he was preoccupied with his emotions does not prove that they were profoundly affected, but only that he was young. He is indulging in the pose of passion. It is the artist more than the man that loves.

With the rebuke of Beatrice a deeper note in Dante's nature is touched. He found himself in that "part of life beyond which no man can go with the intent to return." He realizes that his love is not in the centre of the circle. His lady is no longer a toy for his fancy to fondle, nor his love for her a sentiment to be held in the interests of his art; it now becomes a genuine passion. The grace of her character reveals the goodness of God. She is a spiritual beauty and power hovering over his soul. The actual woman is hidden in the light with which his idealizing imagination has invested her.

Shelley, who in many respects resembled Dante, conceived for Emilia Viviani a similar Platonic and ideal love. He scarcely knew her, saw her rarely, and his feeling was not affected by her marriage. Such love is the familiar dream of poets. But Dante's imagination first swept into its heights and depths, and gave it noblest expression. With this new experience his verse became sincere, natural, beautiful.

At the death of his lady the spell was broken. The power that stirred the deeps of his soul was withdrawn. As a result the poems included in the third section are distinctly inferior to those of the second, with the exception of the one beginning:

"The eyes that grieve with pity for the heart,"

and the closing sonnet where the familiar theme calls forth and sustains his power.

The originality of the volume is found neither in the subject-matter nor in the poetical apparatus. Dante differed from the school of poets of which he was a member in the intensity of his imagination, his subtler truthfulness of expression, and the sustained nobility of his passion. He was also more deeply religious. By uniting a series of poems, which are milestones in the progress of his inner life, he produced not only the first book of artistic prose in the Italian language, but also its first introspective biography.

VII. THE SLOW DEVELOPMENT OF DANTE'S GENIUS

The "Vita Nuova" gives us ample evidence of the slow development of Dante's genius. In a hardy plant the blossom comes late. The poet was eighteen years of age when he wrote the first sonnet he cared to preserve. He was about twenty-seven when the last sonnet of the book was completed. The early metrical pieces are stiff with conventionality and show scarcely a sign of unusual poetic merit. His most beautiful rhymes were written in the interval between his twentieth and twenty-fifth years. Of the lyrics composed before the death of Beatrice, and therefore before Dante's twenty-sixth year, we have preserved to us in the "Vita Nuova" and elsewhere some twenty-nine of undoubted authenticity, and three about which there is some dispute. At twenty-five he had written less than a thousand lines which he or his friends thought fit to perpetuate. Keats in his twenty-fourth year produced four times as many lines as Dante wrote in seven years; at twenty-six he ended his life-work, having given the world three volumes of verse, and "by the faultless force and profound subtlety of his deep and cunning instinct for the absolute expression of absolute beauty" won a place with the high immortals. At the age when Keats died Dante had struck one note with purity and force, but he had displayed no such manifold richness and maturity of genius as Keats.

Shelley at twenty-eight had written "Queen Mab," "Alabaster," "The Revolt of Islam," "Cenci," and "Prometheus Unbound." Before he was thirty his feet had been caught in the snare of the dark Fowler, yet he had won enduring fame. Dante at the same age was just formulating his life-work.

At twenty-four Byron had published "Childe Harold," and had awakened to find himself famous. "The Ancient Mariner" was in print when Coleridge was twenty-six. Browning at twenty-three had given the world "Paracelsus," in which the finished outlines of his philosophy of life appear. Tennyson at twenty-three had published two volumes of poems on a large variety of themes, and at twenty-four his mind began to brood upon "In Memoriam."

If we climb still higher the Mount of Song to the summits occupied by those who are more usually compared to the Florentine in genius, we find that at twenty-five Goethe had given to the world "Götz" and "Werther." Milton had written in his twenty-first year that incomparable ode "On the Morning of Christ's Nativity." In his twenty-fifth he had given classic expression to both the joyous and persuasive moods. Before he was thirty he had uttered the strong notes of "Arcades," "Comus," and "Lycidas."

Shakespeare's genius ripened slowly. At thirty he was far more of an apprentice than Dante. "Venus and Adonis" — "the first heir of my invention" — written before his twenty-seventh year, manifests his nimbleness of wit, his joy in beauty, the vigor and playfulness of his fancy, but gives no hint of a mind of amazing resource and masterful power. "The Rape of Lucrece," published when the poet was thirty, although containing lines "all gold seven times refined," has all the faults of youth.

The slow unfolding of Dante's gift of song was partly due to the conditions under which he lived. He stood at the close of one era and at the beginning of another. There was not a multitude of poets immediately about him and before him, celebrating every phase of beauty, and early awakening to life every chord of his sensitive nature. On the contrary, between him and any singer of imperishable name stretched many dark centuries. The Tuscan air was not vibrant as our own with the notes of many singers. He was born into no such dazzling and stimulating heritage as greeted Tennyson and Browning.

The slenderness of Dante's poetical output was due in part also to his theory of poetry. He was not provoked to burst into song at the sight of an urn, or a sunset, or a daffodil. Such objects in his judgment might be the ornaments of poetry, not its subject-matter. One theme only was worthy of the muse, and that was Love. This theory limited his interests and restricted the exercise of his talents.

But especially is the explanation to be found in the nature of Dante's own genius. He was introspective. The beauty of the external world struck the soul of Keats into music. Shelley would have written a Marseillaise to cheer a liberty-loving people in those tremulous times. But it was the world within that inspired Dante, and he must needs wait upon the slow footsteps of experience. An introspective poet of necessity matures as slowly as a metaphysician. But slow as was the unfolding of his genius, these early lyrics are not without their prophecy of coming power. "Throughout the 'Vita Nuova,'" says Rossetti, "there is a strain like the first falling murmur which reaches the ear in some remote meadow, and prepares us to look upon the sea."

VIII. CHARACTER AND ABILITY

As the death of Beatrice closes a distinct period of the poet's life, it may be well to pause a moment to form a judgment of his character and abilities, ere we follow him into the stormy and perplexing years which ensue.

His nature as he reveals it to us is one of singular elevation and purity. In the book which records what he calls his true life there is no bitterness, no enmity. His dream world is unshadowed by evil thoughts or envious impulses. Every woman he cares to write about is a "gentil donna," every man a chivalrous friend. Unstained was the love which he cherished for his lady. The beauty which attracted him in her and in

PERIOD OF YOUTH

all women was spiritual. The virtues he most admired in them were humility, gentleness, and the "ornaments of a meek and quiet spirit."

He asserts that the dominant power that ruled his inner life was love, but it was such love as dwells only in a heart "pure, true, and clean from guile." "Love and the gentle heart are the same thing." This love which stirs his own breast and whose glory is revealed in Beatrice is a ray of light from God, the source of all love. Only the virtuous can feel its lordship and reveal its splendor. Shakespeare at the same period of his life — the period of the sonnets — was concerned with the transitoriness of love. It cannot abide. It is "scarred by Time's imperious hand." Dante also reflected upon this phase, but what impressed him most was the divine nature and the redeeming power of love. It is of God and cleanses the heart of all impurity.

At this period he displays no unusual intellectual ability. In his verses there is no weight of original thought; they contain scarcely a quotable line; their power lying almost entirely in the sustained and elevated intensity of his passion. In these early pages he is a spirit "ethereal, flushed and like a throbbing star." The masculine strength so evident in the "Comedy" is not apparent here. Trouble will ere long transform this fine sensibility into fierce indignation and volcanic energy, but at present this young poet reveals himself as a dreamer, eager, gentle, full of loftiest aspirations.

Although abnormally sensitive his emotions are under the steady curb of his will. He writes as reason, as well as love, dictates. The qualities of literary expression which he cultivates are sincerity and delicate beauty. Yet now as ever afterwards he delights in technical subtleties and in finding and hiding meanings in facts and words. For even in these early years Dante is a mystic. The seen is the thin veil hiding the supreme spiritual realities, and the divine intention is half-revealed and half-concealed in all things.

The characteristic quality of his imagination is disclosed in these early days. The very first sonnet is a description of a vision. Love appeared to him, not as a sentiment, or a mood of mind, but visibly as a shining god, holding a flaming heart and a sleeping lady. Again Love comes "like a pilgrim lightly clad and in mean raiment." At another time he sat by Dante's bed in the form of a youth "clothed in white raiment, and very thoughtful," weeping piteously. And at last there came a vision so wonderful that it sealed his lips and won the consecration of his life. His imagination was more than insight, it spontaneously visualized his emotions, thoughts, memories, and ideals, so that they stood before him in crystalline clearness and compelling power.

IX. AS HE APPEARED TO THE FLORENTINES

One would err in thinking of Dante during this period as a lovelorn recluse, moodily brooding over his emotions. Both tradition and a few established facts give us a very different impression of him. "He did not," says his biographer Lionardi Bruni, "renounce the world and shut himself up to ease, but associated and

PERIOD OF YOUTH

conversed with youths of his own age. Courteous, spirited, and full of courage, he took part in every youthful exercise; and in the great and memorable battle of Campaldino, Dante, young but well esteemed, fought vigorously, mounted and in the front rank. Here he incurred the utmost peril, for the first engagement was between the cavalry, in which the horse of the Aretines defeated and overthrew with such violence the horse of the Florentines that the latter, repulsed and routed, were obliged to fall back on their infantry. . . . Dante gives a description of the battle in one of his letters. He states that he was in the fight, and draws a plan of the field. . . . Dante fought valiantly for his country on this occasion. And I could wish that our Boccaccio had made mention of this virtue rather than of love at nine, and the like trivialities which he tells of this great man. But what use is there in speaking? 'The tongue points where the tooth pains,' and 'Whose taste runs to drinking, his talk runs to wines.' When Dante returned home from this battle, he devoted himself more fervently than ever to his studies, yet omitted naught of polite and social intercourse. It was remarkable that, although he studied incessantly, none would have supposed from his happy manner and youthful way of speaking that he studied at all."[1]

Probably Dante followed the fortunes of this campaign and was present at the capitulation of the fortress of Caprona in August, 1289. Two passages in the "Divina Commedia" seem reminiscent of his military

[1] Dinsmore: *Aids to the Study of Dante*, pp. 117-18.

experiences;[1] while in the "Inferno" he explicitly declares that he was with the troops before Arezzo. "I have seen ere now horsemen moving camp, and set out to charge and make their muster, and sometimes fall back in their retreat. I have seen skirmishers overrun your land, O Arentines, and I have seen the starting of raids, the onset of tournaments, and the running of jousts, now with trumpets, and now with bells, with drums and with signals from strong-holds."[2]

"From the aforesaid victory," writes Villani, "the city of Florence was much exalted, and rose to good and happy state, the best which it had seen until these times, and it increased greatly in people and in wealth, for every one was gaining by some merchandise, art or trade; and it continued in peaceful and tranquil state for many years after, rising every day. And by reason of gladness and well being, every year, on the first day of May, they formed bands and companies of gentle youths, clad in new raiment, and raised new pavilions covered with cloth and silk and with wooden walls, in divers parts of the city; and likewise there were bands of women and of maidens going through the city dancing in ordered fashion, and ladies, two by two, with instruments, and with garlands of flowers on their heads, continuing in pastimes and joyance, and at feasts and banquets."[3]

We cannot doubt that Dante entered with zest into the joy and activities of those eager days.

---

[1] *Inferno*, XXI, 94–96. *Purgatorio*, v, 92.
[2] *Inferno*, XXII, 1–8.
[3] *Chronicles of Villani*, Selfe and Wicksteed, pp. 293–94.

NOTE ON
THE IDENTITY OF BEATRICE

THE identity of Beatrice, who cast such a powerful spell over Dante's mind and heart, has caused much animated debate.[1] Boccaccio, writing about 1350, certainly not later than 1364, declares that she was the daughter of a near neighbor. His description merits a full quotation:

"In that season wherein the sweetness of heaven reclothes the earth with all its adornments, and makes her all smiling with varied flowers scattered among green leaves, the custom obtained in our city that men and women should keep festival in different gatherings, each person in his own neighborhood. And so it chanced that among others, Folco Portinari, a man held in great esteem among his fellow citizens, on the first day of May gathered his neighbors in his house for a feast. Now among these came the aforementioned Alighieri, followed by Dante, who was still in his ninth year; for little children are wont to follow their fathers, especially to places of festival. And mingling here in the house of the feast-giver with others of his own age, of whom there were many, both boys and girls, when the first tables had been served he boyishly entered with the others into the games, so far as his tender age permitted.

"Now amid the throng of children was a little daughter of the aforesaid Folco, whose name was Bice, though he always called her by her full name, Beatrice. She was, it may be, eight years old, very graceful for her age, full gentle and pleasing in her actions, and much more serious and modest in her words and ways than her few years required. Her features were most delicate and perfectly proportioned, and, in addition to their beauty, full of such pure loveliness that many

---

[1] *Vide* Moore: *Studies in Dante*, vol. 11, art. "Beatrice." Also Toynbee's *Dante's Studies and Researches*, and Del Lungo's *Beatrice nella Vita e nella Poesia del Secolo XIII*.

thought her almost an angel. She, then, such as I picture her, or it may be far more beautiful, appeared at this feast to the eyes of Dante; not, I suppose, for the first time, but for the first time with the power to inspire him with love. And he, though still a child, received the lovely image of her into his heart with so great affection that it never left him from that day forward so long as he lived." [1]

In his commentary on "Inferno," II, 70, Boccaccio states that his information about Beatrice Portinari was derived by him from a person worthy of trust, who not only knew her, but was very closely connected with her (fu per consanguintà strettissima a lei).[2] He also affirms that she was the wife of Simone de' Bardi, and died in 1290.

The association of the name of Beatrice Portinari with Dante justifies us in recording what knowledge of her and her family the patient research of scholars has obtained. The records show that Folco Portinari was a prominent and philanthropic citizen of Florence. His will dated the 15th day of January, 1288, reads as follows: "Humbly do I commend my soul unto the living and true God, and I do desire to be buried in the chapel of my hospital of Santa Maria Nuova. Unto God, unto the Lord Jesus Christ, and unto the blessed Virgin Mary, His Mother, do I offer the aforesaid hospital and chapel, or church, as an atonement for the sins of myself and my family, and for the service of the sick and the poor." He then bequeaths certain sums to brotherhoods, monasteries and hospitals, both in the city and country. Provision is also made for his wife Madonna Cilia dei Caponsacchi, and for his sister Nuta. Each of his four unmarried daughters, Vanna, Fia, Margherita, and Castoria are remembered. Then follows the clause all important to us: "Also to Mistress Bice, my daughter, the wife of Messer Simone de' Bardi, I leave fifty Florentine pounds (libras L ad florenos)." The other daughter, Madonna Ravignana, being dead, he bequeathed an

---

[1] Dinsmore: *Aids to the Study of Dante*, p. 77. [2] *Ibid.*, p. 67.

equal sum to her son Nicola. He next names his sons Manetto, Ricovero, Pigello, Gherardo, and Jacopo, as his heirs. The three latter being minors, are entrusted together with the younger daughters to the guardianship of the two elder brothers, associating with them Messer Bindo de' Cerchi, Messer Vieri di Torrigiano de' Cerchi, and two of his own kindred. He asserts at the end that he is "healthy in mind and body, thanks be to God."

"A few months later, on June 23d, Folco himself first opened his beloved hospital, with solemn ceremony, assigning to it lands, furniture, and sacred vessels and vestments, causing himself and his descendants to be invested as perpetual patrons by Andrea de' Mozzi, Bishop of Florence, and installing the first rector with the ringing of bells and the chanting of the Te Deum in the new church. A year and a half later, on the last day of 1289, the good Folco was lost to his children and his poor forever. His tomb, bearing the coat of arms and an inscription in Gothic lettering, remained in the church for several centuries, watched over by a picture of the Virgin, by Cimabue, which Folco himself had placed over the altar. To this, in course of time, succeeded an 'Annunciation' by Andrea del Castagno, and eventually a painting by Alessandro Allori, representing the Virgin Mother surrounded by the saints. Neither the chapel nor the original hospital, afterwards called the Hospital of San Matteo, are in existence at the present day, and traces of both the one and the other have been lost sight of beneath the mass of notarial documents preserved in the Archives of Contracts. The only one of all the Portinari tombs which has survived is that of Folco himself, and well it deserved to escape destruction. Reconstructed with reverent care in modern times this has been placed in the church of Sant' Egidio, the church of the now existing hospital of Santa Maria Nuova. Yet, while the scene of his charity thus once more possesses the presence of its tutelary genius, but few know of this tomb, or rather cenotaph, which bears the following inscription; *His iacet Fulcus de Portinarius qui fuit fundator et edificator (h)uius ecclesie et ospitalis S. Marie Nove et decessit anno MCCLXXXIX die XXXI decembris. Cuius anima pro Dei misericordia requiescat in pace.*" [1]

Besides his philanthropies we know that Folco Portinari was actively interested in the political fortunes of the city, and his name appears among the "fourteen" elected March, 1282, by Cardinal Latino to cement the peace between Guelf and Ghibelline. In August of the same year he represented the quarter of Porta San Piero and the Guild of Merchants in the Priori delle Arti. Again his name is found among the Priors in 1285 and 1287.

It is only in the will of her father that Beatrice emerges into the clear light of history. This establishes her existence, her husband's name, and her social status in January, 1288. We have no record of the date of her marriage, nor of the time of her death. The fact that her father in his will made no reference to her children would lead us to surmise that she had none at the time. This supposition is strengthened by what knowledge we have of her husband. There are records to show that one Messer Simone di Geri de' Bardi, in 1290, during the Guelf war with Arezzo was councilor of the Commune with Messer Amerigo di Nerbona. He was of the Donati faction and their representative with the Conti Guidi. Of him records exist until 1315. Isidoro del Lungo, who has examined the mercantile books of the Bardi, thinks that beyond doubt this Simone was the husband of Beatrice and he further affirms that no record or document of any kind has yet been found to prove him possessed of offspring. Associating the first supposition that Folco's daughter had no children in 1288 with the fact that the Bardi records contain no mention of offspring to Messer Simone di Geri, the

---

[1] Isidoro del Lungo: *Women of Florence*, pp. 119, 120; translated by Mary C. Steegmann.

THE TOMB OF FOLCO PORTINARI

supposed husband of Beatrice Portinari, and we have an argument, or the atmosphere for an argument, that the lady of the "Vita Nuova," whose death occurred two years and a half after 1288, in June, 1290, is identical with the Beatrice of the will. Yet there is no document to prove that the wife of Messer Simone died on this date, and there is no evidence to the contrary.

The date of Folco Portinari's death, December 31, 1289, harmonizes well with the passage in the "Vita Nuova" which describes the death of Beatrice's father.

A further argument adduced to establish the identity of Folco's daughter Beatrice with the lady of the salutation is the statement contained in a commentary on the "Divina Commedia," supposed to have been written by Dante's own son Pietro. Among the manuscripts in the collection of Lord Ashburnham was discovered a recension of this commentary, containing these words: "It must first be said, however, that a certain lady, named Madonna Beatrice, greatly esteemed for her manners and her beauty, did actually dwell in Florence during the life time of the author, being born of a family of certain Florentine citizens called Portinari. Whilst she lived this lady was admired and loved by the author Dante, who composed many songs in her praise: and after that she was dead, in order to exalt her name, it is thought she appeareth many times in his poem in the allegory and type of Theology."

If the recension was by Pietro's own hand, and he is here stating the belief of Dante's family, then his testimony is decisive. But in his original work the identity of Beatrice is not mentioned. If, therefore, this recension is by him, he would seem to have been ignorant of the solution of so interesting a problem in the earlier book, and to have added the information on Boccaccio's authority, or on the authority of Boccaccio's informant. It is more probable, however, that some unknown person inserted the positive statement while copying the original. The passage quoted above is of such doubtful authority, and even if authentic conveys information which was evidently acquired not from Dante himself but from some third person, that it can hardly be credited as an independent authority.

The chief justification for identifying Beatrice Portinari with the lady of Dante's mind is the trustworthiness of the person who gave Boccaccio his information. Isidoro Del Lungo [1] claims that among the agents of the bank of the Bardi from 1336 to 1338 was a certain "Boccaccio Ghellini (Chellini) of Certaldo." Another was a member of the Portinari family, Ubertino di Gherardo di Folco, who lived in Paris to look after the Bardi affairs, and died there in 1339. Gherardo was the name of a brother of Beatrice, thus making Ubertino her nephew. Giovanni Boccaccio was probably in Paris at several periods prior to 1339, and if, as Del Lungo believes, the Boccaccio of Certaldo above mentioned was his father, he might have obtained from Ubertino the statement or the surmise that the glorious symbol in the "Divina Commedia" was Beatrice Portinari. This is all the more credible for Boccaccio states in his commentary on the Inferno that he received the identification from a near relative of the lady.[2]

Even if the facts are as stated, the credibility of the witness is somewhat impugned by his close kinship with Beatrice. The pride of the Portinari family would be flattered by the tradition that one of their number has been so nobly celebrated by a famous poet. Furthermore, as the Portinari and the Alighieri were near neighbors, and there was a Beatrice Portinari who might have incited this passion in Dante, what was at first a mere surmise might easily have become a cherished belief. Yet this would scarcely have been made

---

[1] *Beatrice nella Vita e nella Poesia del Secolo XIII*, p. 52.
[2] *Inferno*, II, Lez 8 (vol. I, p. 224). See also Dinsmore: *Aids to the Study of Dante*, p. 67.

and accepted unless the age of Beatrice Portinari and the date of her death corresponded very closely with the dates chronicled in the "Vita Nuova." Certitude in the matter cannot be reached. We may have opinions but not convictions. If Dante's contemporaries were puzzled about the identity of the lady of his mind, six hundred years have done little to enlighten us.

It is quite settled, however, that it was a maiden of flesh and blood who stirred the deeps of the lad's soul. This is assured by Dante's well-known habit of using the actual as a gateway into the spiritual, and by the extraordinary pains he takes to compel events and dates to fit into his scheme. A single illustration will suffice. Nine in Dante's system of thought is a sacred number. He was nine when he first met Beatrice. Nine years later her salutation led him to the bounds of bliss. But the date of her death caused him some difficulty. It occurred on the 8th of June, 1290. The year presents no problem, since 1290 is the year in which the perfect number ten was completed for the ninth time in that century. To have June appear the ninth month he had recourse to the reckoning of the Syrian calendar which makes the first month begin with the month Tisrin, which is our October. But to make the evening of the 8th of June appear as the ninth day he appeals to the Arabian calendar in which the evenings and the mornings make up each day, so that after sunset on June 8 it is the ninth day. Dante surely would not go to the elaborate trouble of appealing to calendars, the Arabian for the day, the Syrian for the month, and the Italian for the year, to secure the mystical number nine, were he not endeavoring to whip an uncompromising fact into his adopted scheme of thought.

Some basis of fact is necessary for an artist, but too many facts cramp his genius. "To have seen Beatrice two or three times," says Matthew Arnold, "to have spoken to her two or three times, to have felt her beauty and her charm; to have had the emotion of her marriage, her death — this was enough. Art requires a basis of fact, but it also desires to treat this basis with the utmost freedom; and this desire for the freest handling of its object is even thwarted when its object is too near, and too real. To have had his relations with Beatrice more positive, intimate, prolonged, to have had an affection for her into which there entered more of the life of this world, would have even somewhat impeded, one may say, Dante's free use of these relations for the purpose of art." [1]

Dante's Beatrice is as enigmatic as the "Mr. W. H." to whom Shakespeare's sonnets were dedicated. Both poets choose to hide the names in order to immortalize the influence of their ideal person. Each drew a portrait indistinct in every feature — a bright unlimned presence.

---

[1] Matthew Arnold: *Essays in Criticism*, Third Series, p. 93.

CHAPTER II
PERIOD OF DISCIPLINE: 1290-1313

a. Following False Images of Good
1290-1300

To those citizens of Florence living when the last decade of the thirteenth century was beginning, Dante appeared as a distinguished member of a brilliant circle of favored youths who sauntered through the land "which bards in fealty to Apollo hold." A dilettante in poetry and music, a leisurely student enjoying the companionship of the learned, he was not unskilled in arms, or lacking in virile qualities. The period of dreams and of dallying now closes and the epoch of storm and stress begins. His life enters upon a phase of discipline and of preparation for his supreme work, extending from 1290 to 1313, from the death of Beatrice to the death of Henry VII of Luxemburg. The twenty-five years of youth are succeeded by twenty-three years of severe training. The first half was spent in Florence, the second in wandering about Italy in poverty and bitterness of soul, exposing everywhere the wounds of grievous fortune. Intense and prolonged study, deep sufferings, stern grapplings with stupid or evil men and with untoward circumstances, changed the soft dreamer, whose delicate face is preserved to us in the Bargello portrait, to the grim prophet whose rugged strength is immortalized in the death mask.

It is necessarily a time of soul trial when a young idealist is hurled against the rugged facts of life, and is compelled either to abandon his exalted visions or to pay the price of adjusting them to the things that are.

I. SIMILARITY BETWEEN THE CAREERS OF DANTE AND MILTON

It is interesting to note how like Dante's was the experience and training of Milton. The career of each was divided into three distinct periods of nearly equal length. Each enjoyed a studious and leisurely youth, rich in opportunities for gathering poetic material and for refining his genius, each early won generous fame for lyrics and sonnets of unusual beauty, each at about the same age dedicated himself to a life-long task by which he hoped to gain terrestrial immortality. At twenty-nine Milton wrote to his friend Diodati: "You make inquiries as to what I am about: What I am thinking of? Why, with God's help, of immortality! Forgive the word, I only whisper it in your ear! Yes, I am pluming my wings for a flight." If the closing words of the "Vita Nuova" were written, as most scholars think, within five years after the death of Beatrice, then at almost precisely the same age Dante was, not whispering, but proclaiming to the citizens of Florence that he was pluming his wings for a flight into the highest ether. "After this sonnet a wonderful vision appeared to me, in which I saw things which made me resolve to speak no more of this blessed one, until I could more worthily treat of her. And to attain to this, I study to the utmost of my power, as she well knows. So that, if it please Him

PERIOD OF DISCIPLINE 111

through whom all things live, that my life be prolonged for some years, I hope to say of her what was never said of any woman."

Then for each there followed approximately two decades of severest discipline. The contemplative singers, dreaming of immortality, were snatched from their gentle, iridescent worlds of ideals and cast violently upon the rocks of actual evil conditions. Each was made fit to write a world poem by experiencing the world's fiercest passions and its elemental struggles.

In 1639, in the thirty-first year of his age, Milton returned from his travels on the continent to bear his part in the civil struggle of the times. "The sad news," he said, "of the Civil War in England called me back: for I considered it base that while my fellowmen were fighting at home for liberty I should be traveling abroad for intellectual culture." Nor could his motive be put in nobler phrase: "I conceive myself to be not as mine own person, but as a member incorporate into that truth whereof I am persuaded." Thereafter Milton gave himself unreservedly to the political fortunes of his country. Mingling with many men he grew in wisdom and sympathy; fighting for civil liberty his will became iron. Yet through all he clung to his earlier purpose. In 1641 he mentions "an inward prompting which now grew daily upon me, that by labor and intent study, which I take to be my portion in this life, joined with the strong propensity of nature, I might perhaps leave something so written to after times, as they should not willingly let it die."

The nineteen muscularizing years of the English

poet were prolonged for the Italian to twenty-three. Thus for two decades at the same period of their lives these two poets held their supreme ambitions in the background while absorbed with concerns of more immediate moment. Each knew instinctively that he could not write an epic until he had lived heroically; that the characters from which issue immortal poems are not fashioned by the splendor of dreams drifting through the mind, but by toil, sorrow, and spiritual victory. During this period of storm and stress each worked unremittingly for a better social order. Equally conspicuous were they for "the untempered fierceness" of their political pamphlets. Milton took practically twenty years from poetry to give to patriotism, but Dante, more fortunate, was not so absorbed in public affairs that he failed to cultivate his poetic gifts. Like the Englishman, believing in God, he waited his appointed hour. Dante at forty-eight, and Milton at fifty, set themselves to fulfill the dreams of youth and the settled purpose of a lifetime. Each looked out upon a chaotic world in which his political ideals had gone down in helpless defeat. In dependency, disillusionment, and faith the one proposed to justify the ways of God to men, the other to reveal to men the true path to God. Milton was engaged for some six years on his "Paradise Lost," beginning in 1658 and finishing in 1665. Dante was absorbed in the "Divina Commedia" for an equal period — from 1314 until his death in 1321. Each had conceived the general theme of his masterpiece in the days of youth, but the method of treatment was left an open question. Milton, in 1640, was contemplating "Paradise Lost" as a dramatic tragedy. Tradition rumors that Dante began the "Comedy" in stately Latin verses in 1300. Each, taught by the ripened wisdom of the years, chose the form best suited to his genius, and amid the ruin of temporal fortunes, wrought an enduring monument to his fame and achieved spiritual serenity and joy for himself. Milton, like Samson, "Eyeless in Gaza at the mill with slaves," could yet write in nearly his last words:

> "All is best, though oft we doubt,
> What th' unsearchable dispose
> Of highest wisdom brings about,
> And ever best found in the close." [1]

And Dante, in "calm of mind, all passion spent," could sum up his verdict on life's experiences in this glowing sentence, "but now my desire and will, like a wheel that is moved evenly, were revolved by the Love that moves the Sun and other stars." [2]

II. INTELLECTUAL AWAKENING

This middle period of Dante's life falls quite naturally into two divisions. The first extends from 1290 to 1300. During these years the dominant mood of the poet is one of joy, for his mind is awakening to the delights of study, his poetic genius is receiving recognition, public affairs are luring his interest and bringing their honors, and the satisfactions of home also are his.

From 1300 to 1313 his prevailing mood is stern and sad. The shadows cast by responsibility, exile, poverty, political disaster darken his spirit.

[1] *Samson Agonistes.*   [2] *Paradiso*, XXXIII, 143–45.

If we consider Dante's life as it shaped itself in his thought, the year 1300 is for him a turning-point. The preceding ten years, filled with the satisfactions of growing wisdom and power, were yet years when his feet were unconsciously straying from the right way; the following thirteen were spent in a vain endeavor to reach a true goal by a false and impossible way.

In his own words we have a description of his emotions and of his consolations when his dream-world dissolved and he faced the prosaic facts of existence:

"I say that as the first delight of my soul, of which mention is made above, was destroyed I remained pierced with such sadness that no consolation availed me. However, since I could not console myself, nor could others console me, after some time my mind, which was striving to be healed, bethought itself to have recourse to a method which a certain disconsolate man had employed for his own consolation. And I set myself to read that book of Boëthius, with which few are familiar, wherein when captive and exiled he found solace. And hearing besides that Tully had written another book, in which when discoursing *On Friendship* he had introduced words of consolation for Laelius, a most excellent man, on the death of his friend Scipio, I set myself to read that. And although it was hard for me at first to enter into their meaning, yet finally I entered into it, as far as the knowledge of Latin which I possessed, and such slight ability as I had enabled me to do, by which ability I already perceived many things as it were in a dream, as may be seen in the 'New Life.'

PERIOD OF DISCIPLINE 115

"And as it often happens that a man goes in quest of silver succeeds beyond his intention in finding gold, which some hidden cause puts in his way, not perchance without the divine behest, so I who sought to console myself discovered not only a remedy for my tears, but also the words employed by authors and sciences and books."[1]

The "De Consolatione Philosophiæ" of Boëthius was a favorite with thinking men for a thousand years. Its author knew life well, and he knew it in the extremes. One day the opulent and powerful minister of Theodoric, the next in prison unjustly charged with treason and condemned to death. The thoughts which consoled him as he awaited his doom he wrote down for the world in a book which Gibbon calls "a golden volume, not unworthy the leisure of Plato or Tully, but which claims incomparable merit from the barbarism of the times and the situation of the author." Here the eager and plastic mind of Dante found the great world problems — the Ultimate Good, the fickleness of Fortune, the emptiness of temporal affairs, the way of happiness, the nature of evil, the relation of free will to foreknowledge — discussed by a capacious and virile intellect, trained in affairs and rich in that deep wisdom which heroic virtue learns in a rough world. In his later works Dante has fourteen direct quotations from the volume, and in some fifteen passages he discusses the thoughts contained therein. Both the "Vita Nuova" and the "Convivio" imitate "De Consolatione" in connecting verse with prose explanation

[1] *Convivio*, II, 13; Jackson's translation.

and narrative. The lines upon Fortune in the seventh canto of the "Inferno," the reproach of Beatrice upon the Purgatorial Mount, the personification of Philosophy in the "Convivio," seem to be directly suggested by Boëthius. From his plunge into so profound a work, the young poet must have emerged with his mind invigorated by grappling with a matured intelligence, expanded by a contemplation of the soul's deepest problems, and persuaded of the real sources of permanent satisfaction. But Dante's temperament was reverse in essential particulars from that of his new-found guide. His mental habitude was not, and never became, philosophical. The study of philosophy stimulated his intellectual appetite, but it did not radically change his ways of thinking. His fiery spirit never rested in that calm zone where the truly philosophic mind finds joy and strength. Consequently the monument which he reared to Philosophy is an unfinished column.

Cicero's "De Amicitia" appears to have exerted no lasting influence, as there is only one clear reference to the essay in Dante's writings.[1] Dante acknowledges that he read the volumes of Boëthius and of Cicero with difficulty, his knowledge of Latin being limited. This leads us to infer that until his twenty-sixth year his insatiable intellectual appetite had not been awakened. He was doubtless familiar with the rudiments of the *Trivium* — grammar, logic, and rhetoric, and of the *Quadrivium* — music, arithmetic, geometry, and astronomy. Now he sets himself to that prolonged

[1] *Convivio*, I, 12, 19–24.

PERIOD OF DISCIPLINE

study of which he says, "Greatly taxing my sight in eagerness for reading, I so weakened the visual spirits that all the stars appeared to me to be shadowed by a kind of halo." [1]

In his passion for knowledge he endured cold, vigils, and fastings. The results of this arduous study soon appear, for if we place the date of the compilation of the "Vita Nuova" at 1295, he had by that year made great progress. "He shows," says Mr. Toynbee, "some familiarity with the 'Ethics' and 'Metaphysics' of Aristotle (not of course in the original Greek — a language he never knew — but through the medium of Latin translations) and quotes Homer twice, once from the 'Ethics' of Aristotle, and once from the 'Ars Poetica' of Horace. Ovid, Lucan, Horace, and Virgil are all quoted directly, the last several times, but there is not much trace of intimate acquaintance with any of them. Dante also displays a certain knowledge of astronomy in the 'Vita Nuova,' Ptolemy being quoted by name, while to the Arabian astronomer, Alfraganus, he was certainly indebted for some of his data as to the motions of the heavens, and for his details as to the Syrian and Arabian calendars. If we add to these authors the Bible, which is quoted four or five times, and the works of Cicero and Boëthius, we have practically the range of his reading up to about his thirtieth year, at any rate as far as may be gathered from his writings, which in Dante's case is a fairly safe criterion." [2]

---

[1] *Convivio*, III, 9, 150.
[2] Toynbee: *Dante Alighieri*, p. 66. The extent of Dante's studies is nowhere set forth with such thoroughness as in Dr. Moore's *Studies in Dante*, vols. I, II, III.

III. FALSE IMAGES OF GOOD

But serious study was not engaging all of Dante's attention. Other influences less elevating than the noble thoughts of Boëthius and Cicero were impressing his mind. With consistent honesty he describes how he allowed himself to be possessed with desire for a gentle lady who looked piteously upon him from a window. Sometime after the "year was complete since this lady (Beatrice) was made one of the denizens of the life eternal . . . happening to be in a place where I was reminded of the past time, I stood deep in thought, and with such doleful thoughts that they made me exhibit an appearance of terrible distress. Wherefore, I, becoming aware of my woebegone looks, lifted up my eyes to see if any one saw me: and I saw a gentle lady, young and very beautiful, who was looking at me from a window with a face full of compassion, so that all pity seemed gathered in it." [1] This new love which seemed to him at one time mean and at another pleasing, as memory or present passion prevailed, was at its flood some thirty months later when he composed an ode beginning: "Ye who by understanding rule the third heaven." [2] This passion soon afterwards appears to Dante most base and he dismisses it in a sonnet which declares: "Love is not there." [3] As this episode of the lady at the window takes place at the time he is giving his attention assiduously to the study of philosophy, a mind like Dante's, prone to see subtle connections be-

---

[1] *Vita Nuova*, XXXVI. [2] *Convivio*, II, 1.
[3] Sonetto XLIII, Oxford Dante.

PERIOD OF DISCIPLINE 119

tween the outer and the inner life, would not fail to make this lady a symbol of some experience. When in after years he wrote the "Convivio," wishing to praise Philosophy, he naturally used this lady in allegorical figure, seeking thus to explain away this discreditable infatuation. But the earlier narrative is doubtless the better statement of the facts.

Among the odes which Dante wrote before the year 1300 there are four which indicate that at this period he had other passing fancies, perhaps a genuine passion, for some fair one. As they are lyrics of strong sentiment, and play repeatedly upon the word *pietra* or stone, they must have been inspired either by a lady named Pietra, or some one who was to the poet as frigid and as unresponsive as a stone. Her unfriendliness evidently cut deep, for Dante in revenge wrote to her an ode as harsh "as in her bearing is that beauteous stone." [1] In Canzone xv she is called "pargoletta" and it may well be that she is the "young girl" to whom Beatrice refers so scornfully when she calls Dante to an accounting in their meeting on the summit of Purgatory.

But fickleness in love is not the only fault of these years to which Dante confesses. Meeting in Purgatory, on the ledge of the gluttons his friend Forese Donati, who died in 1296, he remarks: "If thou bring back to mind what thou wast with me, and what I was with thee, the present remembrance will even now be grievous." [2] Boccaccio says that in "this wondrous poet licentiousness found a large place." Benvenuto

[1] Canz. XII. [2] *Purgatorio*, XXIII, 115-17.

adverts to the poet's too great love for women, and Dante himself recognizes the need of passing through the flames upon the highest ledge in Purgatory ere he is fit to look into the pure eyes of Beatrice.

Guido Cavalcanti also reproves him in a sonnet which indicates that Dante at this time suffered a moral lapse:

"I come to thee by day time constantly,
  But in thy thoughts too much of baseness find:
  Greatly it grieves me for thy gentle mind,
And for thy many virtues gone from thee.
It was thy wont to shun much company,
  Unto all sorry concourse ill inclined:
  And still thy speech of me, heartfelt and kind,
Had made me treasure up thy poetry.
But now I dare not, for thine abject life,
  Make manifest that I approve thy rhymes;
  Nor come I in such sort that thou mayst know.
Ah! prithee read this sonnet many times:
So shall that evil one who bred this strife
  Be thrust from thy dishonored soul and go." [1]

The standards of social life in Florence were lamentably low, and while the poet in none of his works confesses sexual immorality, yet we cannot affirm that he maintained during this period of divided loyalty a stainless purity. No charge of immorality is proven, nevertheless he admits levity and faithlessness to his highest ideals. Later he grew in moral cleanness and integrity as he meditated eternal themes.[2]

[1] Rossetti, *Dante and his Circle*, p. 105.
[2] Moore: *Studies in Dante*, vol. III, p. 247.

IV. MARRIAGE

Sometime between 1291 and 1296 Dante was married to Gemma di Manetto Donati, a member of the powerful house of Donati. Boccaccio says that this union was brought about by the planning of friends, and creates the suspicion that the marriage was not a happy one. Aside from the fact that Gemma is not directly mentioned in the "Divina Commedia" and did not share his exile, we have no reason to accept the tradition which Boccaccio's garrulity originated. Both the author of the "Ottimo Commento" and Benvenuto da Imola, the former a contemporary of Dante, and the latter lecturing on the "Comedy" in 1374, infer that Cacciaguida's words to Dante: "Thou shalt abandon everything beloved most dearly," [1] indicates the poet's affection for his wife. These authorities certainly show that there was no open breach between the two.

Boccaccio informs us that when Dante was exiled, "under the title of her dowry the wife with difficulty defended a small portion of his possessions from the fury of the citizens, and from the fruits thereof obtained a meagre support for herself and her children." Gemma was living in 1332, and as in that year her sons Jacopo and Pietro paid the largest of Dante's debts, let us hope that her last years were devoid of hardship. There were four children born of this union, — Pietro, Jacopo, Beatrice, and Antonia. Pietro about 1340 wrote a commentary on the "Divina Commedia." He "studied law and showed himself a

[1] *Paradiso*, XVII, 55.

man of ability," writes Lionardo Bruni in his narrative. "Thanks to his own powers and to the remembrance in which his father was held, he attained to great distinction and wealth, and maintained his position at Verona with considerable state. This Messer Pietro had a son named Dante, who in turn had a son Lionardo, who is still living and has several children. A short time ago Lionardo came to Florence with the other young men of Verona, well and honorably appointed, and visited me as a friend to the memory of his great-grandfather Dante. I showed him the houses of the poet and his ancestors, and called his attention to many things that were new to him because he and his family had been estranged from their fatherland." [1]

In 1563 this branch of the family died out. Jacopo "wrote a commentary on the 'Commedia' (or at any rate on the 'Inferno') and a didactic poem called 'Il Dottrinale,' entered the church, became a canon in the diocese of Verona, and died before 1349. Of Antonia [2] it is only known that she was still alive in 1332. Beatrice became a nun in the Convent of Santo Stefano dell' Uliva at Ravenna, where in 1350 she was presented by Boccaccio with the sum of ten gold florins on behalf of the Capitani di Or San Michele of Florence. She died before 1370, in which year there is a record of the payment of a bequest of hers of three gold ducats to the convent where she had passed her days." [3]

[1] Dinsmore: *Aids to the Study of Dante*, p. 128.
[2] Antonia and Beatrice may be the same person, one name being that assumed as a nun.
[3] Toynbee: *Dante Alighieri*, p. 71.

V. ORDINANCES OF JUSTICE

Let us turn for a moment from the consideration of the poet's personal career to glance at important events which were taking place in Florence. In the Battle of Campaldino (1289) the strength of the Ghibellines had been broken throughout Tuscany. The returning Guelf nobles, made confident by the successes of their arms in the battle, behaved violently toward the persons and the goods of the people. Strong measures were necessary to secure popular rights, and a champion of the citizens appeared in the person of Giano della Bella, rich, powerful, and of the ancient nobility. Under his efficient leadership the Ordinances of Justice were passed in 1293 by which the nobles were deprived of all part in the government, stringent laws were enacted to restrain their violence against the people, and a special magistrate, known as Gonfaloniere of Justice, was appointed and given command of a formidable body of troops to enforce the laws against the nobility. Giano, with his fierce love of justice, was for a time immensely popular, but finally the rich burghers and the nobility conspired against him, and on the 5th of March, 1295, he withdrew from the city and went into exile. Upon this event Villani thus moralizes: "And it has been seen and experienced truly in Florence in ancient and modern times, that whosoever has become leader of the people and of the masses has been cast down; for as much as the ungrateful people never give men their due reward. From this event arose great disturbance and change amongst the people and in the city of Florence, and from that time forward the artificers and common people possessed little power in the commonwealth, but the government remained in the hands of the powerful *popolani grassi*."[1]

Of these events Dante was no uninterested spectator. To qualify himself for public office, the political power being in the hands of the guilds of Florence, he joined the Guild of Physicians and Apothecaries, one of the wealthiest and most influential. On the codex containing the names of the members of the *Arte de' Medici e Speziali* is the entry *Dante d' Aldighieri degli Aldighiere poeta fiorentino*. That Dante at this early period should describe himself as "Florentine poet" is singular, and it is a relief to learn that we have not here an instance of youthful vainglory, but the interpretation of a scribe, for the document in which the signature occurs is a late compilation, dated 1446–47, and not the original record. As the names are arranged alphabetically, are in Italian and not Latin, and the record is defective for the years 1282–97 it is probable that the compiler, having written Dante's name, added the words "poeta fiorentino" to identify him![2] This membraneous codex Fraticelli says he saw and read. The date of the entrance he is inclined to believe was 1295.[3] Probably Dante was drawn toward this guild because the shops of the apothecaries were the bookstores of those days and provided the natural meeting-places for artists and writers.

[1] *Chronicles of Villani*, Selfe and Wicksteed, p. 312.
[2] Moore: *Studies in Dante*, vol. III, p. 239 n.
[3] *Vita di Dante*, 112–13.

PERIOD OF DISCIPLINE

It was in the spring of this year, 1295, that Carlo Martello, the eldest son of Charles II of Naples and Anjou, and the crowned King of Hungary, visited Florence, remaining for some three weeks. Villani [1] is stirred to unwonted enthusiasm in writing of the regal splendor of his coming; "with his company of two hundred knights with golden spurs, French and Provençal and from the kingdom, all young men, invested by the king with habits of scarlet and dark green, and all with saddles with one device, with their palfreys adorned with silver and gold, with arms quarterly, bearing golden lilies and surrounded by a bordure of red and silver, which are the arms of Hungary. And they appeared the noblest and richest company a king ever had with him. And in Florence he abode more than twenty days, awaiting his father, King Charles, and his brothers; and the Florentines did him great honor, and he showed great love to the Florentines, wherefore he was in great favor with them all." With the brilliant circle that surrounded the prince Dante mingled. That there was some degree of intimacy between the two is proved by the words with which Charles addressed the poet when they met in Paradise: "Much didst thou love me," said the prince to Dante, "and hadst good reason why; for had I stayed below I had shown thee of my love more than the leaves."[2] These gracious words throw a significant light on Dante's prominence in Florence and on his personal attractions. Carlyle has said that probably Dante would not be a welcome guest

---

[1] *Chronicles of Villani*, Selfe and Wicksteed, p. 316.
[2] *Paradiso*, VIII, 55.

at dinner, but it was otherwise in the days before the fires of his bitter wrath had been kindled.

VI. POLITICAL INTERESTS AND DEBTS

The musty records give us a few insights into Dante's political interests during this tumultuous period. On December 14, 1295, he voted in the election of Priors. On the fragment of the codex containing the minutes of the Council of the Hundred, for June 5, 1296, are the words "Dante Alagherii consuluit secundum propositiones prædictas."[1] Between the years 1297 and 1300 Dante was either seriously embarrassed financially, or else engaged in extensive speculations to better his fortunes. There are documentary records showing that on April 11, 1297, Dante and his brother Francesco borrowed from Andrea di Guido de' Ricci 277½ florins, full Florentine weight, equal to about $682 of our money. On the 23d of December, 1297, they borrowed 480 golden florins ($1160) from Jacopo Lotti and Pannocchia Riccommani. Another 90 florins from Perso Ubaldino and 46 florins from Filippo di Lapo Bonaccolti — for these last three obligations Manetto Donati, Dante's father-in-law, went security. From Francesco on March 14, 1299, he received a loan of 125 florins and again on June 11, 1300, four days before he became Prior, he asked and received another loan of 90 florins. A debt of some 1100 florins — over $2700 of our money — was a considerable sum in those days. Witte, upon the authority of Peruzzi, calculates that Dante's debts amounted to more than

[1] Dante Society (Cambridge, Mass.), *Report*, 1891.

PERIOD OF DISCIPLINE 127

37,000 francs, but he surely has been misled as to the value of the florin of the thirteenth century, whose worth modern writers place at from 10s. to 10s. 3d. or $2.42 to $2.48. These debts were not fully paid until 1332, eleven years after the poet's death, by his sons Pietro and Jacopo, and Francesco, the half-brother.[1] "Previous to his banishment from Florence," writes Lionardi Bruni, "although he was not a man of great wealth, yet he was not poor, for he possessed a moderate patrimony, large enough to admit of comfortable living. . . . He owned good houses in Florence, adjoining those of Gieri di Messer Bello, his kinsman; possessions also in Camerata, in the Piacentina, and in the plain of Ripoli: and, as he writes, many pieces of valuable furniture."[2] "Domestic cares," says Boccaccio, "drew Dante to public ones, where the vain honors that are attached to state positions so bewildered him that, without noting whence he had come and whither he was bound, with free rein he almost completely surrendered himself to the management of these matters. And therein fortune was so favorable to him that no legation was heard or answered, nor, in short, was any deliberation of weight entered upon, until Dante had first given his opinion relative thereto. On him all public faith, all hope, and, in a word, all things human and divine seemed to rest."[3] Doubtless Boccaccio has exaggerated Dante's influence in political matters, yet he was evidently a man

[1] Toynbee: *Dante Alighieri*, pp. 86, 87; see also Dante Society (Cambridge, Mass.), *Report*, 1891, for documents.
[2] Dinsmore: *Aids to the Study of Dante*, pp. 125-26.
[3] Dinsmore: *Aids to the Study of Dante*, p. 86.

of importance. In the "Liber Reformationum et consiliariorum Comunis sancti Gemignani" it is recorded that on the "Die Vij° Maij," the 7th of May (the year 1300 instead of 1299 is now chosen as correct), "the general council of the Commune and the men of San Gemigno having been called together in the palace ... the most noble Dante Alighieri, ambassador of the Commune of Florence, on the behalf of said Commune, in the assembled council explained that at the present time it was expedient for all the commonwealths of the Tuscan League to hold in a certain place a parliament and discussion for the election and confirmation of a new captain, and moreover it was expedient for the hastening of said business that the syndics and appointed embassadors of the aforesaid communes should at once convene." [1]

In this mission, unlike the subsequent ones to Rome and Venice, Dante was successful and his propositions were approved.

The years 1290–1300 were to the poet years of character-forming. His supersensitive nature was being toughened and broadened by contact with practical affairs. War, study, amours, marriage, parenthood, political interests, and responsibility, all set their mark upon him. To us they seem prosperous and happy years, for he was walking in the way of his ambition, growing in wisdom, power, and fame: yet to Dante when he

[1] Dante Society (Cambridge, Mass.), *Report*, 1891, p. 36. See note, p. 59. Fraticelli (*Vita di Dante*, p. 138) gives the date as May 8, 1299. Scartazzini accepted and later questioned the document. It is defended by Fiamazzo in *Cultura* (1892), 182, and by Biagi e Passerini, *Cartulario Dantesco*, 1895.

PERIOD OF DISCIPLINE

wrote the "Comedy" they appeared to be years when he was ignorantly wandering from the true way.

During this period the civic pride of Florence was at full tide, and her eager citizens were conceiving liberal plans for her glory. In 1295 the church of Santa Croce was begun; the following year the Piazza San Giovanni was enlarged to accommodate the growing crowds that participated in her public ceremonials and festivities. Within twelve months a cathedral was projected and the services of Arnolfo secured, and in the following year, 1298, the foundations of both the Duomo and the Palazzo Vecchio were laid.

It is not strange that in a city of such seething creative energy men of permanent fame should be produced.

VII. THE CRITICAL YEAR

The year 1300 marks the culmination of Dante's political influence in Florence, and a crisis in his career. He could well designate it as the significant date of the "Divina Commedia." It was in this year that a storm which had long been brewing burst forth in fury. "In the said time (1300) our city of Florence," writes a contemporary chronicler,[1] "was in the greatest and happiest state which it had ever been since it was rebuilt, or before, alike in greatness of power and in number of people, forasmuch as there were more than thirty thousand citizens in the city and more than seventy thousand capable of bearing arms in the country within her territory, and she was great in nobility

[1] *Villani*, Book VIII, § 39.

of good knights, and in free populace, and in riches, ruling over the greater part of Tuscany; whereupon the sin of ingratitude, with the instigation of the enemy of the human race, brought forth from the said prosperity pride and corruption, which put an end to the feasts and joyaunce of the Florentines. For hitherto they had been living in many delights and dainties, and in tranquillity and continual banquets; for every year throughout almost all the city on the first day of May, there were bands and companies of men and women, with sports and dances. But now it came to pass that through envy there arose factions among the citizens; and one of the chief and greatest began in the sesto of offence, to wit of Porta San Piero, between the house of Cerchi, and the Donati; on the one side through envy, and on the other through rude ungraciousness. The head of the family of the Cerchi was one M. Vieri dei Cerchi, and he and those of his house were of great affairs, and powerful, and with great kinsfolk, and were very rich merchants, so that their company was among the largest in the world; these were luxurious, inoffensive, uncultured and ungracious, like folk come in a short time to great estate and power. The head of the family of the Donati was M. Corso Donati, and he and those of his house were gentlemen and warriors, and of no superabundant riches, but by many were called Malefami. Neighbors they were in Florence and in the country, and while the one set was envious the other stood on their boorish dignity, so that there arose from the clash a fierce storm between them."

To the natural friction between the two houses representing the burghers and the ancient aristocracy another element of feud was added. In the neighboring city of Pistoia was a noble and powerful family called the Cancelliere. The founder of the house, Ser Cancellieri, had two wives, and by them many sons. Between the two branches of this house there was contempt and enmity. "One part took the name of the Black Cancellieri, and the other of the Whites, and this grew until they fought together, but it was not any very great affair. And one of those on the side of the White Cancellieri having been wounded, they on the side of the Black Cancellieri, to the end they might be at peace and concord with them, sent him which had done the injury and handed him over to the mercy of them which had received it, that they should take amends and vengeance for it at their will; they on the side of the White Cancellieri, ungrateful and proud, having neither pity nor love, cut off the hand of him who had been commended to their mercy on a horse manger. By which sinful beginning, not only was the house of the Cancellieri divided, but many violent deaths arose therefrom, and all the city of Pistoia was divided, for some held with one part, and some with the other, and they called themselves the Whites and the Blacks, forgetting among themselves the Guelf and the Ghibelline parties; and many civil strifes and much peril and loss of life arose therefrom in Pistoia; and not only in Pistoia, afterwards the city of Florence and all Italy was contaminated by the said parties."[1]

[1] *Chronicles of Villani*, Selfe and Wicksteed, pp. 322-23.

Florence by virtue of suzerainty over Pistoia interfered, and compelled the leaders of both factions to live within her walls. It was a fatal error. Once before she had made the same mistake in forcing the nobles to leave their castles in the country and reside in the city; thus introducing a ceaseless cause of friction. To take these firebrands from an adjacent commune into her own house could not but prove disastrous. The Cerchi, being connected with the White faction of Pistoia, espoused their cause, while the Donati championed the side of the Blacks. Thus were these two distinctive names introduced into Florentine politics.

Although both the Whites and the Blacks were Guelfs, their political interests were different. The former, being largely of the merchant class, upheld the established democratic order, while the latter, representing the nobility, were against the Ordinances and the authority of the middle class.

The situation was made even more difficult by the efforts of the Blacks to induce the Pope to champion their cause. This Boniface was not loath to do, it apparently being his ambition to add Tuscany to the Papal States. In the year 1300 all the elements of a political convulsion — class hatred, family feud, political passion, and intrigue — were conjoined. The first spark fell into this magazine of explosives on April 18. Upon that day three Florentines were sentenced for plotting against the State in the interest of the Pope. Six days later Boniface demanded that the sentence be revoked and the case tried before him. This order the Priors refused to obey.

BONIFACE VIII
By Arnolfo di Cambio

PERIOD OF DISCIPLINE

While the citizens were still dazed by the thunder of this detonation, passion threw a firebrand, producing a greater upheaval. On May Day the young gallants of both factions were "watching a dance of ladies which was taking place on the piazza of Santa Trinità; one party began to scoff at the other, and to urge their horses one against the other, whence arose a great conflict and confusion, and many were wounded ... and through the said scuffle that evening all the city was moved with apprehension and flew to arms." [1] To restore order in the turbulent city full power was given to the Priors to defend the commonwealth from danger within and without. The latter were evidently the more pressing. On May 15 the administration received a bull from the Pope threatening reprisals, both spiritual and temporal, if the sentence was not removed from his three agents and they together with the most violent accusers and representatives of the republic sent to him. A month later, on the 15th of June, 1300, Dante was elected one of the six Priors of Florence, an office which was the highest within the gift of the citizens, and was held for two months. To the political activities of his priorate he attributed all the subsequent woes. This he states in a letter quoted by Bruni: "All my troubles and hardships had their cause and rise in the disastrous meetings held during my priorate. Albeit in wisdom I was not worthy of that office, nevertheless I was not unworthy of it in fidelity and in age." [2]

One of his acts on the day he entered office was to

---

[1] *Chronicles of Villani*, Selfe and Wicksteed, p. 326.
[2] Dinsmore: *Aids to the Study of Dante*, p. 119.

confirm the sentence against the three agents of Boniface.[1] The Pope's legate, Cardinal Matteo d' Acquasparta, was then in the city, seeking to remove the causes of strife. Dante, who belonged to the White Party, suspecting that the Pope's real design was to take away the liberty of the city, joined with his colleagues in refusing the papal demands. Whereupon the legate withdrew, leaving Florence excommunicate and under interdict. The most important action of Dante and his fellow Priors, during the two months in which they held office, was to banish the heads of both the Black and the White Parties. In adopting this drastic measure we see how Dante's patriotism and loyalty to justice triumphed over all feelings. Prominent among the Whites whom he voted to banish was Guido Cavalcanti, "his first friend," while the leader of the Blacks was Corso Donati, the distinguished head of the house to which his wife Gemma belonged. The Whites obeyed this mandate of expulsion, but were recalled soon after the close of Dante's term of office. Not in time, however, to save the life of Guido, who, contracting malarial fever in exile, died in the latter part of August after his return to Florence. In thus subordinating personal friendship and family ties to the interests of the State Dante reveals that stern and lofty patriotism which ever distinguished him.

Crowded as was this year 1300 with fierce political passion, there were religious events taking place which made it memorable in history, and probably also in Dante's experience. Beginning with Christmas Day,

[1] Dante Society (Cambridge, Mass.), *Report*, 1891, p. 38.

PERIOD OF DISCIPLINE 135

1299, and extending through 1300, the Catholic Church celebrated the first of its jubilees. The Pope decreed that "whatever Roman should visit continuously for thirty days the churches of the Blessed Apostles Saint Peter and Saint Paul, and to all other people who were not Romans who should do likewise for fifteen days, there should be granted full and entire remission of all their sins, both the guilt and the punishment thereof, they having made or to make confession of the same." Rome was thronged with devout worshipers. So impressive was the Eternal City and the thronged churches to Giovanni Villani, that he resolved to chronicle the events of Florence, even as Sallust and Livy had written the history of the parent city. Although Dante was bitterly opposed to the reigning Pope and to his temporal pretensions, there is no evidence that he was ever sceptical of the spiritual claims of the Church. There is no proof that he made a pilgrimage to Rome, but in "Inferno," XVIII, 28, we have a description of the throng crossing the bridge of Castello Sant' Angelo which indicates that he witnessed the crowds of the faithful who at this time visited Rome. If he did so, it is not improbable that there he had a spiritual experience which led him to select Easter week of the year 1300 as the time when he awoke to his perilous condition. Kneeling before the altars in the solemn stillness of the churches, Florence with its turbulent factions would seem far away. The vaster issues of life would loom large before him, and assert their supremacy. Reviewing his life in the presence of these symbols of the eternal realities, it would be natural for the poet to feel that he had wandered from the true way and to resolve to exert every energy to climb the sunlit mountain.

The man revealed to us in the zenith of his political fortunes compels our admiration. In a city given over to factional strife he sides with neither faction, but patriotically puts the welfare of the city above the interests of party. Set amid extremists, he is moderate. Loyal to liberty, he steadily resists the partisanship that would call in the aid of the Pope or of France, thus giving the city over to be but a pawn in the larger world game. Valuing justice, peace, and order more than popularity or even friendship, he does not hesitate to subordinate personal considerations to the public welfare. He stands for the freedom of his native city against the intrigues of Rome, and for its peace and order against the powerful passions of his own party.

b. THE PATH IN THE SAVAGE WOOD
1300–1313

VIII. POLITICAL ACTIVITIES

We have brief records of Dante's activities during the year 1301. On April 13 we learn that he voted in the Council of the Consuls of the Arts on the mode of procedure in the election of future priors. On April 28 he was appointed to superintend certain works on the streets of San Procolo, "so that the common people may, without uproar and harassing of magnates and mighty men, have access whenever it is desirable to the Lord Priors and the Standard Bearer of Justice." On June 19, in the Council of the Hundred on the ques-

PERIOD OF DISCIPLINE

tion of supplying a hundred soldiers to join the Papal forces for the war in Sicily, "Dante Alagherij consuluit, quod de servito faciendo domino Pape nichil fiat." (Dante Alighieri advised that in the matter of giving aid to the Pope nothing be done.)[1] There are also records of his voting on September 13 and September 20 of the same year. On September 28, in regard "to the conservation of the Ordinance of Justice and the Statutes of the People," appears his last recorded vote.

To make clear the direct causes of Dante's exile, let us resume the consideration of the debate which Florence was having with Boniface. In April, 1300, three Florentines had been arrested and condemned for plotting against the liberties of the city, and for working in the interests of the Pope. Boniface sent Cardinal Matteo d' Acquasparta to Florence to act as peacemaker between the Blacks and the Whites, and to demand that the three men be turned over to him for trial. A Florence independent of the Pope's temporal power was with Dante a guiding political principle. One of his first acts on becoming Prior was to confirm the sentences of the three emissaries of the Papal Court. The Cardinal legate returned in anger to Rome, leaving Florence excommunicate. Boniface, in order to reduce the city to submission and to further other political designs, invited Charles of Valois, brother to the King of France, to come into Italy. Boccaccio tells us that when Charles was about to be appointed peacemaker of Florence, "All the chiefs of the party to which Dante held were assembled in council to look to this matter,

[1] Dante Society (Cambridge, Mass), *Report*, 1891.

and there among other things they provided that an embassy should be sent to the Pope, who was then at Rome, in order to persuade him to oppose the coming of the said Charles, or to make him come with the consent of the ruling party. When they came to consider who should be the head of this embassy, all agreed on Dante. To their request he replied, after quietly meditating on it for a while, 'If I go, who stays? And if I stay, who goes?' as if he alone was of worth among them all, and as if the others were nothing worth except through him." [1]

Dino Compagni, who was active in the political life of Florence at the time, writes in his chronicle that the White Guelfs sent a joint embassy from Florence and Bologna to the Court of Rome for the purpose of averting the coming of Charles. "When the ambassadors arrived in Rome the Pope received them alone in his chamber, and said to them secretly, 'Wherefore are ye thus obstinate? Humble yourselves before me. And I declare to you in truth, that I have no other intention but to promote your peace. Let two of you go back, and let them have my blessing if they can cause my will to be obeyed.'" [2] The two who returned were Maso di M. Ruggierino Minerbetti and Corazzo of Signa,[3] while Dante remained. Why was Dante retained? Did Boniface recognize in the stern face and incisive sentences of this ambassador an unyielding and dangerous foe to his policy of bringing Tuscany within the Papal See?

[1] Dinsmore: *Aids to the Study of Dante*, p. 101.
[2] *Chronicle of Dino Compagni*, Temple Classics, pp. 82-83 n.
[3] *Ibid.*, p. 100.

PERIOD OF DISCIPLINE

If so, it was good policy to keep Dante in Rome. Perhaps, as has been suggested,[1] it was during these three months that Dante acquired the "fine scorn for the venal and simonical Roman Curia" that left his heart at a white heat of indignation even after Boniface was dead. Dante himself evidently believed that the Pope entertained toward him a personal enmity, and that his exile was due in part, at least, to the papal malignity. Cacciaguida in his prophecy very clearly states this: "So must thou needs sever thee from Florence. This is willed, this is already sought for, and will soon be brought to pass by him who meditates it there where every day Christ is bought and sold."[2]

IX. THE DECREE OF EXILE

On November 1, 1301, Charles of Valois entered Florence, with twelve hundred men at his back. Having received from the commonwealth the lordship and charge of the city, he openly espoused the cause of the Blacks. In the midst of the tumult which followed, Corso Donati returned, opened the prisons, and gave the city over to plunder. "After Charles had restored the Black party to Florence," says Dino, "he went to Rome, and when he had demanded money from the Pope, the latter answered, 'that he had put him in a fountain of gold.'"[3] Widespread confiscation of property followed. Messer Cante de' Gabrielli was made Podestà, and entered so vigorously into his office that hundreds of the Whites were punished and ban-

[1] Ragg: *Dante and his Italy*, p. 33.   [2] *Paradiso*, XVII, 48–51.
[3] *Chronicle of Dino Compagni*, p. 134.

ished. In the "Libro del Chiodo," preserved in the Archives of Florence, we can read the decree written in the quaint medieval Latin under the date of January 27, 1301 (as formerly the year began in Florence with March 25, the date would be 1302 according to our reckoning), how "Dante Alleghieri de sextu Sancti Petri maioris," together with four others, is condemned for fraud, corrupt practices in office, peculation, rebellion against the Pope and his representative, Charles of Valois, and against the peace of the state of Florence and the Guelf Party. Having been summoned by herald and having failed to appear, they were condemned to pay fines of five thousand gold florins each, besides the repayment of all the money illegally extorted. Restitution must be made within three days from the issue of the sentence. Failing in this all their goods would be forfeited and destroyed. Moreover, they were exiled beyond the boundaries of Tuscany for two years, and that the record may be perpetual their names were to be written on the public statutes as peculators and defrauders, and never again were they to hold office or benefits within the commonwealth of Florence.[1]

As Dante was absent from Florence when his enemies triumphed, and as he could not appear before the tribunal without danger of immediate death, the charges against him were left unrefuted. His early biographers had no question of his innocence. His contemporary Villani declares that he was banished "without any other fault" because he was of the

[1] Del Lungo: *Dell' Esilio di Dante*, pp. 97–103; also Dante Society (Cambridge, Mass.), *Report*, 1891, pp. 48–52.

PERIOD OF DISCIPLINE 141

White Party, and subsequent biographers have believed that the criminal assertions were made in order perpetually to disqualify him for office.

On March 10 of the same year the sentence was reaffirmed against these four and ten others. This second sentence even went to the savage extreme of condemning them to be burned alive if they should ever come within the boundaries of the commonwealth — "ut si quis predictorum ullo tempore in fortiam dicti Communis pervenerit, talis perveniens igne comburatur sic quod moriatur." [1]

X. WANDERINGS

Our precise knowledge of Dante's wanderings during his exile is meagre. Bruni declares that, "When Dante heard of his ruin, he at once left Rome, where he was ambassador, and, journeying with all haste, he came to Siena." Here he learned more definitely of his misfortune, and seeing no recourse, decided to throw in his lot with the other exiles. He first joined them in a meeting held at Gorgonza, where among the many things discussed they fixed on Arezzo as their headquarters. There they made a large camp, and created the Count Alessandro da Romena their captain, together with twelve councilors, among whom was Dante.[2]

On June 8, 1302, Dante is known to have met with his fellow-exiles in the church of San Godenzo, about

[1] Del Lungo: *Dell' Esilio di Dante*, pp. 104–06; and Dante Society (Cambridge, Mass.), *Report*, 1891, pp. 52–54.
[2] Dinsmore: *Aids to the Study of Dante*, p. 124.

twenty miles from his native city, plotting with the Ubaldini an attack upon Florence.

On July 20, 1304, the exiles, supported by allies, attempted to enter Florence by surprise. A part even succeeded in forcing the gates, carrying their banners as far as the Piazza of San Giovanni. "But God saved the city," says Villani. In the attacking party was the father of Petrarch, who, when he returned to Arezzo, found that a son had been born to him upon the very day of the disastrous battle, a son whose studious talents and lyric gifts would make that ill-starred day memorable after the defeat and all the contestants were forgotten. Dante does not appear to have been in the attack, for disgusted by the folly and wickedness of his fellow-exiles, he had withdrawn from them, and formed a "party by himself." The poet's first refuge was "the courtesy of the great Lombard, who on the ladder beareth the sacred bird." The great Lombard was Bartolomeo della Scala of Verona, with whom he tarried some time, endeavoring in all humility, "by good deeds and upright conduct," says Bruni, to "obtain the favor of returning to Florence through the voluntary action of the government. Devoting himself resolutely to this end, he wrote frequently to individual citizens in power and also to the people, among others one long letter which began, "Popule mee, quid feci tibi?"[1] It is supposed that he was in Padua, in August, 1306, as a Paduan document dated August 27, 1306, was witnessed by "dantino q' alligerii de florentia et nunc stat paduæ."[2] But as the name "Dantinus"

---

[1] Dinsmore: *Aids to the Study of Dante*, p. 124.
[2] Dante Society (Cambridge, Mass.), *Report*, 1891, p. 55.

PERIOD OF DISCIPLINE 143

appears in other Paduan documents after Dante's death the proof is not certain.[1] In October[2] of that year he was in the district of Lunigiana with Franceschino, Marchese Malaspina, by whom he was commissioned special envoy to establish terms of peace with the Bishop of Luni. Dante acknowledges his gratitude to the Malaspini by his noble tribute to a race that "strips not itself of the glory of the purse and the sword," "and alone goeth straight, and scorns the path of evil." [3]

It is not improbable that in 1308 Dante was at Forli. The historian of that place, Flavio Biondo (d. 1463), declares that letters dictated by Dante were preserved in his time. That Dante was at one time in Forli is to be inferred from a passage in the "Purgatorio" which seems to have a reminiscent value.[4] We can trace his steps to Lucca,[5] and Villani states that he went to the University of Bologna and afterwards to Paris and many parts of the world. Probably he remained in Paris studying philosophy and theology until 1310 when the expedition of Henry VII called him back to Italy.

"In 1311 the mists which obscure the greater part of Dante's life in exile are dispelled for a moment by three letters of unquestioned authenticity, and we gain a clear view of the poet. In 1310 Henry of Luxemburg, a man who touched the imagination of his contemporaries by his striking presence and his chivalric accomplishments as well as by his high character and

[1] Toynbee: *Dante Alighieri*, p. 91.
[2] Dante Society (Cambridge, Mass.), *Report*, 1892.
[3] *Purgatorio*, VIII, 129 ff. [4] *Ibid*, XXIV, 31. [5] *Ibid*, XXIV, 45.

generous aims, 'a man just, religious, and strenuous in arms,' having been elected Emperor as Henry VII, prepared to enter Italy with intent to confirm the imperial rights and to restore order to the distracted land. The Pope, Clement V, favored his coming and the prospect opened by it was hailed not only by the Ghibellines with joy, but by a large part of the Guelfs as well; with the hope that the long discord and confusion, from which all had suffered, might be brought to end, and give place to tranquillity and justice, Dante exulted in this new hope; and on the coming of the Emperor, late in 1310, he addressed an animated appeal to the rulers and people of Italy, exhorting them in impassioned words to rise up and do reverence to him whom the Lord of heaven and earth had ordained for their king. 'Behold, now is the accepted time; rejoice, O Italy, dry thy tears; efface, O most beautiful, the traces of mourning; for he is at hand who shall deliver thee.'

"The first welcome of Henry was ardent, and with fair auspices he assumed at Milan, in January, 1311, the Iron Crown, the crown of the King of Italy. Here in Milan Dante presented himself, and here with full heart he did homage upon his knees to the Emperor. But the popular welcome proved hollow; the illusions of hope speedily began to vanish; revolt broke out in many cities of Lombardy; Florence remained obdurate, and with great preparations for resistance put herself at the head of the enemies of the Emperor. Dante, disappointed and indignant, could not keep silence. He wrote a letter headed 'Dante Alaghieri, a Florentine and undeservedly in exile, to the most wicked

Florentines within the city.' It begins with calm and eloquent words in regard to the divine foundation of the imperial power, and to the sufferings of Italy due to her having been left without its control to her own undivided will. Then it breaks forth in passionate denunciation of Florence for her impious arrogance in venturing to rise up in mad rebellion against the minister of God; and, warning her of the calamities which her blind obstinacy is preparing for her, it closes with threats of her impending ruin and desolation. This letter is dated from the springs of the Arno, on the 31st of March.

"The growing force of the opposition which he encountered delayed the progress of Henry. Dante, impatient of delay, eager to see the accomplishment of his hope, on the 16th of April addressed Henry himself in a letter of exalted prophetic exhortation, full of Biblical language, and of illustrations drawn from sacred and profane story, urging him not to tarry, but trusting in God, to go out to meet and to slay the Goliath that stood against him. 'Then the Philistines will flee, and Israel will be believed, and we, exiles in Babylon, who groan as we remember the holy Jerusalem, shall then, as citizens breathing in peace, recall in joy the miseries of confusion.' But all was in vain. The drama which had opened with such brilliant expectations was advancing to a tragic close. Italy became more confused and distracted than ever. One sad event followed after another. In May the brother of the Emperor fell at the siege of Brescia; in September his dearly loved wife Margarita, 'a holy and good woman,' died at

Genoa. The forces hostile to him grew more and more formidable. He succeeded, however, in entering Rome in May, 1312, but his enemies held half of the city, and the streets became the scene of bloody battles; Saint Peter's was closed to him, and Henry, worn and disheartened and in peril, was compelled to submit to be ingloriously crowned at St. John Lateran. With diminished strength and with loss of influence he withdrew to Tuscany, and laid ineffectual siege to Florence. Month after month dragged along with miserable continuance of futile war. In the summer of 1313, collecting all his forces, Henry prepared to move southward against the King of Naples. But he was seized with illness, and on the 24th of August he died at Buonconvento, not far from Siena. With his death died the hope of union and peace for Italy. His work, undertaken with high purpose and courage, had wholly failed. He had come to set Italy straight before she was ready.[1] The clouds darkened over her. For Dante the cup of bitterness overflowed.

"How Dante was busied, where he was abiding, during the last two years of Henry's stay in Italy, we have no knowledge. One striking fact relating to him is all that is recorded. In the summer of 1311 the Guelfs in Florence, in order to strengthen themselves against the Emperor, determined to relieve from ban and to recall from exile many of their banished fellow-citizens, confident that on returning home they would strengthen the city in its resistance against the Emperor. But to the general amnesty which was issued on the 2d of

[1] *Paradiso*, XXXI, 137.

September there were large exceptions; an impressive evidence of the multitude of the exiles is afforded by the fact that more than a thousand were expressly excluded from the benefit of pardon, and were to remain banished and condemned as before. In the list of those thus still regarded as enemies of Florence stands the name of Dante.

"The death of the Emperor was followed eight months later by that of the Pope, Clement V, under whom the papal throne had been removed from Rome to Avignon. There seemed a chance, if but feeble, that a new Pope might restore the Church to the city which was its proper home, and thus at least one of the wounds of Italy be healed. The Conclave was bitterly divided; month after month went by without a choice, the fate of the Church and of Italy hanging uncertain in the balance. Dante, in whom religion and patriotism combined as a single passion, saw with grief that the return of the Church to Italy was likely to be lost through the selfishness, the jealousies, and the avarice of her chief prelates; and under the impulse of the deepest feeling he addressed a letter of remonstrance, reproach, and exhortation to the Italian cardinals, who formed but a small minority in the Conclave, but who might by union and persistence still secure the election of a pope favorable to the return. This letter is full of a noble but too vehement zeal. 'It is for you, being one at heart, to fight manfully for the Bride of Christ; for the seat of the Bride, which is Rome; for our Italy, and in a word, for the whole commonwealth of pilgrims upon earth.' But words were in vain; and after a struggle kept up for two years and three months, a pope was at last elected who was to fix the seat of the Papacy only the more firmly at Avignon. Once more Dante had to bear the pain of disappointment of hopes in which selfishness had no part."[1]

XI. LITERARY ACTIVITIES
a. Il Convivio [2]

During these dreary and eventful years Dante was neglectful neither of serious study nor of the Muses. However distressing the circumstances of his life might be, he had the power and the inexpressible consolation of withdrawing into that inner sanctuary where he could find peace in the contemplation of truth, and joy in the exercise of his gift of song. Amid trying conditions he never seems to have forgotten that he was an elect man, richly endowed for service, nor to have ceased to feel the imperative of the teacher's instinct to distribute his treasures to those less fortunate. Out of the richness of his inner life issued many sweet rhymes of love, and canzoni on severer and more ethical themes. These odes of passion and of conduct, together with some of his earlier poems, he determined to collect and publish that he might exalt philosophy and share with others the truths which had given him both insight and joy. The proposed volume he entitled

[1] Charles Eliot Norton. See Dinsmore: *Aids to the Study of Dante*, pp. 140–44.

[2] From 1723 this work was called *Il Convito*, but this title does not rest on sufficient authority. Of the thirty known manuscripts, *Convivio* occurs in twenty-six, including the only six which are assigned to the fourteenth century.

PERIOD OF DISCIPLINE

"Il Convivio" (The Banquet), for it was to be a feast of good things. "All men," he says, "by nature desire to know," yet many are bereft, and live all their lives famished for the universal food. "And blessed are those who sit at the table where the bread of angels is consumed, and wretched are those who share the food of cattle. . . . I, who do not sit at the table of the blessed, but having fled the pasture of the common herd, gather up at the feet of those who sit at the other table, what falls from them, and through the sweetness I taste in that which little by little I pick up, perceive how wretched is the life of those whom I have left behind, and moved with pity for them, not forgetting myself, have reserved something for those wretched ones."[1]

He had also another motive, more personal, for publishing the little volume, namely, to clear his own name from stain. Many of the odes which he had published, interpreted literally, revealed him yielding to earthly passion. To set himself right before the world he determined to allegorize these lyrics into a praise of his lady Philosophy. "I fear the infamy of having pursued so great a passion as he who reads the above-named odes conceives to have had dominion over me. Which infamy is entirely quenched by this present discourse concerning myself, which shows that not passion but virtue was the moving cause. I purpose also to reveal the true meaning of the said odes, which none may perceive unless I relate it, because it is hidden under figure of allegory."[2]

[1] *Convivio*, I, 1.   [2] *Ibid.*, I, 2; Wicksteed's translation.

Besides these two prime considerations Dante wished to magnify the Italian tongue.

The banquet was to have fourteen courses, the viands being fourteen odes treating of love and of virtue, and the bread being the exposition of their significance. But the task was never completed. Four only of the treatises were written and three of the odes commented upon. The roots of the failure were in Dante's own nature. Wishing to separate himself from those experiences and utterances which were contrary to his better nature, he endeavored to allegorize his amatory verses into praise of divine philosophy. Untruth makes a poor cement. The carefully designed structure would not hold together. The integrity of Dante's mind would not allow him to explain away what the angels of his better nature told him needed to be repented of. The deepening sincerity of his life made his task impossible and it was abandoned.

The "Convivio" is the literary monument of this second period of Dante's life, as the "Vita Nuova" has made imperishable his youthful love. Its pages attest the growing maturity of his mind, his insatiable thirst for truth, and his firm grasp on the philosophy and theology of his day. Even the modern reader cannot fail to be impressed with the many passages of profound thought expressed in sentences of lofty eloquence. But the extreme care of the author to subtly analyze his subject according to the exact processes of logic, its burden of scholastic lore, the remoteness of many of its discussions from the interests of to-day prevent one from reading its pages except with enforced attention. Not artificial and difficult, however, did it appear to his contemporaries. Villani gives it an enthusiastic reference. "And he began a comment on fourteen of the above-named moral canzonets in the vulgar tongue, which in consequence of his death is found imperfect except on three, which, to judge from what is seen, would have proved a lofty, beautiful, subtile, and most important work; because it is equally ornamented with noble opinions and fine philosophical and astrological reasoning."[1] Boccaccio also calls the "Convivio" "a very beautiful and admirable little work." Its chief biographical interest lies in the exquisite passage in which the exile describes his wanderings. "O that it had pleased the disposer of the universe that the occasion of my excuse had never been! For then neither would others have sinned against me, nor should I have unjustly suffered penalty, the penalty, I mean, of exile and poverty. Since it was the pleasure of the citizens of the most beauteous and the most famous daughter of Rome, Florence, to cast me forth from her most sweet bosom (wherein I was born and nurtured until the culmination of my life, wherein with their good leave I long with all my heart to repose my wearied mind and end the time which is granted me), through well-nigh all the regions whereto this tongue extends, a wanderer, almost a beggar, have I paced, revealing against my will the wound of fortune, which is often wont to be unjustly imputed to him who is wounded. Verily have I been a ship without sail and without rudder, drifted upon ports and straits and

[1] Dinsmore: *Aids to the Study of Dante*, pp. 62–63.

shores by the dry wind that grievous poverty exhales. And I have seemed cheap in the eyes of many who perchance have conceived of me in other guise by some certain fame; for in the sight of whom not only has my person been cheapened, but every work of mine, already accomplished or yet to do, has become of lower price."[1]

The date of this important work can be fixed with some degree of certainty. As Gherardo da Cammino, who died in 1306, is referred to as dead, and King Charles of Naples, who died in 1309, is mentioned as living, we are justified in assigning the date of the "Convivio" between 1306 and 1309. The poet's absorption in the political fortunes of the German Emperor distracted his thoughts from the task of philosophical instruction, and his altered mood after Henry's death made him disinclined to pursue further discussions of such nature. He felt the compulsion of a greater mission than to gather crumbs falling from the table of the wise to feed hungry minds. Upon him lay the weightier burden of making plain to an indifferent world the just judgments of God.

During this period Dante was engaged also in a serious study of his native tongue. In the "Convivio" he tells us of his discovery of the beauty and meaning of words: "And as it often happens that man goes in quest of silver and beyond his intention findeth gold . . . so I, who sought to console myself discovered not only a remedy for my tears, but also the words employed by authors and sciences and books." The de-

[1] *Convivio*, I, 3; Wicksteed's translation.

light in the significance and music of words, which comes to every one of literary tastes, was supplemented in Dante's case by a desire to set forth the resources of the vulgar tongue. He had already proved his faith in the national speech by writing the "Vita Nuova" in the vernacular; when he wrote the "Convivio" his appreciation had so far increased that his loftiest odes to virtue were sung in the speech of his native country, and the profoundest questions in philosophy were discussed in Italian. In this insight Dante was not alone. He was a member of a brilliant group of poets who were releasing literature from the bondage of Latin and giving it the freedom of the living speech of Italy. That they were clear-visioned men in advance of their times is seen by contrasting them with Petrarch who, coming later, gave preference to the Latin, with the result that his most cherished works are buried in an ancient tongue, while only his Italian verse lives. In the interests of this study of the merits of the Italian tongue Dante was preparing a volume entitled "De Vulgari Eloquentia."

b. *De Vulgari Eloquentia*

That this unique and learned critique belongs to the period under consideration is indicated by the following reasons. In the first book there is an allusion to John of Montferrat [1] as to one then living. As this marquis died in 1305, the early pages of the treatise must ante-

[1] *De Vulgari Eloquentia*, I, 12, 38. The second book may have been written later. The opening sentence indicates that work was resumed after having been laid aside.

date that year. At this period of Dante's life the odes were his chief claim to literary distinction, and in both the "Convivio" and the "De Vulgari Eloquentia," the poet is dealing with this form of verse. Both treatises also are concerned with the relationship between the Latin and the vulgar tougue, and both refer to the bitterness of exile. In the "Convivio" also Dante mentions a prospective work in the vulgar tongue, "This will be more fully treated in another place, in a book which, with God's help, I mean to write concerning the vulgar speech." [1] This reference indicates that the material of this work belongs to the epoch of the "Convivio." Some interruption stayed the author's pen in the middle of the fourteenth chapter of the second book, and the task was never completed, although the original plan contemplated at least four books. It is not improbable that the death of Henry and the consequent change of mood and purpose in Dante's life were the reasons why this work, so original in observation and analysis, was never finished.

The intention of the volume is to teach the correct use of the vernacular, which the author distinguishes from the "Grammatica," or artificial speech of the learned. Of these two kinds of speech the vernacular is the nobler, because it is universal and natural. Originally there was but one language, Hebrew, spoken by Adam, which was preserved by the Hebrews after Babel, and became the language of grace used by the Redeemer. The Romance languages in Dante's opinion did not come from the Latin, but are variations of the

[1] *Convivio*, I, 5, 69.

PERIOD OF DISCIPLINE

idiom spoken by the men who settled in Southern Europe after the confusion of tongues. Of the three Romance languages the Italian is awarded precedence. Of the many dialects of Italy which is the noble Italian tongue? He answers: "Not one of them." The vernacular for which Dante labored was the common speech freed from "rude words, involved construction, defective pronunciation, and rustic accents, chosen out in such a degree of excellence, clearness, completeness, and polish as is displayed by Cino of Pistoia and his friend in their canzoni." [1] This friend is Dante himself. This selected language is illustrious, cardinal, courtly, and curial. Dante's originality is seen in this: that in a land possessing no standard speech, but only dialects, he affirmed it to be possible to construct a language at once stately, rhythmical, glorious, and further declared with a confidence, which would appear to be inexcusable conceit had not time vindicated his claim, that Cino and he by genius and learning had achieved this noble vernacular and had established a standard deserving imitation.

In the second book it is maintained that only the loftiest subjects, such as arms, virtue, and love, are the appropriate themes of this illustrious vernacular. The canzone being the most exalted and solemn form of poetry is the proper vehicle to clothe noble thoughts, while the ballad and sonnet are humble forms of poetry, and suited to lighter themes. The author then deals with style, the rules of versification, and is beginning the treatment of the number of lines and syllables in

[1] *De Vulgari Eloquentia*, I, 17.

the canzone when he lays down his pen, never afterward to find the mood and time conjoined to complete his task. Professor Saintsbury, in his "History of Criticism," declares that we have here a document of the very highest value, giving us the first critical treatise on the literary use of the vernacular, by the greatest creative writer of Europe: "I am prepared to claim for it, not merely the position of the most important critical document between the Longinus and the seventeenth century at least, but one of intrinsic importance on a line with that of the very greatest critical documents of all history." [1]

Fragmentary though this book is it reveals to us the originality and boldness of Dante's mind. He was the first to conceive for the common speech of Italy a standard of excellence, and to subject his mother tongue to scientific treatment. Thus through his initiative the latest of the Romance languages was the first to be tested by the principles of art.

c. De Monarchia

Some time in this second period of Dante's life now under consideration he wrote and completed a treatise on government entitled "De Monarchia": a volume unadorned in style, giving in full his political ideals. As the book contains no definite personal reference and no undisputed allusion to contemporary events, it is impossible to assign the exact date of its composition. Because, like the "Vita Nuova," it makes no reference

[1] *History of Criticism*, vol. I, Book III, c. ii. Also Dinsmore: *Aids to the Study of Dante*, p. 209.

THE TOMB OF CINO DE' SINIBALDI AT PISTOIA

The relief shows him lecturing to his pupils

PERIOD OF DISCIPLINE

to his exile, and because in the opening chapter Dante expresses the fear lest he some day be convicted of the charge of the buried talent unless he bears fruit for the public weal, some authorities think the volume was written prior to his banishment in 1302. Others even affirm that the serenity of the author's mood and the maturity of his judgments indicate that he was engaged on the treatise as late as the period of calm between 1318-21 when he had triumphed over outward evil and was writing the "Paradiso." On the whole, however, the weight of evidence seems to date this treatise about the year 1309.[1] One curious bit of internal testimony helps us in this conclusion. In the fourth section of the "Convivio" Dante attacks with severity the Emperor Frederick of Swabia's definition of nobility as "ancient wealth and gracious manners."[2] It happens that the Emperor in this instance was quoting, without acknowledgment, Aristotle's statement that nobility consists of "ancient wealth and virtue,"[3] and surely Dante would not have been at such pains to show that the Emperor was not to be taken seriously, if he had known at the time of writing the fourth book of the "Convivio" this statement of the Greek philosopher. Evidently he was then ignorant of the source of Frederick's declaration. But in the "De Monarchia"[4] he quotes this definition of Aristotle's to substantiate an argument. If the reader will consult Dr. Edward

---

[1] For a full and accessible discussion of the date of the *De Monarchia* see Henry's translation (Houghton Mifflin Co.), p. xxxiii; Temple Classics *Convivio*, p. 425, and Latin Works, p. 281 ff.

[2] *Convivio*, IV, 111, 44.   [3] Aristotle: *Politics*, IV, VIII.

[4] *De Monarchia*, II, 3.

Moore's essay on "Dante and Aristotle," [1] in which are tabulated the references in Dante's works to the philosopher, he will note that there is no allusion to the fourth book of Aristotle's "Politics" in any of Dante's works save the "De Monarchia"; thus leading us to infer that he had not read this fourth treatise with its illuminating definition at the time of writing the "Convivio." Perhaps he had read and forgotten it, but this supposition does not seem likely as the definition is so prominently used in his treatise on Monarchy. Hence we have some warrant for placing the composition of the "De Monarchia" after the writing of the "Convivio."

The confession in the first chapter of the volume under consideration, that the writer was conscious of having borne but little fruit for the public advantage hitherto, does not militate against the date we have assigned, for at that time the poet had published nothing but the "Vita Nuova" and some fugitive poems. Yet it does prohibit us from assigning it a date after the "Inferno" and the "Purgatorio" had brought the author fame.

In 1309 there was an adequate occasion for writing the treatise and the mood of the author might well have been that which is so clearly reflected in his pages. In 1308 Henry of Luxemburg was elevated to the throne of the Roman Empire. The reigning Pope looked upon the newly crowned Emperor with favor and the opposition to the imperial coronation at Rome had not become formidable. To prepare the way for this Messiah

[1] *Studies in Dante*, vol. I, pp. 343, 386.

PERIOD OF DISCIPLINE 159

of his hopes Dante wrote this discussion of the nature and functions of the Empire and its relations to the Church. In lofty exaltation of mood he for once forgot to pity himself for his undeserved misfortunes and uttered his convictions in a spirit of personal detachment. If, as we have stated above,[1] he was in Paris for some months previous to 1310, both his surroundings and the habits induced by study would invite him to write a learned treatise which omitted any personal complaint. The late date further has the sanction of Boccaccio. "At the coming of the Emperor Henry VII," he says, "this illustrious author wrote another book, in Latin prose, called the 'De Monarchia.'"[2]

The bold governmental theories which Dante advocates in this volume are rooted in his religious philosophy. Man, he asserts, has a dual nature, a soul and a body, one incorruptible and the other corruptible. His life therefore has two goals; happiness on earth and happiness in heaven. To attain these he needs two guides, the Emperor and the Pope, the one to direct him in temporal affairs, the other to lead his soul into the presence of God. The chief source of the evils of the day arose, in Dante's opinion, from joining the sword to the crozier, from the intrusion of the Church into secular affairs.

The work is divided into three books. In the first the necessity of universal empire to the well-being of the world is proved. The broad premise is laid down that the goal of civilization is "to keep the whole capacity of the potential intellect constantly actualized"

[1] Page 143.   [2] Dinsmore: *Aids to the Study of Dante*, p. 108.

in thought and action. "Whence it is manifest," says Dante, "that universal peace is the best of those things which God has ordained for our beatitude." Peace was the burden of the song of the angel host; peace was the parting salutation of the Saviour of men, for "it befitted the supreme Saviour to utter the supreme salutation." This universal peace longed for through all the suffering centuries can be secured only under the rule of one supreme monarch.

In the second book it is maintained that the Romans by the will of God acquired imperial authority; their right being attested by Christ, who acknowledged Roman rulership by being born under it and by submitting to death under the agent of Tiberius. As all humanity was punished in the flesh of Christ, our Lord confirmed the universal jurisdiction of Rome by accepting its decision. "Wherefore let those who pretend that they are sons of the Church cease to defame the Roman Empire, to which Christ the bridegroom gave his sanction both at the beginning and at the close of his warfare." [1]

In the third book it is argued that the imperial authority is derived directly from God and is not dependent upon any earthly minister or vicar of God. Yet let it not be asserted that the "Roman Prince is subordinate in naught to the Roman Pontiff: inasmuch as mortal felicity is in a certain sense ordained with reference to immortal felicity. Wherefore let Cæsar honor Peter as a first-born son should honor his father, so that, refulgent with the light of paternal grace, he

[1] *De Monarchia*, Book II, 13.

may illumine with greater radiance the earthly sphere over which he has been set by him who alone is ruler of all things spiritual and temporal."[1]

The theory here set forth is idealized Ghibellinism. Powerful and eloquent as the treatise is it bears all the characteristic medieval defects of reasoning: ingenious arguments are based upon fanciful premises, little discrimination is shown in the valuation of authorities and no appreciation of what constitutes evidence.

The book did not give the author the immediate and widespread fame he anticipated, remaining comparatively unknown until the controversy between Louis, Duke of Bavaria, and Pope John XXII, which occurred some years after Dante's death. "The Duke and his followers," says Boccaccio, "having found this book by Dante, began to make use of its arguments to defend themselves and their authority; whereby the book, which was scarcely known up to this time, became very famous." Afterwards Cardinal Beltrando of Poggetto "seized the book and condemned it in public to the flames, charging that it contained heretical matters. In like manner he attempted to burn the bones of the author, and would have done so, to the eternal infamy and confusion of his own memory, had he not been opposed by a good and noble Florentine knight by the name of Pino della Tosa."

It is now six hundred years since Dante conceived and defended his political theories and time has applied its acid test. His contention that both Church and State would be purer and more efficient if the temporal

[1] *De Monarchia*, Book III, 16.

power be separated from the spiritual has been amply vindicated; but his dream of universal peace under a divinely ordained monarch having world-wide authority has revealed itself to be unsubstantial. Italy has come to unity, not through the weight of a single power imposed upon her from above, but through a spirit of nationality created by the many, and the foundations of her peace rest upon the law-abiding habits of a free people trained in self-government, and not on the sword of a conqueror.

In the fierce controversy between Florence and Henry, Dante was on the wrong side. The hope of Italy was in the rising strength of its free cities, not in the benevolent despotism of the German monarch. The poet utterly failed to appreciate at its true worth the chief political movement of his day. The promise of peace and national greatness was in that spirit which impelled the Florentines to defend their city with desperate courage and enabled them to make a defensive league with other Italian cities — a spirit which Dante did not understand and which he bitterly denounced. The future was with the allied cities maintaining liberty through union, and not with the representative of the Holy Roman Empire. Italy has come to that condition for which Dante yearned by doing that which he condemned — throwing off the foreign yoke and uniting for mutual defense. But he was not wrong in his essential insight that a contentious world could find peace only by all nations yielding obedience to some wise and impartial supra-national power. Thinking in the familiar terms of his century, Dante thought of this supreme arbiter as a divinely ordained monarch. We to-day, thinking in the terms of our democratic traditions, conceive of the sovereign power as an international court, whose decrees are to be sustained by international force; but with the war-weary poet we agree "that universal peace is the best of those things which God had ordained for our beatitude," and the bitter experience of six centuries has taught us that this blessedness is not to be obtained by such chimeras as "the balance of power" or invincible alliances, but that it can come only through a sovereign power that is above all nations.

XII. MIND AND CHARACTER

Reviewing the section of the poet's life from 1290 to 1313, which we would denominate as the muscularizing period, we find that although our knowledge of his movements is small, he has given us in the works written at this time a clear delineation of his essential character and his prevailing moods. The decade from 1290 to 1300 was a period of maturing powers, increasing influence, and widening fame. In those years, rich in experience and valuable in the discipline they brought, Dante won for himself a distinguished position in his native city. We cannot affirm that he was happy; he was too sensitive for happiness; the fires in his breast were too hot and the urge of his ambitions was too strong; but he had found a fountain of joy compared with which mere happiness seemed trivial. We refer to his almost ecstatic delight in study. He experienced a depth of satisfaction in searching for truth to which the modern student is almost a stranger. In the Middle Ages the intellect of Europe, awakening from prolonged lethargy, had not yet learned its limitations, and to it all things seemed possible. Absolute and complete knowledge appeared to be within the grasp of the eager mind, and the student, pursuing truth with a religious rapture, saw in the written page the "very sparkling of the Holy Ghost." Such keen and confident joy has gone largely from scholarship to-day, but to Dante, according to the measure of his transcendent genius, came this abounding and exultant delight.

After the death of Beatrice, in seeking for the silver of consolation in philosophy he found gold — the gold of "words of authors and of sciences and of books," and he "began to feel so much of her [Philosophy's] sweetness that the love of her expelled and destroyed every other thought."[1] What modern student could write of philosophy: "Oh, most sweet and unutterable looks, of a sudden ravishing the mind, which appear in the demonstrations in the eyes of Philosophy when she discourses to her lovers!"[2] So eager was he that his eyes grew dim with his vigils.[3] Even the familiar Scriptures seemed to him "a star charged with light."

After the tragedy of his exile we are not to think of him as an embittered and vindictive man. Doubtless he was deeply wounded by the undeserved infamy, realizing that both himself and his works were cheapened in the eyes of men. Doubtless the rude and boisterous courts of the lords of Italy were extremely distasteful to him. Often he cried out in anger and self-pity; often

[1] *Convivio*, II, 13.   [2] *Ibid.*, II, 16.   [3] *Ibid.*, III, 9, 147.

he was homesick and despondent and wretched, but these moods were not habitual. Athanasius had said of his own exile, "It is a little cloud and will soon pass." And while Dante may have thought the cloud to be bigger and blacker than it appeared to the great theologian, he too saw it permeated and gilded by the sun. The odes written during this period reveal him in a kindly light. In the one with which he intended to close the "Convivio" he declares that "this exile which is awarded me I count mine honor." Again in his treatise on the power of language he utters his sense of victory over the misfortunes of his life: "How glorious it [language] makes its familiar friends we ourselves know, who for the sweetness of this glory cast even our exile behind our back."[1] So thoroughly was he chastened by the lofty discipline of writing the "Comedy" that, when his spirit was lifted to the vision and courage experienced in the planet Mars, he could represent his destiny as coming to the sight as sweet harmony comes to the ear from an organ. In the mind and purpose of God he was persuaded that his exile was wholly good. For fifteen years, he claimed in a letter to a Florentine friend, he had borne his exile patiently. These comforting convictions which consoled the closing years of his life were not absent entirely during this season of storm and stress.

The opening pages of the "Convivio" give us a very pleasant presentation of his prevailing mood at this middle period of his life. It is amiable, generous, lofty; far other than the fierce scorn which popular imagina-

[1] *De Vulgari Eloquentia*, I, 17.

tion has considered to be the author's habitual temper. "Oh happy are those few who sit at that table where the bread of angels is eaten, and wretched are those who share the food of cattle. But since a man is naturally the friend of every man, and every man grieves for the defect of him whom he loves, they who feed at so lofty a table are not without pity for those whom they see go about eating grass and acorns on the pasture of beasts."

The introduction to the "De Monarchia" reveals Dante's innate nobility of soul, his craving for fame, his sense of mission, his instinctive and ever-present desire to share with others what of good has been disclosed to him:

"All men on whom the Higher Nature has stamped the love of Truth should especially concern themselves in laboring for posterity, in order that future generations may be enriched by their efforts, as they themselves were made rich by the efforts of generations past. For that man who is embued with public teachings, but cares not to contribute something to the public good, is far in arrears of his duty, let him be assured; he is, indeed, not a 'tree planted by the rivers of water that bringeth forth his fruit in his season,' but rather a destructive whirlpool, always engulfing, and never giving back what it has devoured. Often meditating with myself upon these things, lest I should some day be found guilty of the charge of the buried talent, I desire for the public weal, not only to burgeon, but to bear fruit, and to establish truths unattempted by others. For he who should demonstrate from a theorem of

Euclid, who should attempt after Aristotle to set forth anew the nature of happiness, who should undertake after Cicero to defend old age a second time — what fruit could such a one yield? None, forsooth; his tedious superfluousness would merely occasion disgust.

"Now, inasmuch as among other abstruse and important truths, knowledge of temporal Monarchy is most important and obscure, and inasmuch as the subject has been shunned by all because it has no direct relation to gain, therefore my purpose is to bring it out from its hiding place, that I may both keep watch for the good of the world, and be the first to win the palm of so great a prize for my own glory. Verily, I undertake a difficult task and one beyond my powers, but my trust is not so much in my own worth as in the light of the Giver 'that giveth to all men liberally and upbraideth not.'" [1]

The reader will notice Dante's eagerness to do something that has not been attempted by others. This passion of the pioneer for the untried is eminently characteristic. It appears in his purpose to say of Beatrice what never was said of any other woman, in this effort to establish the right, the sanctity and the independence of the imperial power, in his attempt to make the first critical study of the dialects of Italy, in his confidence that he was setting the standard of a noble Italian tongue superior to all the dialects, and finally in a masterpiece so unique in design and execution that it imitated no predecessor and has left no successor.

In the introduction to the third book of the "De

[1] *De Monarchia;* Henry's translation.

Monarchia" the heroic temper of his mind finds clear expression. Knowing that the truth about to be discussed may bring him enemies he exclaims: "The truth may be a cause against me, since it cannot be brought forth without causing certain men to blush. But since Truth from her immutable throne demands it . . . I will engage in the present conflict, and by the arm of him who with his blood liberated us from the power of darkness, I will cast out the ungodly and the liar from the arena, while the world looks on. Wherefore should I fear, when the Spirit, co-eternal with the Father and the Son, says by the mouth of David, 'The righteous shall be in everlasting remembrance, he shall not be afraid of evil tidings.'"

It is interesting to note Dante's curious sense that whatever he does has universal significance — "I keep watch for the good of the world": and "while the world looks on!" But it is more interesting to reflect that this apparently vainglorious boast has been made good by unparalleled achievement.

The letters written during this period, to which we have already referred, reveal the same man that is disclosed in the more elaborate treatises — one who feels deeply his personal wrongs and the evils of his day, intense in his patriotism, eager to share with others the delights of knowledge, craving an imperishable name, profoundly convinced of a prophetic mission, a lover of philosophy, but never attaining the calm poise of the philosophic mind, serene at the core of his being, at peace with God and resting upon Him, experiencing a rapturous joy which ever and anon breaks forth in the most unexpected places, a militant, bleeding soldier of the ideal, drinking deep of the primal fountains of satisfaction.

Disdainful and withering in his scorn, Dante is also passionately intemperate in many of his utterances, even affirming that the sentiments of his opponents should be answered with daggers and not with words. All this is evident enough, yet there are some considerations which must be borne in mind if one would rightly estimate his character. First, he believed it a virtue to hate shams with an intense hatred. He wrote in italics that his words might be powerful against evil. Moreover, the Middle Ages, as has been well said, had every virtue except moderation, and he should be judged by the standards of his times. The fallibility of the mind was not so clear to men of those days as to us. Truth seemed so accessible and authoritatively revealed, and error so much a matter of willfulness, that the need of charity was not so evident. Again it was the woe of the world and not his personal wrongs that called forth his hottest indignation. Finally it must be remembered that Dante was an artist as consciously following a model in uttering his fiercest outbursts of indignation as when he was celebrating the nature and influence of love. The Hebrew seers were his models; he imitated them as closely in forging his thunderbolts of wrath as he did Aristotle in formulating his philosophy. If he prophesies against Florence, it is in the style of Jeremiah. His wrath is never unrestrained fury, but is constrained to those excellences of form which shall delight the wise and confer lasting honor upon the author. If he exhorts Henry to greater activity, he speaks with such a display of learning that others shall be incited to study and he himself shall win a name among the learned. Toleration was not considered a virtue in his day; to smite all shams and to lighten against all evil was his ideal; truth was so clearly revealed that only the stupid and the perverse could fail of righteousness, and against them the prophet had thundered; therefore Dante rejoiced that he could utter words that glowed with the same fires that burned in the sentences of the ancient seers.

CHAPTER III

THE CRUCIAL YEAR : 1313

THE year 1313 apparently marks a distinct epoch in Dante's spiritual experience. It is quite as crucial as the years 1290 and 1300. It is a time of collapsing hope, of deep heart-searching and of high resolve.

The first period of the poet's life, according to the divisions which we have ventured to adopt, ended with the death of Beatrice. Until this twenty-fifth year — 1290 — Dante affirms that his true life was in a dream-world, which was shattered when "the Lord of Justice called the most gentle one to glory." Then follow some twenty-three years of discipline which quicken his insight, broaden his sympathies, and toughen the fibres of his intellectual and moral character. The sensitive lover becomes the man of affairs, deeply interested in the political struggles of the time; the student eagerly exploring all the realms of knowledge; the exile, brooding indeed over his personal wrongs, but still more over the follies and wickedness of the world. Whatever the moral lapses of which he was guilty during this middle period of his life they were due to the fact that he was under the spell of no compelling object of devotion. His personality was divided; he had not found himself. Pronounced as was Dante's individuality he must needs be in servitude of a guide. His powers could be expanded and unified only as they came into subjection to an ideal or a truth comprehensive and glorious enough to enslave both imagination and will.

The events of the year 1313 left him a disappointed and disillusioned man. His fierce advocacy of Henry had closed to him the gates of Florence forever; the Emperor's death had dissolved his dream of a peaceful and ordered world; the Papacy afforded him no consolation, for it was in his view a ravening wolf, the devourer and not the guide of men.

When one's world dissolves in black disaster a deep-souled man turns either to pessimism, or to God. The problem which confronted Dante was first of all a personal one, how to save his own life from utter ruin! Is there no way for a man to live victoriously when all the conditions of his life are hopelessly wrong? Dante's spirit was too virile and positive for pessimism, and to God he turned to find that peace which a frenzied world could not give. As neither Pope nor Emperor could lead in the way of felicity out of the world's dark wood he retired to the Inner Light. His guides would be right reason and that divine revelation which even a corrupt church could not hinder. His restless heart, not finding peace in the polluted and broken order of the world's affairs, turned to that Light above

> "which visible
> Makes the Creator unto every creature,
> Who only in beholding Him has peace." [1]

But personal considerations were never the weightiest with one in whose heart the fires of ethical passion

---

[1] *Paradiso*, xxx, 100 ff.

burned with steady intensity. Dante felt that he was sent to keep "watch for the good of the world." On him had fallen the mantle of the Hebrew prophets. From his mother's womb he had been called to a sacred mission. The very stars had foretold it; impregnate with great virtue their fire had endowed him with lofty virtue. To him was entrusted the dread task of showing to a lost and bewildered world the true path to peace and righteousness. The same impulse that from the first had led him to share with men the delights of his information now with great urgency put him under bonds to make known the true way to peace and liberty.

It is instructive to note how Dante looked upon his past life in this critical hour of heart searching and new resolve. We find this interpretation of his previous career in the first canto of the "Inferno." As there are thirty-three cantos each in the "Purgatorio" and the "Paradiso" — symbol of the years of the earthly life of Christ — and thirty-four in the "Inferno" we are justified in the conclusion that the first canto is an introduction, written after the manner of authors to explain their purpose and motives. While one need not deny that even in this preface Dante writes allegorically as a representative of humanity, yet the chief note is a distinctly personal one. Surely Dante's own interpretation of his life is authoritative. He had too great respect for the facts of experience and too genuine a love for fitting them into a consistent scheme not to make the outline of his moods and adventures as here recounted substantially accurate.

In his own inimitable style Dante tells us that "midway in the journey of our life I found myself in a dark wood, where the right way was lost. . . . I cannot well recount how I entered it, so full was I of slumber at that moment when I abandoned the true way." At the end of the Woeful Valley rose a high hill, lighted by the sun. After a little rest he began ascending the slope, "so that the firm foot was always the lower. And lo! almost at the beginning of the steep a she leopard . . . so hindered my road that I often turned to go back." Then a lion came against him, giving him great fear. Most terrible of all, a she-wolf pushed him back, "thither where the sun is silent." Then Virgil appears, offering to be his guide along the better way. After a period of hesitation and explanation which the poet recounts in Canto II, the two set out at evening "along the deep and savage way."

Of this much-discussed allegory the following interpretation is, I think, a reasonable one. Dante assigns Easter week of the year 1300 as the period of a thorough spiritual awakening. Perceiving himself miserable and lost in the tangled and dark forest of Italian political and ecclesiastical conditions, his aroused mind conceived a lofty ideal and formed a fixed purpose. He would find a way out of the dreadful forest to virtue and happiness for himself and of good government for Florence and Italy. As the woodland on the summit of Purgatory undoubtedly represents the ideal condition of a world rightly governed where the individual attains true liberty and temporal happiness, we are justified in interpreting the delectable mountain in the first canto of the "Inferno" as the poet's ideal of a temporal condition, which, if attained, would mean escape from the savage wood in which he now finds himself. At the very beginning of the ascent the poet encounters a leopard. It is the morning of Good Friday, the sun is just rising and the moon is full. The inexperienced and hopeful pilgrim attacks this spotted beast, but she hindered him so that he often turned to go back. Then appeared the lion and the wolf. A spiritual interpretation is that these beasts represent respectively the sins of incontinence, violence, and avarice. And this may well be true in an allegorical interpretation of the life of man. But Dante at thirty-five would not be hopefully attacking the personal sins of incontinence, neither was avarice an unconquerable passion in him. If we are right in finding in this canto a record of personal experiences, then the political interpretation of these symbols is preferable. This being assumed, Dante affirms that soon after his moral awakening he encountered the hostility of Florence, mottled by the political division of the Blacks and the Whites. More terrible still was the lion of France and the political hunger of Charles of Valois. Worst of all was the wolfish Papacy with its insatiable avarice. The factions of Florence impeded Dante in his efforts to achieve his political ideals: France dismayed him by her violent opposition; but it was the Papacy whose malign and evil nature drove him back to despair. If the twelve or thirteen hours occupied in fighting the beasts, discoursing with Virgil, and in deciding to follow him, represent years, then Dante informs us that it was some thirteen years after his awakening before he was persuaded to change his methods of attaining his ideal and seriously began his mystical journey.

What we know of the poet's life makes plausible the interpretation we have given. If he is recording a fact that it was in Easter week in the year 1300 that he came to himself, then it is equally true that immediately he was set upon by the factional passions of Florence. Good Friday of 1300 was April 8. On June 15 he assumed the office of Prior and grappled with the fierce antagonism of the Blacks and the Whites. In 1301 France, in the person of Charles of Valois, came to Florence and closed the way to liberty, and in 1302 Dante felt the hostility of Boniface VIII. Yet he did not despair entirely. He continued his political activities for some years longer, but with the ever-increasing conviction that although his ideal was true the way in which he was walking was not the right road for him, or indeed for any. He had consistently tried to bring in better government and juster conditions by his active interest and efforts, yet he was being driven back to where "the sun is silent." The conviction was growing within him that, unlike Boëthius and Cicero, he could not be an active man of affairs, indulging in literary pursuits as a pastime. Poetry, not politics, was his exclusive vocation; Virgil, not Aristotle, his guide. He was a seer, as well as a poet and the Almighty had called him. Not by militant self-assertion could he or any other climb the heights of freedom. Only by self-surrender and obedience to a higher will is the soul redeemed. Yet like every prophet who has assumed a tremendous task, Dante experienced a period of hesitation and held with himself a prolonged debate, which he has faithfully recorded in Canto II of the "Inferno." I do not think that Dante was ever seriously unsettled in his Catholic faith, or that he had ever forgotten his purpose to write an immortal work in honor of his lady, or that there was ever a time when the way of life as he describes it in the "Comedy" would not have seemed to him a truer way than self-reliant struggle for an unattainable mountain. Beatrice and his purpose were ever in the background of his consciousness. Nevertheless, present duties were urgent. The call to strenuous activity for a better Italy was imperative. His purposes were high and good. He was acting as a patriot and a practical man, yet he was disturbed by an ever-increasing realization that he was pursuing an impossible way. By another path, under another guide, must he seek liberty and joy.

Moreover, his prevailing mood had changed during these thirteen years of struggle with the beasts. In 1300, when he set out to climb the sunlit mountain, it was in a self-reliant spirit. He fought the beasts in his own strength. Not in this mood can the mountain be climbed. When in the "Purgatorio" he would ascend the holy mountain he is girded with the reed of humility, his face is washed with the dews of repentance, and he is trusting to a Power higher than his own will. This definite change from good works to faith, from trust in self to trust in God, is the familiar experience of the mystics. And it was in this mood that Dante turned away from active participation in the world's affairs and gave himself to his "mystic, unfathomable song." It was in the year 1313, if I am not mistaken, that Dante definitely outlined his poem and thought out its marvelous structure. Not that it was shapeless in his mind before that date. Its general nature may have been determined in that memorable vision to which he refers in the closing pages of the "Vita Nuova." [1]

Boccaccio, who was born in this epochal year, 1313, and who affirms that he conversed with Dante's nephew, Andrea Poggi, with Dino Perini, who claimed the greatest possible intimacy and friendship with the poet, and with Dante's daughter Beatrice, from whom he derived much information, is authority for the following not improbable story.

Some one in Florence, he says, searching (about 1307) among the chests containing Dante's belongings which had been concealed when his house was looted, found seven cantos of an unfinished poem. Greatly admiring them, he brought them to Dino di Messer Lambertuccio, who pronounced them Dante's. Finding that he was then with Marquis Moroello in Lunigiana, they forwarded the manuscript to the Marquis, who urged Dante "not to leave so lofty a beginning without its fitting end." "I naturally supposed," said Dante, "that,

[1] In the *Bulletina della Società Dantesca Italiana* (N.S.) xv, Parodi endeavors to show that the *Inferno* and *Purgatorio* were practically completed before 1313. I cannot but think that his opinion is erroneous. His reasoning rests heavily on the assumption that Henry is the *Veltro*, and that the different moods displayed in the two compositions reflect the events of the times; whereas, the themes themselves are sufficient to account for the moods of the writer.

THE CRUCIAL YEAR

in the general ruin of my things, these and many other books of mine were lost. Both from this belief and from the multitude of other troubles that came upon me, by reason of my exile, I had utterly abandoned the high design laid hold of for this work. But since fortune has unexpectedly restored the work to me, and since it is agreeable to you, I will try to recall the original idea and proceed according as grace shall be given me!"[1]

A tradition has come down to us, on the authority of Frate Ilario's letter, long supposed to be a forgery, but now regarded more favorably by many scholars, that Dante began the Comedy in Latin after the following manner:

> Ultima regna canam, fluido contermina mundo,
> Spiritibus quæ lata patent quæ præmia solvunt
> Pro meritis cuicumque suis.[2]

Some such production Dante may well have begun about 1300 and left unfinished to be resumed in other form about 1307 at the suggestion of Marquis Moroello Malaspina. "When Dante," continues Boccaccio, "had thus recommenced the great work, he did not finish it, as many think, without frequent interruption. Indeed, many times, according as the seriousness of supervening events demanded, he put it aside, sometimes for months, again for years, unable to accomplish anything on it." Poor Dante! Those little interruptions endear him to the whole tribe of writers and excuse some hot outbursts of wrath!

[1] Dinsmore: *Aids to the Study of Dante*, p. 105.
[2] The Latin text of Frate Ilario's letter is given in Fraticelli's *Storia della Vita di Dante*, and translations in Toynbee's *Dante Alighieri* and elsewhere.

During the years between 1307 and 1313 as he studied and traveled, he doubtless made many notes and perchance wrote whole sections which afterwards were inserted in the "Comedy": but certainly he would not declare, as he does in "De Vulgari Eloquentia" (II, III), that forms of verse other than canzoni, ballads, and sonnets are irregular and illegitimate, and that arms, love, and virtue are to be treated only in the lofty tragic style, if at the time when the second book of the treatise was composed (probably about 1308) he was meditating the "Comedy" in terza rima.

It is eminently characteristic of him that he should in this tragic hour of unsettlement search for surer foundations upon which to rest his hopes and endeavors. He had done the same at every critical period of which we have record. In early youth his joy was in the salutation of his lady. When this was withheld he determines to place his happiness on more secure basis than the moods of his gentil donna. Henceforth he will rejoice in the praise which he himself offers. After the death of Beatrice, when the sentiment of adoration had exhausted itself, he turned to the study of philosophy as a safer rest for mind and spirit. So now, when all temporal supports had fallen from him, he seeks to build on a Reality which cannot be removed. His support is in the Eternal and in the consolations which come from the contemplations and expressions of truth.

The temptation must have been strong to Dante at this hour of thaw and dissolution to abandon the world and seek the consolations of study. Plato speaking of

THE CRUCIAL YEAR

the lovers of true wisdom says: "Now, he who has become a member of this little band, and has tasted how sweet and blessed his treasure is, and has watched the madness of the many, with the full assurance that there is scarcely a person who takes a single judicious step in public life, and that there is no ally with whom he may safely march to the succor of the just; nay, that, should he attempt it, he will be like a man that has fallen among wild beasts, — unwilling to join in their iniquities, and unable singly to resist the fury of all, and therefore destined to perish before he can be of any service to his country or his friends, and do no good to himself or any one else; — having, I say, weighed all this, such a man keeps quiet and confines himself to his own concerns, like a man who, in a storm of dust and spray driven by the wind, takes shelter behind a wall; and when from his retreat he sees the infection of lawlessness spreading over the rest of mankind, he is well content if he can in any way live his life here untainted in his own person by unrighteousness and unholy deeds, and when the time for his release arrives takes his departure with noble hope and with a cheerful and serene mind."[1]

Although Dante's ethical passion was too intense to allow him to retire from the world for philosophic contemplation, he must have felt the need of a quiet retreat where he might have uninterrupted leisure to think out his message and perfect his verses. As his theme was a deeply spiritual one, and he himself was one of the most learned theologians of his day, it would

[1] *Republic*, 496 c.

seem but natural that he should bend his steps to some monastery for the necessary calm and sympathy. This experiment he seems to have tried, but without much satisfaction. There is a credible tradition that, after the death of Henry, he sought peaceful asylum in the monastery of Santa Croce di Fonte Avellana, on the slopes of Monte Catria, in the territory of Agubbio. Peter Damien's vivid description of the monastery [1] would indicate that the poet had intimate knowledge of the place. From this high seat among the Apennines he looked down upon this little threshing-floor and laid the grand design of his reconstructed masterpiece. But the atmosphere of this religious haven was certainly not congenial to him, for he made its founder to say: "That cloister of old bore a fertile harvest for these heavens, but is now found so barren that its shame will soon be laid bare."

Even if the conditions in this monastery were unfavorable for meditation and its air sterile of spiritual vigor, one would conjecture that Dante would have sought asylum in some other cloister, or better still that he would have domiciled in some university town where he might have the association of minds ripe in learning and piety. The astonishing fact, however, is that although he was meditating and constructing a poem of infinite subtlety and range, requiring, one would suppose, unbroken leisure in order to keep its many parts in proper relation, Dante wended his way to the courts which were the centres of the political intrigues and military activities of the day; where the

[1] *Paradiso*, xxi, 106 ff.

THE CRUCIAL YEAR

clamor was loudest and political passion the hottest; where life was intensest and the hound of the Ghibellines was straining at the leash to attack the wolf of the Papacy — first to the camp of Uguccione at Lucca and then to the bustling court of Can Grande went the poet for peace to elaborate his song.

Milton could not have written under such conditions. During the period of his political engrossment the springs of his song were entirely choked with public cares. "His soul was like a star and dwelt apart." Like the hermit thrush he could sing only in the silent places.

Shakespeare probably wrote his supreme dramas under pressure and amid constant interruptions. They must be ready at a certain date, the lines must fit the talents and the peculiarities of the contemplated actors, corrections were made in the confusion behind the scenes while the play was being rehearsed. When the external compulsion was removed the English bard stopped writing. His genius was a fountain gushing up under the weight of waters.

Two reasons among lesser ones may account for Dante's strange selection of abiding-places in which to write his masterpiece, for bread and quiet would not have been wanting either in the religious houses or at the universities. In the first place, he was not a dreamy contemplative, but a man of active temperament, an agitator and a reformer. Literature was more than an opiate for personal disappointment, it was a decalogue. Even if his hope of a peaceful world had died with the lofty Henry, still he was passionately zealous to do his part in bringing the just judgments of God upon an avaricious Papacy and an evil Florence. The hound of God and the impending day of recompense were ever in his thought, and where the hosts of retribution were gathering there he was eager to be.

Again his genius was at its best when under restriction, like a river whose current flows strongest where its channel is narrowed. His song was sweetest and his thoughts most original when he voluntarily shackled his muse with difficult metres, symbolic meanings, limited space. Obstacles aroused him; adverse conditions kindled the fires which favorable surroundings would allow to die out. He seems to have needed for the best workings of his mind the stimulus of active life, the excitement of affairs. Evidently he found relief from his exacting studies in the society of practical men rather than in the company of scholars.

That the "Inferno" and the "Purgatorio" were written in the midst of stirring events has given to them a vitality and a realism which they would not have had had they been written in a cloister. The "Paradiso," composed in greater quiet is cumbered with medieval lore which often weighs down the wing even of Dante's imagination.

If his mind needed the stimulus of affairs for its best activities, he was saved from mental dissipation by his truly marvelous power of concentration. Boccaccio says that "if any pleasing contemplation came upon him when in company, it mattered not what was asked of him he would never answer the question until he had ended or abandoned his train of thought." No news would divert him from his studies. "Once when he chanced to be at an apothecary's shop in Siena, there was brought to him a little book, very famous among men of understanding, but which he had not seen. . . . So lying breast downward upon a bench in front of the apothecary's he laid the book before him and began to read with great eagerness." A grand tournament of young noblemen created great uproar, there was noise of instruments and applause, fair ladies danced and boys played numerous games, yet "none saw Dante move from his position, or once lift his eyes from his book." For three hours he remained absorbed in his reading, and declared to an astonished questioner that he had heard nothing of the confusion.[1] With such powers of mental abstraction it mattered little whether he was in the wilderness or whether the gaunt soldiers of Uguccione wrangled o'er their spears under his very window.

The sovereign sense of a prophetic mission that now clothes Dante as a garment, the vast task he assumes, cause him to change his whole poetical apparatus. The mightier theme releases hitherto unused energies. Perhaps the most distinctive and prominent of all the gifts of the man is the visualizing power of his imagination. The preternatural energy of this faculty has made the "Inferno" one of the imperishable books of literature. Yet this remarkable talent seems to have been full-born. If the reader will recall all that Dante had written up to the present moment, he cannot fail to observe how little indication the poet had given

[1] Dinsmore: *Aids to the Study of Dante*, pp. 97, 98.

of his ability to think in vivid pictures. During the period in which he was composing the "Vita Nuova," Love, indeed, appeared before him in visible shape; he also tells us that he had a very wonderful vision. But this most precious of his talents lies buried during the middle period of his life. Either its value to poetry he did not rightly estimate, or this power displayed itself only when his nature was powerfully stirred. Nothing in his previous writing prepares one for that splendor of imagination which bursts upon us in the very first page of the "Inferno." Heretofore he has been a lyrist, celebrating truth and beauty; now thoughts and experiences are externalized in vivid imagery.

Not only does Dante change the form in which he expresses thought, he radically modifies his attitude toward his work. He reaches a conclusion which is ultimately forced upon every great teacher of men. He is convinced that education is not a banquet, but a discipline. Man's chief need is not varied and delightful information, but insight and self-mastery. He realizes that he can best serve humanity not by spreading a pleasant feast, but by revealing a way — hard and glorious — along which educated wills may climb to liberty and vision. Therefore he lays aside his singing robes and becomes an interpreter. He is no longer a celebrant but a seer. He harnesses new horses to his chariot of the Sun. The conscience and passion of a prophet control his ambitions as an artist. Neither love nor philosophy is sufficient for his song, but the whole sphere of truth. For his purpose neither ballads nor

THE CRUCIAL YEAR 187

sonnets with an interpretation in prose are now adequate for his larger theme. Neither Guido Guinicelli, Brunetto Latini, nor Boëthius are his models. He has outgrown them. He casts off much of his medievalism and takes his place consciously among the universal masters, Homer, Virgil, Lucan, Horace, and Ovid, the sixth among the lords of fairest song.

When Dante at last definitely set himself to produce a work of lasting greatness, how little he had done to prove himself capable of fulfilling an ambition so lofty! He had to his credit the "Vita Nuova," of which, if we may believe Boccaccio, he was somewhat ashamed, a group of lyrics, a number of published letters, the "De Monarchia," and two unfinished volumes — the "Convivio" and "De Vulgari Eloquentia." He has yet to prove that he was able to constrain his genius to sustained majestic effort. That faith in his powers which permitted him in the very beginning of the "Comedy" to number himself with the world's greatest poets, was not justified by anything which he had yet achieved.

If he had not proved his ability to sustain his creative imagination through patient, arduous years to the accomplishment of a gigantic task, yet in wealth of intellectual material he was not lacking. Of his native Italian he was completely a master, and he had critically studied the works of the Italian poets who preceded him. He wrote Provençal with ease and was familiarly acquainted with the songs of southern France. Less intimately he knew the poetry of the north of France. Latin he could read and use with facility. He had learned his "Æneid" as thoroughly as he had learned his Latin Bible. Cicero and Boëthius were cherished friends and counselors. Greek being to him practically a sealed language he knew Aristotle only through Latin translations, but to him the great Greek was "Magister sapientium." Homer was only the shadow of a great name. He had studied the "Ars Poetica" of Horace, and carefully read Ovid, Lucan, Statius. Livy he knew and Paulus Orosius; something also of Seneca and Juvenal. Lover of stars, he had studied astronomy with eager thoroughness in the "Elementa Astronomica" of Alfraganus, an epitome of the great works of Ptolemy by an Arabian scholar, which had been translated into Latin. Dante's knowledge of theology was profound. The system of Saint Thomas Aquinas he knew from beginning to end. Scarcely less was his intimacy with Saint Augustine and Albertus Magnus. In the writings of the great mystics, Bernard, Hugh and Richard of Saint Victor, Saint Bonaventura, he delighted. Professor Edward Moore, than whom no one is more competent to speak, expresses "amazement at the variety and extent of Dante's learning. No doubt the Middle Ages furnish many other examples of such prodigies of industry. But they occur among professional students, and teachers; it would be difficult to find a parallel to the literary activity and extensive reading of Dante in any life of such perpetual distraction and unrest."

CHAPTER IV

YEARS OF THE DIVINE COMEDY: 1314-1321

WHILE Dante was giving absorbed attention to the work which was to show the only way by which a defeated man or the bewildered nations could find temporal and spiritual happiness, an event occurred which for a moment drew his thoughts from his task and caused him to lift up his voice in wrathful admonition. Probably it also added an intensity of wrath to the "Inferno."

I. LETTER TO THE ITALIAN CARDINALS

Clement V, the Gascon Pope, who never entered Italy and who had transferred the papal court from Rome to Avignon, died April 20, 1314, eight months after the Emperor. Dante believed that the death of the Pope was a divine judgment for his treachery to Henry, and that his soul was thrust into hell for simony. There was now an opportunity for the Cardinals to elect a true shepherd of the people, and restore to Rome the chair of Peter, thus healing one of the wounds of Italy, and bringing holiness to the Church. How thoroughly the King of France had brought the Church under French influence is seen by the fact that when the Cardinals met to elect a successor to Clement, of the twenty-four only six were Italians, the others being French, Gascons, and Provençals. The Conclave was hopelessly divided, the French siding with the Italians.

Month after month went by without an election. The division in the Conclave reappeared in the populace. "The Gascons attacked the homes of the Italian Cardinals and pillaged them. The rabble cried, 'Death to the Italian Cardinals!' A fire broke out which threatened the hall of the Conclave, and finally the Cardinals, bursting through the back wall fled in dismay. For more than two years the papal throne was vacant." To us the Italian Cardinals seem to have put up a brave fight for Italy and the purity of the Church; but at the time Dante evidently feared that the jealousies of the prelates and their lust of gain and power which had betrayed the Church in the past, might be manifest at this crisis. Therefore from his seclusion he addressed to them a letter, too stilted and heavily ornamented for our modern taste, too severe in its castigation of offenders bitterly repentant of what they considered past mistakes of judgment, but which Dante called sins; yet withal a letter full of noble sentiment and deep feeling. "Yet the wound will be healed, if ye, who were the authors of this transgression, will all with one accord fight manfully for the Bride of Christ, for the Throne of the Bride, which is Rome, for our Italy, and in a word for the whole Commonwealth of Pilgrims upon the earth." But his hope was not realized. After two years of struggle a pope was elected who continued the Babylonian exile, and in Dante's opinion drank the blood of Peter.[1]

Where the poet was abiding when he wrote his vehement epistle to the Italian Cardinals is not known.

---

[1] *Paradiso*, XXVII, 58.

Perhaps he thought out its fiery sentences in the seclusion of Fonte Avellana, but probably it issued from the stirring political activity of Lucca. In the June following the death of Clement that city came under the dominion of the famous Ghibelline chief Uguccione della Faggiuola. Dante, finding the monastery no longer congenial, and urged by what seems a temperamental necessity to find peace in a storm centre, turned his steps toward the seat of the most promising political energies of the day. Of this visit he has left a record. In Purgatory Bonagiunta of Lucca prophesies that "A woman is born, and wears not yet the veil, who will make my city pleasant to thee, however men may blame it." [1] As Lucca was an ally of Florence, and Dante would there be in the power of his enemies, he could only have visited it when it was in the possession of his Ghibelline friends, that is, from June 14, 1314, to April 10, 1316.

Some commentators have seen in this reference to Gentucca a confession on Dante's part of a guilty liaison, but Buti, writing in the fourteenth century, states that Madonna Gentucca was of the family of Rossimpelo, and that the poet became attached to her "on account of her great virtue and integrity, and not with any other love." Later research has identified her with Gentucca Morla, wife of Cosciorino Fondora of Lucca, who mentions her with respect in his will dated December 15, 1317.[2] Dante seems to have had

---

[1] *Purgatorio*, XXIV, 43 ff.
[2] Toynbee: *A Dictionary of Proper Names and Notable Matters in the Works of Dante*, art. "Gentucca."

small liking for the men of that city, thieves and money-mad; hell was well furnished with them.[1]

II. LETTER TO A FLORENTINE FRIEND

Uguccione won a brilliant victory over Florence and the Tuscan chiefs at Monte Catini, August 29, 1315. In retaliation the Florentine authorities in October summoned Dante, his two sons, and others to appear in Florence before the royal vicars of King Robert. Failing to appear they were condemned, in a sentence issued November 6, to be beheaded if ever they should come into the power of either the Vicar or of the Commune of Florence; "And lest they glory in their contumacy, we put them all and each under the ban of the city of Florence and district, giving license to any one to offend all and any one of them in goods and in person, with impunity, according to the form of the statutes of Florence."[2]

This document would indicate that Dante was in some degree sharing the fortunes of Uguccione, and that his two sons had joined him. In April, 1316, the Ghibelline leader lost Lucca and retired to Verona, taking service under Can Grande della Scala, the greatest Ghibelline chieftain of his day. Florence, seeing her enemies thus broken, softened her heart toward her exiles, and on June 2, 1316, proclaimed an amnesty, permitting most of the wanderers to return to the city on condition of paying a fine and suffering "the stigma of oblation," that is, allowing themselves to

---

[1] *Inferno*, XXI, 40.
[2] Dante Society (Cambridge, Mass.), *Report*, 1892.

be presented as an offering to Saint John at the high altar of his church. From this amnesty were excluded all who had borne arms against Florence, all who were condemned by Cante Gabrielli from November, 1301, to July, 1302, and all who were banished for malversation of office. Dante was thus excepted by each one of these three specifications, but his many friends in Florence were working faithfully for his recall. Some of them evidently inquired of the poet if he would return on the same conditions offered to the other exiles. To a priest who wrote more delicately and affectionately, Dante replied in a noble letter which has been preserved to us in a manuscript written by Boccaccio's own hand:

"From your letter, which I have received with due reverence and affection, I have learned with a grateful heart, and after diligent consideration, how dear to your soul is my return to my country; and you have thus placed me under so much the greater obligations, in that it happens very rarely to exiles to find friends. But I will answer its import; and if my answer is not such as perchance the pusillanimity of some might look for, I heartily pray that before judgment is passed it may be submitted to the examination of your wisdom.

"Behold then what in the letters of your nephew and mine, and also in those of many other friends, has been made known to me in regard to the ordinance just now made in Florence relative to the pardon of the banished: that if I were willing to pay a certain amount of money and if I were willing to suffer the stigma of oblation, I should be pardoned and could return forthwith. In this, in very truth, there are two laughable and ill-considered things, O Father. I say ill-considered by those who gave them expression, for your letter, more discreetly and advisedly conceived, contained nothing of the sort.

"Is this then the glorious recall wherewith Dante Alighieri is summoned back to his country after an exile patiently endured for almost fifteen years? Did his innocence, manifest to whomsoever it may be, deserve this — this, the sweat and unceasing toil of study? Far be the rash humility of a heart of earth from a man familiar with philosophy, that like a prisoner he may be offered up after the manner of a certain Ciolo and other criminals. Far be it from a man who preaches justice after having patiently endured injury to pay his money to those inflicting it, as though they were his benefactors.

"This is not the way to return to my country, O my Father. If another shall be found by you, or by others, that does not derogate from the fame and honor of Dante, that will I take with no lagging steps. But if Florence is entered by no such path, then never will I enter Florence. What! Can I not look upon the face of the sun and the stars everywhere? Can I not meditate anywhere under the heavens upon most sweet truths, unless I first render myself inglorious, nay ignominious, to the people and state of Florence? Nor indeed will bread be lacking." [1]

The authenticity of this delightful and illuminating

[1] Latham's translation.

letter has been called in question. But it has come down to us on the authority and in the writing of Boccaccio. It is highly improbable that so Dantesque a letter is merely a literary exercise of the poet's biographer. Moreover, Dante's nephew, Andrea Poggi, who may have been the nephew referred to in the letter, was afterwards known to Boccaccio, and, being so closely identified with this incident, may have related it to the biographer, and given him the letter which checked the hopes of Dante's friends for his recall.

III. VERONA

The Ghibelline stronghold at this time was Verona, where the great Lord Can Grande della Scala ruled in power and held court in princely magnificence. Hither Uguccione had returned after his defeat, and hither Dante now quite probably turned his steps, and

> "at the same guest table far'd
> Where keen Uguccio wiped his beard."

Verona was the natural gathering-place of exiled Ghibellines. Can Grande, renowned for his princely patronage of art and letters, was head of the Ghibelline League. A mere lad when Dante made his first visit to Verona, now his renown was filling Italy. With him all the eminent men of the day found a royal welcome. "You might hear," says Cipolla, "Germans, Latins, Frenchmen, Flemings, Englishmen, speaking together; there you might hear disputes on astrology, philosophy, and theology." We have abundant evidence of the generous qualities and splendid achievements of this prince. Of his life Ruskin, in "Verona and its Rivers," gives an interesting summary:

"First he won his wife, Joanna, by a *coup de main;* he fell in love with her when she was a girl, in Rome; then, she was going to be sent into Scotland to be married; but she had to go through Verona, to the Adige gate. So Can Grande pounced upon her; declared she was much too precious a gem — *preziosa gemma* — to be sent to Scotland, and — she went no further. Then he fortified Verona against the Germans; dug the great moat out of its rocks; built its walls and towers; established his court of royal and thoughtful hospitality; became the chief Ghibelline captain of Lombardy, and the receiver of noble exiles from all other states; possessed himself by hard fighting of Vicenza also; then of Padua; then either by strength or subtlety, of Feltre-Belluno-Bassano; and died at thirty-seven of eating apples when he was too hot, — in the year 1329."

A Veronese chronicle describes him as tall and handsome, most gracious in manner and speech, and of martial beauty. How magnificent was his hospitality we infer from the glowing description of an exile who was himself a guest, which Sismondi quotes: "Different apartments, according to their condition, were assigned to the exiles in the Scala palace; each had his own servants, and a well appointed table served in private. The various apartments were distinguished by appropriate devices and figures, such as Victory for soldiers, Hope for exiles, Muses for poets, Mercury for artists, and Paradise for preachers. During meals musicians, jesters, and jugglers performed in these rooms. The halls were decorated with pictures representing the vicissitudes of fortune. On occasion Can invited certain of his guests to his own table, notably Guido di Castello of Reggio, who, on account of his single-mindedness, was known as the Simple Lombard, and the poet Dante Alighieri."[1] Sismondi further describes him as "a man of unflinching character, he was frank of speech, faithful to his principles, and scrupulously observant of his word. He secured not only the love of his soldiery, but of his people and even of his foes." The splendor of his court, Boccaccio affirms, was rivaled only by that of the second Frederick.

Of the feelings in Dante's breast as he turned toward Verona we have an exquisite portrayal in the opening passage of the letter in which he dedicates the "Paradiso" to Can Grande: "To the magnificent and victorious lord, the Lord Can Grande della Scala, Vicar General of the Most Holy Roman Empire in the city of Verona and the town of Vicenza, his most devoted Dante Alighieri a Florentine by birth, but not by character, desires a life happy throughout the duration of many years, and perpetual augmentation of his glorious name. The illustrious praise of your magnificence, which vigilant fame scatters abroad as she flies, draws men in divers ways, so as to exalt some in the hope of prosperous success, and to cast down others in the terror of destruction. Now this renown, surpassing all the deeds of modern men, I was once wont

[1] Toynbee: *Dante Dictionary*, art. "Can Grande."

to think extravagant, as going beyond the warrant of truth, but lest continued doubt should keep me too much in suspense, even as the queen of the south sought Jerusalem, or as Pallas sought Helicon, so did I seek Verona to scrutinize by the faithful testimony of my own eyes the things which I had heard. And there I beheld your splendors, I beheld and at the same time touched your bounty; and whereas I had formerly suspected excess in what was said, so afterwards I knew that the facts themselves were greater.

"Wherefore it came to pass that as a mere report had already made me your well wisher, with a certain submission of soul, from the first sight of the source itself, I became your most devoted servant and friend. ... Cherishing your friendship then as my dearest treasure, I desire to preserve it with loving forethought and continued care. ... And I have found nothing more suited to your preëminence than the sublime cantica which is adorned with the title of Paradise; which cantica ... I inscribe, I offer, and conclusively commend to you." [1]

This same affectionate admiration is expressed in the beautiful words of Cacciaguida's prophecy; supposed to be uttered in 1300 when Can Grande was a lad of nine years:

"With him thou shalt see one, who was so impressed at his birth by this strong star that his deeds will be notable. Nor yet are the people aware of him, because of his young age; for these wheels have revolved around him only nine years. But ere the Gas-

[1] Wicksteed's translation.

YEARS OF THE DIVINE COMEDY 199

con cheat the lofty Henry some sparkles of his virtue shall appear, in his caring not for money nor for toils. His magnificences shall hereafter be so known, that his enemies shall not be able to keep their tongues mute about them. Look thou to him and to his benefits; by him shall many people be transformed, rich and mendicant changing conditions. And thou shalt bear hence written of him in thy mind, but thou shalt not tell it — and he told things incredible to those who shall be present." [1] On the contrary, Albertino Mussato, who was held by Can Grande as prisoner of war, describes him as harsh and intractable, lacking in self-control, obstinate, yet apparently assuming greater severity than was natural to him.[2]

Three anecdotes which have come down to us would indicate that the bread which Dante ate at his benefactor's table was sometimes salt. We have the first on the authority of Petrarch: "Dante Alighieri, erewhile my fellow-citizen, was a man greatly accomplished in the vulgar tongue; but on account of his pride he was somewhat more free in his manners and speech than was acceptable to the sensitive eyes and ears of the noble princes of our country. Thus, when he was exiled from his native city, and was a guest at the court of Can Grande, at that time the refuge and resort of all who were in misfortune, he was at first held in high honour; but afterwards by degrees he began to lose favour, and day by day became less pleasing to his host. Among the guests at the same time were, according to the custom of those days, mimics

---

[1] *Paradiso*, XVII, 76 ff. [2] Toynbee: *Dante Dictionary*.

and buffoons of every description, one of whom, an impudent rascal, by means of his coarse remarks and broad jests made himself a universal favourite and a person of considerable influence. Can Grande, suspecting that this was a cause of vexation to Dante, sent for the buffoon, and, after lavishing praise upon him, turned to Dante and said: 'I wonder how it is that this man, fool though he be, understands how to please us all, and is petted by every one; while you, for all your reputed wisdom, can do nothing of the kind!' Dante replied, 'You would hardly wonder at that, if you remembered that like manners and like minds are the real causes of friendship.'"

A similar anecdote is told by Michele Savonarola, the grandfather of the famous Florentine preacher and reformer, Girolamo Savonarola: "I will tell you the answer made by Dante to a buffoon at the court of the Lord della Scala of Verona, who having received from his master a fine coat as a reward for some piece of buffoonery, showed it to Dante and said: 'You with all your letters, and sonnets, and books, have never received a present like this.' To which Dante answered: 'What you say is true; and this has fallen to you and not to me, because you have found your likes, and I have not yet found mine. There, you understand that!'"

Another story of Dante and Can Grande turns on his host's name, Cane ("dog"): "Once when Dante was at his table Cane della Scala, who was a very gracious lord, wishing to have a joke with the poet and to incite him to some smart saying, ordered his servants to collect all the bones from the repast and to put them privily at Dante's feet. When the tables were removed, they all began to laugh, and asked him if he were a bone-merchant. Whereupon Dante quickly replied: 'It is no wonder if the dogs have eaten all their bones; but I am not a dog, and so I could not eat mine.' And he said this because his host was called Cane ('dog')." [1]

But as every reference which Dante himself makes to Can Grande is replete with affectionate admiration we are justified in rejecting all the traditions of discourtesy on the part of the lord of Verona. As Dante in the "Convivio" (II, XI) says, "that if courtesy is understood to mean the actual manners of the courts of Italy, it would mean all that was most foul and base," and as in the same treatise (IV, 16) he refers disparagingly to Alboino, Can Grande's brother, there may have been some discourtesy shown Dante on the occasion of his earlier sojourn. To this period belongs Boccaccio's interesting story of the poet's appearance and the rumor to which it gave rise. "Our poet was of moderate height, and, after reaching maturity, was accustomed to walk somewhat bowed, with a slow and gentle pace, clad always in such sober dress as befitted his ripe years. His face was long, his nose aquiline, and his eyes rather large than small. His jaws were large, and the lower lip protruded beyond the upper. His complexion was dark, his hair and beard thick, black, and curled, and his expression ever melancholy and thoughtful. And thus it chanced one day in Verona, when the fame of his works had spread everywhere,

[1] Toynbee: *Dante Alighieri*, pp. 144–46.

particularly that part of his Commedia entitled the Inferno, and when he was known by sight to many, both men and women, that, as he was passing before a doorway where sat a group of women, one of them softly said to the others, — but not so softly but that she was distinctly heard by Dante and such as accompanied him, — 'Do you see the man who goes down into hell and returns when he pleases, and brings back tidings of them that are below?' To which one of the others naïvely answered, 'You must indeed say true. Do you not see how his beard is crisped, and his color darkened, by the heat and smoke down there?' Hearing these words spoken behind him, and knowing that they came from the innocent belief of the women, he was pleased, and, smiling a little as if content that they should hold such an opinion, he passed on." [1]

IV. THE LAST REFUGE

Ravenna, to which he seems to have gone in 1317, was the poet's last refuge. It was the gracious invitation of the podestà of the city which brought Dante to this haven of peace. Boccaccio tells us how delicately the proffer of hospitality was made. "Nor did the good lord wait for this to be asked of him, but reflecting what shame good men must feel in asking favors, he generously came to Dante with proffers, asking as a special favor that which he knew in time Dante must ask of him, namely, that Dante should find it his pleasure to reside with him." [2]

[1] Dinsmore: *Aids to the Study of Dante*, p. 95.   [2] *Ibid.*, p. 91.

Fortunate indeed was Dante to have for his host, one so courteous and appreciative as Guido da Polenta, himself a poet of taste, as one can learn from the sixteen ballads which Ricci has collected and identified. Beside the solicitous care of his host, these closing years of the poet's life were comforted, it is probable, by the presence of at least two of his children.

We have evidence that Pietro shared his father's exile. Ricci has published a document dated January 4, 1321, showing that "Petrus filius Dantis Aldigerii de Florencia" held two benefices in Ravenna, one that of Santa Maria di Zenzanigola and the other that of San Simone di Muro, the latter having been given him by the Contessa Caterina, wife of Guido Novello. As the document mentions reiterated demands for the fees due the Pope from these two benefices, it is probable that Pietro was in Ravenna some years before 1321. As Dante's daughter Beatrice was afterwards a nurse in the Convent de Stefano dell' Ulvia in Ravenna it is not unlikely that she was also with him.

The city to which Dante came is one rich in historical associations. Honorius, Emperor of the West, fleeing from Alaric, had sought refuge here because of its protecting swamps and retreating sea. Just outside the walls is the empty mausoleum of Theodoric, the emperor whose suspicions had thrown Boëthius into prison and accomplished his death. Here is the magnificent Byzantine church of San Vitale, whose wonderful mosaics representing Justinian surrounded by soldiers and priests offering to the gods a consecrated vase has left its impress on the "Comedy." It was "from Ravenna" that the Roman eagle had leaped the Rubicon for "such a flight that neither tongue nor pen could follow."

A degree of pecuniary independence, sweetening the salt bread of exile, probably came to Dante at this time. It is quite generally conceded that there was at Ravenna in those days a studio, or university, in which Dante is supposed to have taught vernacular rhetoric. Boccaccio affirms that "here he taught and trained many scholars in poetry, and especially in the vernacular." Such congenial employment softening the harsh breath of dolorous poverty, would tend to that peace of mind which made possible the composition of the "Paradiso."

The delightful correspondence with Del Virgilio throws a clear light upon Dante's character and condition during these closing years. Giovanni del Virgilio, a professor in the University of Bologna, a lover of Italian poetry and of classic tradition, addressed to Dante from that city a Latin eclogue, expressing regret that he who can sing so marvelously should cast such weighty themes as the regions of threefold fate into the speech of the vulgar, and urging him to dedicate his talents to the celebration of contemporary history, such as the famous battle for the possession of Genoa, using the Latin tongue, the only language fit for a garb of the Muses. If Dante will accede to this request, Del Virgilio promises to present him to the applauding schools to receive the poet's crown; the poem concluding with a confession that Del Virgilio speaks as a cackling goose to a clear-toned swan.

Dante's reply reveals that kindlier aspect of his nature which we are apt to forget in the spell which his terrible earnestness casts over us. Had he been the splenetic and disdainful spirit he is popularly supposed to have been, here certainly was provocation enough for his lightning. Was he not champion of the Italian tongue? Had he not vindicated in a learned treatise its worth as a vehicle of the highest poetic expression? Were the "Inferno" and the "Purgatorio" so inferior that a brother poet presumes to request that he drop his theme, and change his whole poetical machinery?

Dante's answer discloses the serenity of his mind, and affords us a glimpse of a genial humor which doubtless appeared often in his daily intercourse. To his presumptuous friend he responded in Latin hexameter and in the cipher of a Virgilian eclogue. Designating himself as Tityrus and Del Virgilio as Mopsus, he represents himself as conversing with Melibœus on the invitation received. "'What wilt thou do?' saith Melibœus, 'Wilt thou ever wear thy temples unadorned with laurel, a shepherd on the pasture lands?' 'O Melibœus, the glory, nay, the very name of bard has vanished into air. The muse hath taxed her power to give us vigil-keeping Mopsus.' I had then replied, when thus did indignation give me voice: 'What were the bleatings to which hills and pastures would echo, were I to raise the pæan on my lyre, with locks entwined with green! — But let me dread the groves and country-sides that know not the gods. Were it not better done to trim my locks in triumph, and that I, who erst was auburn, should hide them, hoary now, under the twined leaves when, if so be, I come again to my ancestral Sarnus?'"[1] This passage indicates that to Dante the applause of the schools would signify little. Neither did he believe it safe to enter a hostile country. Moreover, the recognition which he craved must come from his native city. The words "erst was auburn" hint that in his youth the poet's hair was not as dark as Boccaccio declares it to have been in later life. He continues, "When the bodies that flow around the world, and they that dwell among the stars, shall be shown forth in my song, even as the lower realms, then shall I joy to bind my brow with ivy and with laurel, if Mopsus will allow." This notable passage is evidence that Dante had finished the "Inferno" and the "Purgatorio" and was working upon the "Paradiso." "'What may we do,' asks Melibœus, 'to win Mopsus to our side?' 'I have,' said I, 'one sheep, thou knowest, most loved; so full of milk she scarce can bear her udders; even now under a mighty rock she chews the late-cropped grass; associate with no flock; familiar with no pen; of her own will she ever comes, ne'er must be driven to the milking pail. Her do I think to milk with ready hands; from her ten measures will I send to Mopsus. Do thou meanwhile think on thy wanton goats, and learn to ply thy teeth on stubborn crusts.'"[2]

This last quotation is invaluable. It discloses the poet's mood while writing the "Paradiso," his affection for the canticle, his sense of its uniqueness, his

[1] Wicksteed and Gardner: *Dante and Del Virgilio*, p. 155.
[2] *Ibid.*, p. 155.

feeling that the material is abundant, and his conviction that the creative mood cannot be coerced. Ten at least of the cantos must have been completed and ready to send to his friends. It is most probable that Del Virgilio's suggestion that Dante receive the laurel crown at Bologna caused him to write the nobly pathetic words which open the twenty-fifth canto of the "Paradiso."

"If it ever happen that the sacred poem to which both heaven and earth have so set their hand that it has made me lean for many years, should overcome the cruelty which bars me from the fair sheepfold, where a lamb I slept, foe to the wolves that give it war, then with other voice, with other fleece, a Poet will I return and on the font of my baptism will I take the crown; because I there entered into the faith which makes the soul known to God."

Del Virgilio responds in the same pastoral form, sympathizing with Dante in his desire to be crowned in Florence, but assuring him it is safe to come to Bologna, and setting forth the delightful intercourse the two would have together.

Whether Dante replied in a second eclogue is somewhat in doubt. There exists a reputed communication in which the poet declares that he would gladly make the proposed journey, did he not fear for his safety. The poem is an account, given by Tolas (Guido da Polenta) of a conversation which he overheard between Dante and his friends. Inasmuch as Dante is always referred to in the third person, and is addressed in terms which he would scarcely apply to himself — such as "old venerated Sire," — it may well be that the reply is his only in a remote sense. A commentator, contemporary to Dante, whose information on most points is proved to be accurate, accepts Dante's authorship and states that this second eclogue was given to Del Virgilio by Dante's son a year after the poet's death.

Before leaving this interesting professor, whose admiration and zeal have given us this pleasant insight into Dante's closing years, we will insert the lines which he wrote as an inscription to the monument which Guido da Polenta proposed to erect to the memory of the divine poet. They are valuable as contemporary testimony to the fame and learning of Dante.

"Dante, the theologian, skilled in every branch of knowledge that philosophy may cherish in her illustrious bosom, glory of the muses, author most acceptable to the vulgar, here lieth and smiteth either pole with his fame; who assigned their places to the defunct and their respective sway to the twin swords, in laic and rhetoric fashion. Lastly he was singing pastoral songs on the Pierian pipes; envious Atropos, alas, broke off the work of joy. To him ungrateful Florence bore the bitter fruit of exile, fatherland cruel to her bard; whom pitying Ravenna rejoices to have received in the bosom of Guido Novello her honored chief. In the years of the Deity one thousand three times a hundred and three times seven on September's ides to his own stars did he return." [1]

The influence of Ravenna appears upon many pages of the "Divine Comedy." The city was alive with the

[1] Wicksteed and Gardner: *Dante and Del Virgilio*, p. 175.

YEARS OF THE DIVINE COMEDY 209

associations of Francesca's happy girlhood and Rimini was near by. Dante's host was a nephew of Francesca, and a brother of Paolo ruled in Rimini. It is not improbable that now the poet may have added the final touches to the story of the two lovers which have made the lines immortal. The famed description of the divine forest in the closing cantos of the "Purgatorio" reveals the influence of the Pineta upon Dante's rested spirit:

"Dreaming beneath the mosaics in San Vitale that set forth the twofold glory of Justinian, wandering by the mausoleum where Galla Placidia rests with Honorius and Constantius, or passing what was once the sepulchral monument of the mighty Ostrogoth, Theodoric, whose successors had fallen before Belisarius and Narses, Dante may well have heard the wings of the golden eagle, the sacrosant bird of God and Rome, beating over the course of the world's history, and caught the sound of that great canto of the Paradiso that opens with Constantine's desertion and closes with an exile's lament. Pondering in Sant' Apollinare Nuovo, where those long lines of white and gold robed saints and virgins move orientwise to Christ and his Mother, he may already in ecstatic alienation have beheld the vast *convento delle bianche stole* in the mystic white Rose of Paradise." [1]

Honor came to him in his closing years. From Venice Giovanni Quirino sent this tribute.

> "Glory to God, and to God's Mother chaste,
> Dear friend is all the labor of thy days:
> Thou art he who evermore uplays

[1] Wicksteed and Gardner: *Dante and Del Virgilio*, p. 91.

> That heavenly wealth which the worm cannot waste:
> So shalt thou render back with interest
>   The precious talent given thee by God's grace:
>   While I, for my part, follow in their ways
> Who by the cares of this world are possess'd.
> For as the shadow of the earth doth make
>   The moon's globe dark, when so she is debarr'd
>   From the bright rays which lit her in the sky, —
> So now, since thou my son didst me forsake
>   (Being distant from me), I grow dull and hard,
>   Even as a beast of Epicurus' sty." [1]

Dante's reply indicates the lofty serenity of his mind.

> "The King by whose rich grace His servants be
>   With plenty beyond measure set to dwell
>   Ordains that I my bitter wrath dispel
> And lift mine eyes to the great consistory;
> Till, noting how in glorious choirs agree
>   The citizens of that fair citadel,
>   To the Creator I his creatures swell
> Their song, and all their love possesses me.
>   So, when I contemplate the great reward
>   To which our God has called the christian seed,
>   I long for nothing else but only this.
>   And then my soul is grieved in thy regard,
>   Dear friend, who reck'st not of thy nearest need,
>   Renouncing for slight joys, the perfect bliss." [2]

He was in heaven with Beatrice, and the storm which swept this threshing floor seemed pitifully insignificant. His mind was filled with the noble conceptions of the "Paradiso," and his soul was glowing with its peace and light. "It was his wont," writes Boccaccio, "when he had finished six or eight cantos, more or

---

[1] Rossetti: *Dante and his Circle*, p. 150.   [2] *Ibid.*, p. 151.

less, to send them, from wherever he might be, before any other person saw them, to Messer Cane della Scala, whom he held in reverence beyond all other men. After he had seen them, Dante would make a copy of the cantos for whoever wished them." [1]

Accompanying these first cantos Dante sent a quaint epistle in which in stately language he dedicated "the sublime Canticle of the Comedy" to the "magnificent and victorious lord, the Can Grande della Scala." After the formal inscription there follows a statement of the general character of the whole poem, especially of the "Paradiso," closing with a minute, and to us, not a very illuminating commentary on the prologue. In the thirty-second section of the dedicatory letter there is a paragraph which shows the poet in the unenviable position of a solicitor of patronage. He refrains from continuing his commentary, "for poverty presseth so hard upon me that I must needs abandon these and other matters useful to the public good. But I hope of your magnificence that other means may be given me of continuing with a useful exposition." Such words must have been penned in a despondent mood when teaching seemed irksome. Ample means and abundant leisure might have dissipated a genius which flowed deepest amidst obstacles.

A sonnet written by Giovanni Quirino has recently been discovered, in which the Venetian poet urges a distinguished person, presumably Can Grande, to publish some of the cantos of the "Paradiso."

Dante's growing fame would be quite likely to draw

[1] Dinsmore: *Aids to the Study of Dante*, p. 106.

the attention of the heresy hunters of that keen-scented age. The accusations which came so readily after his death, seem to have begun in his lifetime. Two fifteenth-century manuscripts preserve the following tradition: "At the time when Dante was making his book, many persons did not understand it, and they said it was contrary to the Faith. There was at Ravenna at that time a wise Friar Minor, and he was Inquisitor; and hearing this Dante mentioned, he resolved in his heart that he would know him, with the intent of seeing if he erred in the Faith of Christ. And one morning Dante was in church to see our Lord at the Mass, and this Inquisitor came to this church, and Dante was pointed out to him, so that the Inquisitor had him called; and Dante reverently went to him. Then the Inquisitor said to him, 'Art thou that Dante, who sayest thou hast been in Hell, in Purgatory, and in Paradise?' And Dante answered, 'I am Dante Alighieri of Florence.' The Inquisitor angrily said, 'Thou goest making odes, and sonnets, and trash; thou wouldst have done much better to write a book in Latin, founding thyself upon the Holy Church of God, and not attend to such rubbish as this that could one day give thee what thou dost deserve.' And when Dante wished to answer the Inquisitor, the Inquisitor said, 'There is no time now, but we shall be together on such a day, and I shall wish to look into the matter'; thereupon Dante answered and said that this pleased him much, and he departed from the Inquisitor and went his way to his room; and then he made that capitolo which is called the Credo, the which Credo is the affirmation of all the Faith of Christ. And upon the day appointed upon which he was to meet the said Inquisitor, he returned to him and placed this capitolo in his hand. When the Inquisitor had read it, it seemed to him a notable thing, and he knew not how to answer Dante. So the aforesaid Inquisitor remained then all confused, and Dante departed from him, and went his way all safe and sound. And from that time onward Dante always remained a very great friend of the aforesaid Inquisitor. And this was the cause for which Dante made the same Credo."

Although the "Credo" which has come down to us is doubtless spurious, it is not improbable that Dante had to defend the orthodoxy of his outspoken poem.

The poet's restless mind was not entirely absorbed during these last days with his instruction in vernacular poetry, or in the construction of the "Paradiso." There comes down to us what purports to be a report, written by his own hand, of a disputation which he had in Verona, January 20, 1320. The manuscript was first discovered and edited by Giovanni Benedetto da Castiglione Aretino in 1508.[1] Unfortunately the manuscript used by him has disappeared, and there is no record of its having been seen by any other person, and no early biographer alludes to it. The genuineness of the work was not called in question for over three hundred years, but since the beginning of the nineteenth century, especially among Italian scholars, there has been a strong tendency to regard it as a forgery of Moncetti's. On the contrary English critics

[1] Moore: *Studies in Dante*, Second Series, p. 306.

including Shadwell, Moore, Toynbee, and Wicksteed, who have made a most minute study of its contents are ardent defenders of the work as authentic. Dr. Moore, after showing the "extraordinary absence of motive in such an aimless forgery," affirms that the treatise is "thoroughly Dantesque in the whole texture of its style, language, and form of thought." The title of the address is "Questio de Aqua et Terra." The "Questio" is, "Can water in its own sphere, or natural circumference, be in any place higher than the dry land or habitable part of the earth?" This was an issue much debated in that day and the treatise opens with an account of the occasion of its production.

"Dante Alighieri of Florence, least among real philosophers, to each and every reader of these words, greeting in His name, who is the source and beacon of truth.

"Let it be known to you all that, while I was in Mantua, a certain Question arose, which often argued according to appearance rather than to truth, remained undetermined. Wherefore, since from boyhood I have been nurtured in the love of truth, I could not bear to leave the Question I have spoken of undiscussed; rather I wished to demonstrate the truth concerning it, and likewise, hating untruth as well as loving the truth, to refute contrary arguments."

The subject is treated in a fashion characteristic of the times, and concludes with a keen thrust at the clergy who absented themselves from the address. "This philosophic inquiry was held, beneath the rule of the unconquered lord, the Lord Can Grande della

YEARS OF THE DIVINE COMEDY 215

Scala, Vicar of the Holy Roman Empire, by me, Dante Alighieri, least among philosophers, in the famous town of Verona in the chapel of the glorious Helen, before the entire Veronese clergy, save a few, who, burning with excess of love do not admit the inquiries of others, and by virtue of their humility, poor in the Holy Spirit, lest they should appear to testify to the worth of others, avoid attending their discourses. And this was done in the year 1320, after the birth of our Lord Jesus Christ, on Sunday, which our predestined Saviour bade us keep holy because of his glorious nativity and his marvelous resurrection; which day was the seventh after the ides of January and the thirteenth before the calends of February." [1]

The clause in the introduction, "hating untruth as well as loving the truth," is characteristic of Dante and throws a flood of light upon his unbending severity towards what he considered evil in word or conduct.

The last act of Dante was in the service of his host. In the summer of 1321 some Venetian sailors were killed in an affray with soldiers of Ravenna. The Doge of Venice made immediate preparations for war. He stated his complaint as "excesses committed against us by Guido da Polenta, by the Commune and men of Ravenna, in taking our ships, slaying our captain and his company, and in wounding others of our men without just cause; and while we were in true peace and concord with them." The Doge, Giovanni Soranzo,

[1] Translation by A. C. White; Dante Society (Cambridge, Mass.) *Report*, 1902.

entered into an alliance, offensive and defensive, with Forli, and secured the neutrality of Rimini, Cesena, Imola, and Faenza. Guido in desperate straits sent an embassy to Venice to make overtures of peace. One of the ambassadors was Dante. Filippo Villani, nephew of the more famous chronicler declares that the "Venetians dreading the power of his eloquence repeatedly refused to grant him an audience. At the last, being sick with fever, he begged them to convey him back to Ravenna by sea; but they, increasing in their fury against him, utterly refused this, so that he had to undertake the fatiguing and unhealthy journey by land. This so aggravated the fever from which he was suffering that he died in a few days after his arrival at Ravenna." [1]

It was more probable that, having received the Doge's terms of peace, he returned to Ravenna by the shortest way. The journey was his last. Fatigued and humiliated, he was stricken with fever and died on the night between September 13 and 14, 1321.

The tradition of the lost thirteen last cantos, which will be told later, indicates that the poet had but just completed the closing portion of his great endeavor when he undertook his embassy to Venice. To sustain imagination, emotion, and utterance on such lofty heights must have exhausted all the resources of his mind and body, and it is not strange, therefore, that the humiliation of his unsuccessful mission, coming after months of severest mental effort, left him unfit to encounter the malaria of the Italian lowlands, and to resist the energy of the fever.

[1] Dinsmore: *Aids to the Study of Dante*, p. 112.

One cannot but wonder if Dante like Virgil left his masterpiece incomplete and died dissatisfied with his supreme achievement. If time had been granted him for further revision, would he have strengthened those passages where his "mortal shoulder trembled" under the supernatural burden? After experiencing the supreme beatitude, would the love that turned his mind and will have induced him to soften some bitter passages and temper some harsh judgments? Powerful as was his genius, the final vision of God which his mind beheld must have so far exceeded even his capacity of expression that he closed his eyes with a keen sense of having failed to accomplish his high ambition. The closing cantos can hardly have been copied and placed with the earlier portions of the poem, else the tradition of the search would not have arisen. That they were kept near his bed suggests that they were held for further revision, and that the poet saw many flaws in his work. These are surmises, but surmises accordant with human nature. If he died with a poignant sense of not having attained, his early biographers give no intimation of it.

Let us trust that his mood was prophetically described in his own noble words: "Just as a good mariner when he draws near to the harbour lets down his sails, and enters gently with slight headway on; so we ought to let down the sails of our worldly pursuits, and turn to God with all our understanding and heart, so that we may come to that haven with all composure and with all peace. And our nature gives us a good lesson in gentleness, insofar as there is in such a death no pain, nor any bitterness; but as a ripe apple lightly and without violence detaches itself from the bough, so our soul severs itself without suffering from the body where it has dwelt.... The noble soul therefore gives itself up to God ... and awaits the end of this life with much longing; she seems to herself to be departing from an inn and returning to her own mansion; to be coming off her journey and returning to the city; to be leaving the ocean and returning to port."[1]

V. DEATH AND BURIAL

"But even as the appointed hour comes to every man," writes Boccaccio, "so Dante also, at or near the middle of his fifty-sixth year, fell ill. And having humbly and devoutly received the sacraments of the Church according to the Christian religion, and having reconciled himself to God in contrition for all that he, as a mortal, had committed against His pleasure, in the month of September in the year of Christ 1321, on the day whereon the exaltation of the Holy Cross is celebrated by the Church, not without great sorrow on the part of his aforesaid Guido and in general of all the other citizens of Ravenna, he rendered to his Creator his weary spirit, the which, I doubt not, was received in the arms of his most noble Beatrice, with whom, in the sight of Him who is the highest Good, having left behind him the miseries of the present life, he now lives most blissfully in that life to whose felicity we believe there is no end.

"The noble-minded knight had the body of Dante

[1] *Convivio*, IV, XXVIII; Jackson's translation.

placed upon a bier and adorned with a poet's ornaments, and this he had borne on the shoulders of the most eminent citizens of Ravenna to the convent of the Minor Friars in that city, with the honor he thought due to such a person. And thereupon he caused the body, followed thus far by the lamentings of nearly the whole city, to be placed in a stone sarcophagus, in which it lies to this day. Returning to the house where Dante had resided, he made, according to the custom of Ravenna, a long and elaborate discourse, both as a tribute to the virtue and high learning of the deceased, and by way of consolation to the friends whom he had left behind in bitter grief. Guido purposed, if his life and fortune should continue, to honor him with so magnificent a sepulchre that if no merit of his own should render himself memorable to posterity, this of itself would do so.

"This praiseworthy proposal became known to certain most excellent poets of Romagna who were living at this time. Thereupon, both to publish their own ability and to show their good will toward the dead poet, as well as to win the love and favor of the lord who was known to desire it, each one wrote verses which, placed for an epitaph upon the proposed tomb, by their fitting praises should testify to posterity who it was that lay therein. They sent these verses to the noble lord, but he, not long after, lost his station through great misfortune, and died at Bologna; and the erection of the tomb and the inscription of the proffered verses thereon were for this reason left undone." [1]

[1] Dinsmore: *Aids to the Study of Dante*, pp. 92–93.

VI. THE LOST CANTOS

Boccaccio also gives us an interesting tradition of the recovery of the last thirteen cantos of the "Paradiso."

"It was his custom, when he had finished six or eight cantos, more or less, to send them, from wherever he might be, before any other person saw them, to Messer Cane della Scala, whom he held in reverence beyond all other men. After he had seen them, he would make a copy of the cantos for whoever wished for them. In such wise he had sent Messer Cane all save the last thirteen cantos — and these he had written — when he died without making any provision whatever. And although his children and disciples made frequent search for many months among his papers, to see if he had put an end to his work, in no way could they find the remaining cantos. All his friends were therefore distressed that God had not lent him to the world at least long enough for him to complete the little of his work that remained. And since they could not find the cantos, they abandoned further search in despair.

"Dante's two sons, Jacopo and Piero, both of whom were poets, being persuaded thereto by their friends, resolved to complete their father's work, so far as in them lay, that it might not remain unfinished. But just at this time Jacopo, who was much more fervent in this matter than his brother, saw a remarkable vision, that not only put an end to his foolish presumption, but revealed to him where the thirteen cantos were that were missing.

"An excellent man of Ravenna by the name of Piero Giardino, long time a disciple of Dante, related that eight months after the death of his master the aforesaid Jacopo came to him one night near the hour of dawn, and told him that in his sleep a little while before on this same night he had seen Dante, his father, draw near to him. He was clad in the whitest raiment, and his face shone with unwonted light. The son in his dream asked him if he were living, and heard him reply, 'Yes, not in our life, but in the true.' Again he seemed to question him, asking if he had finished his poem before passing to that true life, and, if he had completed it, where was the missing part which they had never been able to find. And again he seemed to answer, 'Yes, I finished it.' And then it seemed to him that his father took him by the hand and led him to the room where he was wont to sleep when alive, and touching a spot there, said, 'Here is that for which thou hast so long sought.' And with these words his sleep and his father left him.

"Jacopo said that he could not postpone coming to Messer Piero to tell him what he had seen, in order that together they might go and search the place — which he kept exactly in his memory — and learn whether it was a true spirit or a false delusion that had revealed this to him. While there still remained a good part of the night they set out together, and, coming to the designated spot, they found a matting fastened to the wall. Gently lifting this, they discovered a little opening which neither of them had ever seen or known of before. Therein they found some writings, all mildewed by the dampness of the wall, and on the point of rotting had they remained there a little longer. Carefully cleaning them of the mould, they read them, and found that they were the long-sought thirteen cantos. With great joy, therefore, they copied them, and sent them first, according to the custom of the author, to Messer Cane, and then attached them, as was fitting, to the incomplete work. In such wise the poem that had been many years in composition was finished." [1]

VII. DANTE'S SEPULCHRE

With his bodily dissolution Dante's spirit went "to nobler wars," but his ashes continued their wanderings, not back to Florence, however. Five times his native city petitioned for the bones of her most distinguished son — in 1396, 1430, 1476, 1519, 1865 — and each time she was refused. Before telling the story of the empty sepulchre and the rediscovered dust, a few words regarding the sarcophagus and mausoleum are necessary. The ancient sarcophagus into which Guido Novello put the remains of the poet was restored about the middle of the fourteenth century. According to a manuscript dated 1378 two epitaphs were then inscribed upon the tomb, the one by Bernardus de Canatro, written about 1353, remains until this day. Lowell has thus translated it.[2]

---

[1] Dinsmore: *Aids to the Study of Dante*, pp. 106–08.
[2] It was long supposed that Dante wrote this epitaph, but a fourteenth-century manuscript assigns it to Bernardus de Canatro.

THE TOMB OF DANTE: INTERIOR

"The rights of Monarchy, the Heavens, the Stream of Fire,
   the Pit,
In vision seen, I sang as far as to the Fates seemed fit;
But since my soul, an alien here, hath flown to nobler wars
And happier now, hath gone to meet its Maker 'mid the stars,
Here am I Dante shut, exiled from the ancestral shore,
Whom Florence, the least loving mother, bore."

In 1483 Pietro Lombardi, a famous sculptor and architect, working under the direction of Bernardo Bembo, recarved the epitaph and placed above it the letters "S.V.F." (Sibi Vivens Fecit) and executed the bas-relief of Dante's reading at a desk. The other by Minghino da Mezzano of Ravenna, begins "Inclita fama cuius universum penetrat orbem."[1] In 1692 the papal legate, Cardinal Corsi, restored the mausoleum, calling to his aid forty policemen to keep at bay the angry Frati who doubtless feared that the concealment of the poet's bones, a strange story which we shall tell immediately, might be discovered.

In 1780 Cardinal Gonzaga erected the mausoleum with its rounded dome which remains to this day. To verify the remains the Cardinal ordered the sarcophagus to be opened, and the official account vaguely states that they "found what was needful to establish the truth," but one of the monks of the convent states that "Dante's sarcophagus was opened and nothing found inside, whereupon it was sealed up again with the Cardinal's seal, and silence was observed as to the whole matter."

In 1865 Italy was preparing to celebrate the six

[1] Moore: *Studies in Dante*, IV, p. 173.

hundredth anniversary of Dante's birth and the opening of the tomb and the exhibition of the remains was to be an important feature. In making necessary repairs of the tomb it was necessary to remove part of the walls of the Braccioforte chapel. As the work progressed the pick of a workman struck against wood which gave a hollow sound; eagerly displacing some stones the workmen discovered a wooden chest, which partly fell to pieces disclosing a human skeleton. On the bottom plank was found this inscription:

> Dantis ossa
> Denuper revisa die 3 Junii
> 1677

On the lid was another, reading:

> Dantis ossa
> A me Fre Antonio Santi
> hic posita
> Ano 1677 die 18 Octobris

The city was thrown into great excitement by the news; magistrates hastened to the spot and experts were summoned to examine the skeleton. It was found to be intact with the exception of a few bones, the stature answered to that of the poet, and the skull, it is claimed, corresponded with the death mask brought from Florence for comparison.

With much trepidation the sarcophagus which was supposed to contain the remains was opened, and to everybody's relief was found to be empty. Only a few laurel leaves, a little dusty substance, and a few bones corresponding to those missing from the skeleton. A hole had been knocked through the back of the sarcophagus, the skeleton removed, and then the opening had been stopped with bricks and cement, and plastered on the outside.

One naturally inquires why the remains had been secretly removed from their stone urn and hidden in the wall of the convent. The most plausible theory is that between 1514 and 1519, when leading Florentines were urging Leo X, who was the overlord of Ravenna, to permit the bones to be returned to Florence, and when Michael Angelo himself offered to prepare a fitting sepulchre, the monks of the convent became alarmed and secreted their treasure, to be discovered accidentally at a most opportune moment three hundred and fifty years later.

The skeleton was exhibited for three days during the celebration and upon June 26 was enclosed in a heavy coffin of lead and walnut and replaced in the ancient sarcophagus where Guido Novello had reverently laid it to rest nearly six hundred years before.

PART III
Qualities of Genius and Character

CHAPTER I

THE MEANING OF THE DIVINE COMEDY

HAVING described in the preceding section the external happenings of Dante's life, it is fitting now to study with some degree of minuteness the masterpiece which records his spiritual experiences, and expressed his deepest convictions. The "Comedy" is most difficult reading, not only because it voices an epoch so different from our own in its ideals and opinions, but also because of its extreme complexity. The poet intended every detail of it to be seriously studied, and under its symbolism he veiled many meanings — the literal, the allegorical, the anagogical and the moral. He also wrote it under the compulsion of many motives. It was the fulfillment of a life ambition to write a poem of such power and beauty that Florence, shamed by the renown of his achievement, would welcome him within her walls and give him the poet's crown by that font where he was first made Dante and Christian. By means of it he intended to do for Italy what Virgil had done in the age of Augustus, and thus place himself among the supreme poets of the world. It was also to be the promised monument to Beatrice.

When we recall the many instances in which poems, orations, novels have been struck off in the white heat of inspiration to meet some urgent occasion by authors who were unconscious that their work had in it the breath of endless life; when we remember how carelessly Shakespeare broke his magic wand, allowing his dramas to drift about the London theatres without taking sufficient interest in them to revise and publish them; when we consider how large a part self-forgetting sincerity plays in producing what is imperishable, and how perilous is self-conscious effort — "one never goes farther than when he does not know whither he is going" — when we think of these things, then we wonder at Dante's success in deliberately and consciously writing a poem which has in it the inextinguishable fire. He not only succeeded, he surpassed his loftiest ambition. Yet even his genius would have failed — he would have wrecked himself on that immutable principle that whosoever saveth his life shall lose it — if what is personal in the poem had not been absorbed by what is universal. His sense of mission overshadowed his selfish ambition; he was saved by regarding himself only as a servant of the larger truth.

I. A UNIQUE POLITICAL DOCUMENT

But the "Divine Comedy" is more than a great poem, more than a solemn monument of the loftiness of Dante's artistic genius, it is the most powerful controversial political document ever written. The reformer's zeal had burned steadily and fiercely in Dante's breast since those early days when he had mingled in, and striven to allay, the political antagonisms of Florence. Exile had extended his interests and enlarged his vision. By personal activities, by diplomatic missions, by elaborate letters to the Florentines, to the Cardinals, to the German Emperor, by a volume on the true nature of government, he had endeavored to influence the political thought of his day. In the "Comedy" he employs a novel and more effective method. He not only uses art in the service of political propaganda, but uses it in a most original way. In our own day we are disgustingly familiar with works, aspiring to be literature, which are written to promote some reform or to solve some problem. Dealing with current topics they catch the popular attention for a moment and pass into oblivion. They sink in that dark sea because they are too heavily loaded with the author's opinions and theories. The moral purpose protrudes through the artistic form. The characters are personifications, not persons; automatons to be moved about at the writer's will.

Dante did not entirely escape this infirmity of the reformer who constrains art to the service of some dogma. Even his genius too often fails to make Beatrice more than a stage figure amid the celestial circles. His teaching instinct encumbers many pages of the "Purgatorio" and of the "Paradiso" with the deadwood of discarded theories.

Nevertheless the "Comedy" is the most extraordinary and enduring political pamphlet ever issued. For the author did not deal chiefly with problems and their solution, but with passions and their results; not with party slogans, but with moods, ideals, sins, and the permanent aspirations of the spirit. Man fights under many flags, but the battle is always the same. Interested as he was in the banners floating over Italy, our author was wise enough to direct his attention toward the struggling soul of man.

His characters are often symbols, — he is at his weakest then, — but he crowds his pages with the men he saw in Florence, and as he journeyed about Italy, and he paints them as they appeared to that clear-seeing eye of his. Putting them in hell if he saw them there, even though he honored them, he drew to the life historic personages as they appeared to the imagination of his day. Thus he worked with the eternal and not the ephemeral, and allowed his art to labor close to the springs of life.

But the most unique feature of this political document is the use it makes of the supernatural. Dante as a patriot ardently believed in the perpetuity and the divine authority of the Roman Empire, he abhorred the Babylonian captivity of the Church, he would have the Pope give up temporal sovereignty, and he found no language adequate to express his detestation of the corruption of the Papacy.

About these policies and evils he had reasoned and debated with small effect. What more powerful method conceivable could a reformer invent to bring home to men the sins of the Roman Curia than to show the white light of heaven turn red with anger while Saint Peter himself denounces his successors for turning Rome into a sewer of filth and blood! Could a treatise on simony equal in searching power the picture of those pockets in the floor of hell, containing pontiffs head downwards with perpetual flames licking their feet? What a tremendous way of teaching true political principles to have Virgil show the path, Justinian recount the divine providence through Roman history, and all the righteous rulers of the great past flash forth the imperial eagle in the heaven of Jupiter, with one voice discoursing on God's just purposes? And then that empty seat high up in the Great White Rose where soon shall sit the lofty Henry!

More truth enters the mind of men through the imagination than through the reasoning faculties, and no writer has equaled Dante in ability to turn politics into art, and to invoke the authority of the mighty dead. No one has approached him in power to bring the sanction of the Eternal to bear on the trivial concerns of the earth, and to make the judgment seat of the Almighty turn the noisy currents of history.

He failed of complete success, for in many prolonged explanations and discussions he forsook his method; even he could not put vitality into every line, some of his theories were not true enough to be sung, pedantry encumbered his genius, but no reformer ever adopted a more original method or so successfully capitalized the mystery that surrounds our lives in the interests of righteous government.

II. ITS RELIGIOUS SIGNIFICANCE

It is, however, the religious impulse that is supreme in the "Divine Comedy," dominating its thought and action. Dante's prolonged contemplation of the sublimest truths made all personal ambitions seem trivial, until finally they were absorbed in the controlling purpose to be a faithful interpreter of the Truth. The political significance of the poem perceptibly diminishes with the advance of the journey, while more and more the glory of the spiritual engrosses the writer's attention.

The "Divine Comedy" is a guide to the way of life as understood by the best minds of the Middle Ages, and interpreted by its loftiest genius. It shows the path which leads one out from the savage wood of sin into glorious liberty and celestial beatitude. Let the awakened soul give up the attempt to climb into the light by foolish reliance on the power resident in his own will. The lusts of the flesh, the lusts of the spirit, the pride of the froward will are too strong for him. The Most High has ordained a better way in which right Reason, illuminated by Divine Grace will be the guide. Reason will show the nature of sin and its awful consequences, it will lead one through severe discipline to liberty and happiness. But reason has its limits. It cannot penetrate the divine mysteries, nor discern those truths whose glory is the soul's permanent satisfaction. Therefore a divine Revelation will unfold to the attentive and surrendered spirit the ever-brightening splendor of the heavenly verities, until it gazes in rapturous bliss into the Fountain of the Living Light Eternal.

The "Inferno" is not, as so many judge, a devil's nightmare; a horrible picture of torments devised by the fiendish ingenuity of a medieval schoolman. It is the portrayal of the nature and consequences of sin by one whom Lowell has called "the highest spiritual nature that has expressed itself in rhythmical form."

Dante as a prophet of God would arouse a wretched and misguided world to a true conception of the nature of evil. Theologians might define sin, he would paint it. He would paint it in colors so vivid that it would burn forever in the memory of men. But sin can be known in its real character only when it has brought forth its damnable fruit, therefore the poet must go among the "truly dead" and track the evil into the eternal world to strip it of its false glitter and reveal its essential nature. This he does in three ways: by depicting the sinner given over to his besetting sin, by placing him in an environment which symbolizes his guilt, and by personifying the sin in the demons who preside over the nine concentric circles of the underworld: an underworld, by the way, which he located directly under Mount Calvary and the cross, thus symbolizing in a most impressive manner the defeat of Satan. In general the zones of blackness, and fire, and arctic cold portray most powerfully the blindness, the torment, the spiritual death which follow wrongdoing. The fiery hell which sin creates in the soul has been made familiar to us by many writers; it was reserved for Dante to disclose that deeper torment where even the fires of remorse die out, and the cold of spiritual death freezes every emotion.

The "Purgatorio" makes manifest the way to liberty from the power and effects of sin. The mood must be one of humility. One's face must be washed by the dews of repentance and his body girded with the reeds of submission. The method of purification and discipline is to "set love in order." One must repent of his sin, confess it, and by unremitting practice of the corresponding virtue build up a right character and expiate his wrongdoing. Thus will he fill out the measure of Christ's atonement and become a free man, the crowned and mitred lord of himself. Or as an unlettered man once said: "Religion is thinking about the right thing till you want to do it. Then if you do it long enough, you will do it without thinking — natural-like." This is the philosophy of Dante's "Purgatory" stripped of its theological nomenclature.

In the "Paradiso" Dante fulfills the promise of his youth and says of Beatrice what never was said of any woman. In the beauty of her eyes and the splendor of her smile shine forth the proof and the glory of the Divine Revelation. The "Paradiso" to most lovers of Dante is the supreme achievement of his genius. To them it is the noblest expression of the creative poetic imagination in all literature. Dante keenly felt the inability of his pen to describe the ever heightening glory of truth and the unutterable rapture of redemption. "But he who takes his cross and follows Christ will yet excuse me for what I leave, when he shall see Christ lighten in that dawn." Up the stairway of the successive heavens he moves, noting his ascent, not by conscious motion, but by the more radiant splendor on the countenance of his guide, until he reaches the Empyrean, the timeless, spaceless world glowing in the "Light intellectual, full of love, love of true good full of joy, joy that transcends every sweetness." In the depths of that Light his transfigured mind beheld the beatific vision. He saw life's profoundest secret

MEANING OF THE DIVINE COMEDY 237

and its divine meaning. He learned that all the torn and soiled leaves of human experience are bound together into one volume of love, that God is in all things and that all things are in God. With the "vision splendid" come peace and reconciliation with all life's bitter experiences, and one attains that condition when his will is accordant with the "Love which moves the sun and the other stars."

III. ITS PERMANENT ELEMENT

It will not be inappropriate to close this chapter with a brief consideration of those qualities in the "Divine Comedy" which are of enduring value. In every great book there is the ephemeral and the eternal. Of each one that has escaped oblivion it may be said:

> "Die alte schale nur ist fern,
> Geblieben ist uns doch der kern."

> "The old shell only's passed away,
> The kernel is the same to-day."

Unquestionably Dante's science and most of his formal theology have not only passed away, but are so out of date that only by sedulous effort can the modern mind enter into a sympathetic understanding of them. What is there in this poem which makes an appeal to every generation?

There is an unearthly beauty quivering on Dante's pages that will always arrest the attention of elect minds. Rare as is the melody of the *terza rima*, the power of the poem lies deeper. I have read the "Comedy" scores, perhaps hundreds of times, but the familiar verses glow with an ever-increasing beauty, and when I try to analyze the reason of this fascination I find it in the vivid and ineffaceable pictures, in the lines precise as a statement in Euclid, in sentences now throbbing with terrible passion, and again infinitely delicate, tender and full of grace, such as only a strong man of finest feeling could write. Powerful as are the verses and the scenes of the "Inferno," it is upon the pages of the "Paradiso" that there falls the "splendor of the Living Light Eternal." Human thought and human speech can mount no higher. Such beauty is elemental and everlasting. The flight of time will leave no trace upon it.

Men in every age will turn to this miracle of song for the emotional elevation which comes from reading it. By a most fortunate provision our minds are clothed with the character of the objects which engage their attention. The reader may repudiate every dogma that Dante loved, and be a consistent agnostic concerning all his supreme affirmations, yet he cannot live in the great poet's world and think his thoughts without having created in his mind those exalted and productive moods which make life worth living and all things seem possible. One catches the solemn elevation of mind of the ancient prophets, and the ecstasy of the medieval saint, without the intellectual necessity of believing their creeds.

If we make use of De Quincey's distinction between the literature of knowledge and the literature of power, few Dante students will demur if the "Divine Comedy" is ranked among the highest fountains of creative energy. Mr. William Roscoe Thayer in his able volume entitled "Italica" has shown that, although the number of the students of Greek literature in this country is legion, their literary productiveness has been small. On the contrary, there are few devotees of Dante, but their literary output has been of high quality and abundant. The great Italian fertilizes the mind, he enkindles the imagination, stirs the deep places where powerful emotions are born, he rains the fires of his energy into the will, so that nearly every lover of Dante hies himself to his desk to write a book. Men love power too dearly ever to desert one of the chief springs from whence it flows.

But the "Comedy" to its author had a value far beyond its literary merits. Its supreme importance to his mind lay in the fact that it told men the way of life in a manner that would persuade them to walk therein. If man in his essential nature and necessities is always the same, then the moral insights of a writer of extraordinary spiritual genius will have permanent interest. I once asked Professor Charles Eliot Norton what quality in the "Divine Comedy," other than its beauty, attracted him to Dante. "His powerful exposition of moral penalties and rewards," was the reply.

To produce this impression was precisely the purpose of the great Florentine. "The subject of the whole poem," he declares, "is man, liable to the rewards and punishments of Justice." His enduring interest is the same as that of Shakespeare in the tragedies. To both, character is destiny. The superlative fascination of the "Inferno," like the fearful power of "Macbeth," does not lie in the charm of its episodes, nor in those vivid lines which delineate a character by a word or a gesture, nor in the revelation of the author's tremendous personality, but in its envisagement of a sovereign and inexorable law of retributive Justice. His constant vision was that of Augustine: "How deep are thy ways, O God, Thou only great, that sittest silent on high and by an unwearied law dispenseth penal blindness to lawless desires!" John Morley said of Gladstone: "When he saw nations stumbling into paths of wrong, he felt sure of moral retribution. He had in his soul a vision high in the heavens of the flash of an uplifted sword and the gleam of the arm of an avenging angel. The thought with which he rose in the morning and went to rest at night was of the universe as a sublime moral theatre in which an omnipotent Dematurgist uses kingdoms and rulers, laws and policies, to exhibit universal purposes of good." [1] Dante did not fail in a constant conviction of a "sword on high that is not in haste to smite, nor yet doth linger," [2] and no prophet, or dramatist, or statesman, has surpassed him in ability to make the conviction an abiding possession of mankind.

Yet many lovers of the poet omit the mention of the moral truths of the "Comedy" in assuring its claim to permanent attraction. For instance, a recent writer [3] cites three elements of the "Comedy" as likely to ap-

[1] John Morley: *Recollections*, vol. II, p. 94.
[2] *Paradiso*, XXII, 16.
[3] J. B. Fletcher: *Dante*, Home University Library. A valuable contribution to Dante literature.

peal to men for many centuries, its beauty, its ripe worldly wisdom, and its revelation of Dante's unique personality. All this is true, but utterly inadequate. It is like praising "Hamlet" with Hamlet left out. Is Æschylus read to-day for the beauty and wisdom of his quotable sentences? Is not the hiding of his power in the profound and ineffaceable impression he makes upon the reader of an august and unvarying law which presides over human destinies, a sense of the Mystery which is the background of Life?

Dante called his poem a "Comedy," his readers soon added the adjective "Divine," because its pages were vital with the strength and glory of spiritual realities. It is this divineness which will charm men for unnumbered generations.

"If," says John Tyndall in closing his Belfast address, "the human mind, with the yearning of a pilgrim for his distant home, will still turn to the Mystery from which it has emerged, so to fashion it as to give unity to thought and faith; so long as this is done, not only without intolerance or bigotry of any kind, but with the enlightened recognition that ultimate fixity of conception is here unattainable, and that each succeeding age must be held free to fashion the mystery in accordance with its own needs — then casting aside all the restrictions of Materialism, I would affirm this to be the field for the noblest exercise of what, in contrast with the *knowing* faculties, may be called the *creative* faculties of man. Here, however, I touch on a theme too great for me to handle, but which will assuredly be handled by the loftiest minds, when you and I, like streaks of morning cloud, shall have melted into the infinite azure of the past."

The Mystery shaped by the genius of the loftiest poetical intelligence Europe has produced will not fail of perennial interest.

Besides the attraction of its pervading spiritual atmosphere, there are moral truths stated with unforgettable energy. Carlyle described the French Revolution as "Truth dancing in hell-fire!" a not inept description of the "Inferno." Sin is forever as Dante symbolizes it, a darkness to the mind, sterile as sand, tormenting as the ceaseless rain of flakes of fire, loathsome as Lucifer imprisoned by the lake of frozen tears and blood which his transgressions have caused. Into a real Inferno every man enters when he loses "the good of the intellect" and shifts the responsibility for his evil fortunes upon others.

The "Purgatorio" also contains an imperishable element. Purgatory as a place may not exist in our system of thought, but life is a cleansing process if we take its hardships in a proper spirit. We go seeking liberty, and the end is a free man, crowned and mitred o'er himself, and the way is to "set love in order" by strenuous and unceasing discipline.

In the "Paradiso" there is more of the ephemeral than in either of the two preceding sections, but there is also immortal beauty and immortal truth. Dante gives a clear answer to the mind's profoundest questions. What is the supreme felicity? How can man attain spiritual peace, and power, and joy? There is no equivocation in the reply. Man may have real and satisfactory knowledge of the Eternal; he may know God and rest in Him. The Ultimate Reality is not veiled in impenetrable clouds, but rays forth a light that falling upon the prepared mind quickens a spiritual power of vision which apprehends, partially but certainly, the Truth. This intellectual persuasion enkindles in the disciplined heart a love full of joy, a joy that transcends every sweetness. There are many pathways to this high vision. It is reached by the warrior on the battle-field, by the ruler on his throne, by the contemplative in his cell. Its form is as diverse as the brain and the experience of men; but the highest felicity is only reached by the conviction that man has real, if imperfect, knowledge of the Power that alone is great. He can rejoice in its incomprehensible wisdom and goodness, and espouse its will.

One may find himself unable to accept Dante's confident philosophy that man is a knower, and can receive true light from the Eternal; if so, he may have peace by facing the Inscrutable Darkness with fortitude, but the mind's supreme beatitude is as Dante affirms in the "Visio Dei":[1]

> "Our intellect is never satisfied,
>   I plainly see, unless Truth be its light,
>   Outside of which no truth extends.
> It rests therein, as in his lair a beast,
>   As soon as it is reached; and it can reach it;
>   If not, then each desire would be in vain."

---

[1] *Paradiso*, IV, 124–29; Johnson's ranslation.

CHAPTER II

INFLUENCE OF THE COMEDY UPON DANTE

I. THE INFLUX OF POWER

WHAT impresses a reader who has followed the development of Dante's mind through his various earlier works is the immense influx of power coming to the poet as he sets himself to his supreme task. There is lyrical beauty in the "Vita Nuova" and the "Convivio," marked critical capacity in "De Vulgari Eloquentia," lofty idealism and political acumen in "De Monarchia," hot indignation in the "Letters"; but nothing to prepare us for the vivid description, the sustained effort, the humor, the pathos, the majestic poise, the insight into the human heart, the superhuman imagination, which we find in the "Inferno." The superiority of the "Divina Commedia," even from the first pages, to anything which Dante had previously produced is astonishing. Hitherto he has been conspicuous among the writers of his day, now he steps easily into the first rank of the immortals.

How shall we account for this added depth and range of Dante's genius? Doubtless a part of his augmented power comes from the maturity of mind and broader knowledge of men and truth than had been his when he wrote his earlier works. Besides this natural strength which came to him with years and knowledge, he now receives the inflowing of energy and light which always comes to the surrendered mind. Abandonment of worldly ambition for the accomplishment of an immense moral task strengthens the will and illumines the understanding. The heart cleared of self sees deep, and the strength of the universe is back of the submissive will. Moreover, the immensity of his new theme enlarged and energized every power of his mind. Hitherto this idealist has contemplated the lesser ideals, the truth-lover has been absorbed with minor truths. Mystical love, philosophical truth, the claims of the Holy Roman Empire, were segments of Reality. Now the poet matches his mind to the perfect circle. He comes under the spell of the most stupendous verities that can engage human thought, and he writes under the glowing shadow of God. "I see clearly," he affirms, "that our intellect is never satisfied unless the Truth illuminates it beyond which nothing true extends." He beholds humanity outlined against the gloom and the glory of Eternity. All life, all truth, the depths of woe and the heights of bliss, are his theme, and the strength of these high hills of thought comes into his soul.

But the immensity of these subjects tends to confuse the mind and make language vague and unsatisfying. The universe as we know it to-day is too incomprehensible for clear speech. Our imaginations are lost in the vastness. The lack of ardent and contagious enthusiasm to-day results quite largely from the specialized interest of thinkers. Truth is separated into fragments. Life is seen in broken terms. Fortunately for Dante his mighty predecessors had so circumscribed all experience and accepted truth that they could rise before a lofty imagination as a complete and comprehensible system. From the completeness and vividness of this vision came his quenchless enthusiasm. Catholic truth as he understood it was vast enough to call forth all the energies of the believer's will, and so clearly analyzed and definitely outlined that it could be held as an august entirety by a capacious mind. It was majestic, understandable, and tremendously urgent. An intellect like Dante's, precise, credulous, vividly imaginative, easily lent itself to the science and faith of his day. If ever a mind fitted naturally into all the crevices and angles of a dominant philosophy, that mind belonged to him who gave imperishable utterance to the greatness and the defects of the Catholic system of the Middle Ages. The eternal damnation of virtuous heathen was the only point where the system wounded either his brain or heart. If we add to this congenial philosophy the intensity created by a firm belief that the times were wholly evil, the world ripe for judgment, and the writer called of God to make the whole vision manifest, we need not wonder that in the "Divine Comedy" there is a majesty and a range of power far supasssing the promise of his earlier works, and that with the mightier theme and profounder passion there is an added energy and beauty of utterance.

In the "Comedy" his style also gains in clarity and simplicity. Logic was to Dante the snare of the fowler in which his feet tripped. This schoolman's delight in the subtle processes of reasoning makes his prose commentaries difficult to the modern reader, who detects fallacies in both premises and is impatient of the tortuous methods and suspicious deductions. The subtilties of logic are too attenuated to keep alive the celestial fire which makes literature immortal. Only in those passages in his prose writings where Dante breaks away from his dialectical shackles does his style rise to great beauty. Precise, subtle, analytical, his mind lacked in interest unless it was suffused with the glow of his artistic genius. In the "Comedy" the vision and the passion of the seer subdue in great degree the schoolman's method and temper, and the enduring insights and emotions find utterance. Yet even in the "Paradiso" Pegasus carries much of the soil of earth into the realms of eternal day.

II. SELF-VALUATION

The concentration of all his powers on a stupendous and congenial task not only released undiscovered energies of his mind; the joyous realization of these precious endowments immensely enhanced Dante's sense of personal worth. As he wrote the "Comedy" there glowed in him the conviction, which at times must have become ecstatic, that he was an elect man, fortunate above all others except the highest few, and certain of permanent fame among poets and prophets. Something of this sense of being a privileged vessel of the Most High had comforted him from the beginning, but it is only in this last activity that it appears as an habitual state of mind.

Doubtless from youth he drew lofty hopes from the

fact that he was born when the sun was in the constellation of the Twins, and cherished the conviction that these stars, presided over by the cherubim who draw wisdom from the very lips of God, had rained their virtue into his nature. Such was his confidence in his genius that before he was thirty he was planning a work of remarkable originality to give him enduring fame.

In the "Convivio" he contends that God, who is love, sends his rays into the minds of men in proportion as their purity permits them to receive it, transforming them into his own likeness. Some lofty lovers of wisdom there have been whose condition was scarce other than angels;[1] they were almost incarnate God so exalted had they become through the possession of heavenly wisdom. Dante does not claim to be one of these almost transhumanized persons, but modestly assumes that while they sit at the feast of wisdom he gathers up the crumbs that fall from their table.[2] In another paragraph he states that the apex of life of these sons of Highest Wisdom is the thirty-fifth year of their age, though to ordinary men the culmination is somewhere between the thirtieth and fortieth year,[3] but nowhere in these earlier writings does he assert himself to be one of these incomparable ones to whom is given in this world union with God.

In the "Comedy" there is a marked change in self-valuation. In the first line he places the apex of his own life at thirty-five; in the first cantos he quiets all natural doubts and undertakes to do what only Æneas

[1] *Convivio*, III, 7.   [2] *Ibid.*, I, 1.   [3] *Ibid.*, IV, 23.

and Paul had done before. Unabashed he walks into the company of the world poets;[1] "Follow thy star," says Latini, "thou canst not miss the glorious port";[2] he is confident that he has left behind the two Guidos.[3] His name "as yet makes no great sound," but he is certain that his judgment is to confer an immortality of shame or honor upon those he mentions in his poem. To Cacciaguida, gazing into the mind of God to behold the fortunes of his descendant, there comes a vision "as sweet harmony comes to the ear from an organ."[4] All whom he meets on his mystical journey acclaim him one singularly favored of the Most High.

In girding himself to write the "sublime canticle" he experienced such spiritual exaltation as to assert that Wisdom in her own person breathed upon him, and all the muses were giving him their aid. And in the final pages he claims to have enjoyed a mystical union with God which is "granted only to perfectly endowed souls."

The conviction of having a special mission from the Almighty to men, which is often suggested in his earlier writings, in the "Comedy" becomes a dominant motive. He was making no curious journey into the Eternal World to gather interesting poetic material for a masterpiece. Down through a world of endless bitterness, up over the mountain from whose fair summit the eyes of his lady lifted him, and afterwards through the heavens from star to star he traveled that he might throw the fierce light of truth upon this

---

[1] *Inferno*, IV.
[2] *Ibid.*, XV, 55, 56.
[3] *Purgatorio*, XI, 97 ff.
[4] *Paradiso*, XVII, 43.

earth. The Hebrew prophets were his models and in their succession he stood. Beatrice, Saint Peter, Cacciaguida, repeatedly charge him to make the whole vision manifest. In the very heaven of heavens he does not pause to enjoy the rapt emotion of the mystic, but searches eagerly for authority to condemn the corruptions of the papal court; and his final prayer as he joins his look unto the Infinite Goodness is that he may not fail of his lofty mission: —

"O Supreme Light, that so high upliftest Thyself from mortal conceptions, re-lend a little to my mind of what Thou didst appear, and make my tongue so powerful that it may be able to leave one single spark of Thy Glory for the future people; for, by returning somewhat to my memory and by sounding a little in these verses, more of Thy victory shall be conceived." [1]

Thus power and a sense of eminent worth come to a mind that finds a task great and beloved.

III. MORAL EFFECTS

From youth and for the greater part of his life a steady and compelling motive of the poet was ambition for that just fame which attaches to work of superior excellence performed in the service of righteousness. Like many who are temperamentally shy, he thirsted for distinction, especially among his towns-people. The fond aspiration which did not desert him through all his wanderings was that he might be crowned with the laurel in Florence. His purpose in writing the "De Monarchia" was "to keep watch for the good of the

[1] *Paradiso*, xxxiii, 67-75.

INFLUENCE UPON DANTE

world, and be the first to win the palm of so great a prize for my own glory."[1] The keenest pang of his grievous poverty was the thought that thus not only would his person be cheapened in the eyes of those who had heard of his growing fame, "but every work of mine, already accomplished, or yet to do."[2] His consolation amid the calumnies of his enemies was that he had "a future far beyond their perfidies."[3] Not until he was far up in the celestial circles did the ever-brightening glory of truth free his mind from every other desire,[4] and his passion for fame become absorbed in his greater passion for truth.

But the "Comedy" wrought a still deeper and more important effect upon him. His imagination could not walk in that steep and arduous way of life without his heart and will following. His son Pietro says that the sin of luxury to which his father had hitherto been addicted he now abandoned. He could not lightly sin when traversing those zones of darkness and fire. Naturally he would become more austere both in morals and temper, and his quick wrath would flame all the more intensely against unrighteousness. His sense of God's presence even in seeming evil increased. Fortune, which in the "Convivio" is the capricious dispenser of good things "in which no distributive justice shines forth," in the "Inferno" is described as the agent of God's will.[5] In the "Paradiso" he is continually asserting that "God suffices for everything." "Ah, souls deceived, and creatures impious, who from

[1] *De Monarchia*, I, 1. [2] *Convivio*, I, 3. [3] *Paradiso*, XVII, 97.
[4] *Ibid.*, XVIII, 14. [5] *Convivio*, IV, 11; *Inferno*, VII.

such good turn away your hearts," [1] was his constant reflection. As he journeyed upward the supernal light illumined his mind and its peace rested upon his heart. Bitterness and rebellion depart from him. He realizes that God has been to him "greatly courteous." [2] The harsh experiences of his life now seem to his enlightened mind as a "sweet harmony." In the contemplation of the splendors of divine truth earthly things appear trivial. In the heaven of the Fixed Stars he looks back on earth and he sees this planet "such that I smiled at its mean semblance, and that counsel I approve as best which holds it of least account, and he who thinks of other things may be called truly righteous." [3] He could not well hold in thought the Beatific Vision without experiencing its transforming power. Lifting his eyes so constantly to the "great consistory" he was possessed with the love which inspired the glorious choirs.[4]

To the weary exile there was granted, even in this world, a home for his soul, into the tempestuous spirit there came the peace of God, and the fierce hater experienced the love that passeth knowledge.

[1] *Paradiso,* ix, 10.
[2] *Ibid.*, xv, 48.
[3] *Ibid.*, xxii, 135 ff.
[4] Sonnet to Quirino.

CHAPTER III

THE SECRET OF DANTE

TENNYSON and Fitzgerald were standing one day before a shop-window in Regent Street, looking at the busts of Goethe and Dante. "What is there wanting in Goethe which the other has?" inquired Fitzgerald. "The divine intensity!" answered Tennyson. But that divine intensity is not in the Bargello portrait! What stress of experience put it into the death mask? What wrestlings of soul transformed the gentle, aspiring lyrist of the "Vita Nuova," whose ethereal song has no slightest suggestion of bitterness, into the terrible hater of iniquity whose imagination conceived the world's most awful inferno? Or rather what was the secret of faith and character which enabled the poet to preserve through poverty, calumny, shame, and wrong the beauty and fine delicacy of his spirit?

Two processes went on in Dante's life. One sequence of experiences hardened his nature into massive strength; the other kept alive love and pity and radiant hope. His peculiar discipline gave him the sternest of faces and lighted it with the glory of the divine. The sea of troubles which formed the shell also secreted the pearl. Other Florentines passed through the same fiery trials, the same weariness, yet attained no equal vision of truth or grandeur of character.

To learn how a richly endowed spirit so met the misfortunes of life as to turn tragedy into most glorious comedy is a study of genuine human interest. To discover, if possible, his secret we shall sketch those qualities of mind and will which reacting on his experiences moulded the face whose majestic intensity artists still love to delineate.

I. INTELLECTUAL MYSTICISM

James Russell Lowell states that Dante's nature was "one in which a clear, practical understanding was continuously streamed over by the northern lights of mysticism, through which the familiar stars shine with a softened and more splendid lustre." Quite the reverse is true. The mystical sense was the very core of Dante's nature. Far from being the auroral glow merely suffusing the objects of his thoughts, it was the sacred fire burning on the central altar of his being. By its light he read the meaning of life, and its flame enkindled the other lamps of heart and will when the storms of life extinguished their fires.

He was a great poet because first of all he was a great seer. The conspicuous trait of his mind was its intuitive quality. As a reasoner he was faulty in premise and infinitely labored and uninteresting in his argument. One is tempted to say of him what Goethe said of Byron: "Lord Byron is only great as a poet, as soon as he reflects he is a child." Being sensitive and highly imaginative Dante's mind quickly pierced the heart of an object, or an experience.

One having an intuitive mind which moves easily and powerfully toward the spiritual is inevitably a mystic.

THE SECRET OF DANTE 255

Dante's mysticism was not of the hysterical sort which has brought the name into disrepute; his was what I should call an intellectual mysticism by which the mind sees all things in the eternal and finds their worth, their glory, and their unity in the Unseen. If in God we live and move and have our being, then we touch him on all sides of our nature; the intellect knows him as Truth, the æsthetic sense as Beauty, the heart as Love, and the will as Energy. Dante's preoccupation was with the Truth in which all things are rooted and grounded, and the beauty of Truth enraptured him. The good he sought was the good of the intellect. But Truth to him was not a dry proposition; it shone glorious as the sun! If I might coin a term and refine my definition I should call Dante an æsthetic-intellectual mystic. The spell which held him was the "splendor of the True." He caught Plato's vision of a spiritual order and unity, yet his insight was made incomparably glorious by "a light such as never was on sea or land."

This mystical sense awoke early in his life. The beauty of a maiden enkindled a love which urged his thoughts upward to the Divine Love. To quote the fine words of Sophocles in "Antigone," he perceived that "Love, who keepeth his vigil on the soft cheeks of a maiden, sits enthroned in power beside the Eternal Love." How eagerly Dante studied the books of the great mystics, Mr. Gardner has conclusively shown.[1] Prolonged study made the veil separating the eternal from the temporal seem very thin, and when

[1] *Dante and the Mystics.*

he penned the "Paradiso" the light of his mystical passion cast a lustre on every page. Everywhere on the walls of the temple of the world he beheld the handwriting of God. Light and unity and infinite good formed the background of all things. One having such a vision of God in his world could not be a vindictive misanthrope, for his faith will be too real to give calamity a permanent victory over him.

Walter Pater claims that "all the great Florentines were preoccupied with death. *Outre-tombe! Outre-tombe!* is the burden of their thoughts from Dante to Savonarola." The seriousness of this thought of death to Dante cannot be questioned. The night after the courtesy of Beatrice's salutation there came to him a vision of his beloved rigid in death, and when the most gentle one was called to glory the world was changed and desolate to the poet. But Dante was not preoccupied with death to the extent that he used it for poetic material, or allowed it to clothe him with brooding melancholy. His mind was too fundamentally healthy to dwell long in that shadow. Rather did his contemplation of the frailty of life stimulate in him a sense of the Eternal. He was preoccupied not with death, but with the sacramental nature of the world. Every experience of which he has left record during his early years quickens his sense of the spiritual. This intuition of the Eternal Reality which manifests itself in all forms and explains all experiences I find to be the core of Dante's nature, the key to his character and to his spiritual victories. From this powerful mystical sense issued the dominant idea of his mind, that the temporal is the symbol of the everlasting. And when we have found the dominant idea of a man's mind we have gone far in our understanding of him.

II. IMAGINATION

If Dante's mystical sense fashioned his character and enabled him to take toward life a victorious attitude, his *alta fantasia* made him a supreme poet. The imagination takes the raw material given by perception and intuition and shapes it according to the laws of reason into forms of beauty, glorious ideals, sculptured truth. From these vivid images, from reality thus actualized, issue the inventions, the affirmations of faith, the art and literature of the world.

In creative imagination Dante is unexcelled. Spontaneously his emotions, thoughts, and ideals were visualized in crystalline clearness. His very first sonnet is a description of a vision. Love appeared to him, not as a charming sentiment or tender mood, but visibly as a shining god, holding a flaming heart and a sleeping lady. Again Love appears "like a pilgrim, lightly clad and in mean raiment." At another time, a youth in white graments, thoughtful in aspect and weeping piteously, he sat by the poet's bed. Finally Dante beheld a vision so wonderful that it sealed his lips and won the consecration of his life.

Yet the poet did not fail to hold in check the extraordinary vigor of his envisaging mind at the limits prescribed by reverence and good taste. We can understand why he shrinks from portraying Beatrice in the "Comedy," but it was a delicate artistic instinct which curbed his youthful enthusiasm in his early sonnets and made him content with suggestions of her spiritual beauty. Dante never drew steady lines to configure what was loftiest in his thought. When dealing with comprehensible objects he is amazingly graphic, but, as he approaches those spiritual realities which speech is inadequate to describe, he becomes the vaguest of impressionists. This union of faithful delineation with shadowy suggestiveness is eminently characteristic of Dante's genius, and is seen in his first pages as well as in his last.

Such a visualizing, creative imagination is a master and not a servant, shaping character and coloring all experience. It constructs ideals and is the source of the divinest rapture and of imperishable art. It also creates images out of darkness and magnifies by a hundred-fold the pathos of the common ills of life. Possessing this fateful gift in rare measure, Dante touched the depths of suffering and the heights of joy. It profoundly influenced his character, being the source of that divine pity and exquisite tenderness revealed in all his works. Fancy does not necessitate compassion, but genuine imagination enables one to put himself in another's place. A penetrating and dramatic imagination such as his could not fail to engender in him a fine delicacy of sympathy.

The lucidity and concreteness of his vision determined his written style, making it restrained and exact. Empty declamation and exaggeration became impossible. One who sees clearly will make his speech conform with precision to the picture in his mind. He has but to make the whole vision manifest to write with power.

III. EXTREME SENSITIVENESS

An imagination like Dante's could subsist only in a nature uniquely sensitive. He was so finely strung that he reacted vigorously to every stimulus. One hundred per cent of him went into his hate as well as into his love. The ardor of his nature turned every truth into a passion and every admiration into a longing. Where anything touched him he burned and he burned hot. In his earliest volume he produces his effects not by dramatic incidents or sentences of wise insight. There is scarcely a quotable line in any of his lyrics. The power of his verse lies almost entirely in the sustained and elevated intensity of his passion.

"Our difference of wit," says Emerson, "appears to be only a difference of impressionability, or power to appreciate faint, fainter, or infinitely faintest voices and visions." His feminine impressibility the poet clearly recognized. "I, who by my nature," he declares, "am transmutable in every wise."[1] Influences both tenuous and coarse he felt keenly. Although extraordinarily impressionable, his nature was not plastic. Fine as was his mental texture it did not readily allow its imprints to be effaced. This consistency of mind and will revealed itself in a memory at once accurate and tenacious, and in an individuality of no uncertain outlines. This excessive impressionability reflected itself in his experiences. To him would come

[1] *Paradiso*, v, 98.

ecstasy in joy and extreme bitterness in sorrow. Such a heart was made for suffering, not happiness. In self-defense Dante must wrap himself about with the haughtiness and disdain which have become a tradition. As he must bleed, he will bleed inwardly. His proud reserve was the shield he threw out to protect a heart that quivered too readily.

IV. THE SUPREME NEED OF HIS NATURE TO LOVE

Nothing so clearly reveals to us the essential purity and elevation of the nature of this delicately fibred man as a knowledge of the objects to which he most easily and vigorously responded. Contrary to the common impression that he was a violently vindictive man stands the evident fact that Dante was habitually ruled by his admirations and not by his resentments. He would flame forth in a bitter sentence, but he only followed the glorious and lofty. He is immortal because he was supremely a lover. Love was the first influence that kindled his genius, love was the guiding star during his whole dolorous pilgrimage, love was the centre of his philosophy. The strongest necessity of his nature was to love. Even in that period of his life when his wrongs were most keenly felt, when poverty and exile were most distressing, before he had become absorbed in the "Divine Comedy," he could write in "De Monarchia": "But love, which nature implants in us, allows not scorn to last for long, but, like the summer sun that when it has dispersed the morning clouds shines with full brightness, this love prefers to put scorn aside, and to pour forth the light which shall set

THE SECRET OF DANTE

men right."[1] To pour forth the light, rather than to hurl smoking bolts of wrath, was Dante's characteristic passion.

But it must ever be borne in mind that this lover was a lover of truth, rather than of persons. The splendor of ideals smote his soul, not the lovable qualities of individuals. No Abou Ben Adhem was he, with strong kindly feeling holding to his heart all sorts and conditions of men. There is nothing to indicate that his personal affections were peculiarly intense or lasting. He was indeed the lover of Beatrice. "Despite the distance and the dark," her glorified presence blessed him from the "realms of help." Yet she never would have attained or reasserted her sovereignty over him, unless through her he had seen the glory of truth. Her smile was the beauty of truth, the wonder of her eyes was truth's persuasion. One ascends to God as he beholds "the beauty of truth enkindled along the stairways of the eternal palace." In Heaven he needs the gentle rebuke:

> "Turn thee about and listen;
> Not in mine eyes alone is Paradise."[2]

In that heaven given to the contemplation of truth Beatrice dared not smile lest the effulgence of her glory should destroy his powers of sight; and his imagination could conceive no greater beatitude than to gaze eternally into the essence of truth with unveiled eyes.

One's philosophy interprets his prevailing habits of mind and his intensest experiences. Only an ardent

[1] *De Monarchia*, II, 1.   [2] *Paradiso*, XVIII, 20, 21.

and convinced lover of goodness, truth, and beauty could have held Dante's philosophy that the Divine Love penetrates everywhere through the Universe, and kindles in every soul an instinctive reaching-out after goodness.

Because he was such an ardent lover of the good Dante hated evil vehemently. A witty Frenchman, speaking of a critic famous for his venomous writings, announced that "he died as the result of having accidentally tasted of the tip of his own pen." It is the prevalent notion that Dante was in constant danger of the same retributive death. But it must be remembered that the exquisite sensibilities of the poet would be grievously wounded by incidents which would merely scratch a coarser nature. There is surprisingly little personal spite in the writing of this man so bitterly wronged. The two incidents which have done the most to attach to him the odium of implacable personal resentment are his fierceness with Filippo Argenti,[1] and his apparently malignant treatment of Bocca.[2] One should remember, however, that the journey is a symbolical one. The poet never did those atrocious deeds. Perchance he wishes to show how one is influenced by his environment, for it is in the circle of wrath that he is unable to control his anger, and he acts treacherously among the traitors. In the "Convivio" he states the philosophy of anger which he expresses so dramatically in the circles of hell. "But inasmuch as everything is lovable in itself, and nought is to be hated save for the evil superinduced

[1] *Inferno*, VIII, 32 ff.   [2] *Ibid.*, XXXII, 73 ff.

THE SECRET OF DANTE

upon it, it is reasonable and right to hate not things, but their badness, and to strive to sever it from them. ... I, following her [Philosophy] in deed as in emotion, to the best of my power, abominated and dispraised the errors of men, to the infamy or blame not of the erring ones, but of the errors."[1]

When Prior of Florence he was the leader of the moderate party and exercised his authority impartially for the public good and not to satisfy personal malice. But when he took his pen to portray the wrongness of evil he was governed by his conviction that he should hate evil even as God hates it. "Do not I hate them, O Lord, that hate thee? and am not I grieved with those that rise up against thee? Yea, I hate them with a perfect hatred."[2] Dante's wrath, it is to be remembered, was not purposeless rage. John Stuart Mill once remarked to John Morley that the fatal drawback to Victor Hugo's claim to the world's immense recognition was that he brought forward no practical proposal for the improvement of that society against which he was incessantly thundering. Morley replied: "You have no business to ask a poet to draft bills." Carlyle also indulged in "impassioned caricature against all the human and superhuman elements in our blindly misguided universe. But of direction or any sign-post or way out, not a trace was to be discovered."[3]

Dante also railed and thundered, but he pointed out the way, charted it, and set up guide-posts at every

[1] *Convivio*, IV, 1.   [2] Psalms 139: 21, 22.
[3] John Morley: *Recollections*, vol. I, p. 56.

corner. His wrath was constructive and all the hotter because he saw the way so plainly.

Also his speech was influenced by his artistic ideals. His sulphurous wrath is not the unregulated outburst of bad temper, but studied and fashioned for effect. In his letters he is evidently following closely the rhetoric of the Hebrew prophets. How deliberate and measured it is in the "Paradiso"! In every circle of the heavens, even in the Empyrean, there is a stern denunciation corresponding to the nature of the truths taught in that circle.

V. LOVE OF ORDER

We realize the moral earnestness of Dante's indignation only when we recall how radically evil cut athwart the grain of his mind. Order, which is heaven's first law, was the first law of his nature. His genius was mathematical. He thought with the care and precision of an engineer. In the most chaotic period of history he wrote a poem of matchless symmetry. The whirlwind of his passion never breaks this perfect form. In the "Inferno" he classifies every sin: in the "Purgatorio" every step of ordered ascent had its known and definite purpose: in the "Paradiso" his positions are matters of mathematical calculation. From the first sonnet of the "Vita Nuova" to the final canto of the "Paradiso" all thoughts and emotions are restrained within the appointed bounds. Order was more than a convenient habit of thought and speech, it was the burning passion of his soul. There must be orderly and just government on earth because, as he reminds us in the first canto of the "Paradiso," it is unity which makes the universe most resemble God, who is one. Order is the footprint of the Eternal Goodness; disorder obliterates the divine. The turmoils of Florence were not merely unhappy divisions, they were sins against the Holy Ghost. Civil government being ordained of God, a corrupt city fails of its divine mission as truly as a corrupt church and deserves to be anathematized. He could call the inhabitants on the valley of the Arno "foul hogs," "curs," and "wolves," because to his mind they were tearing the seamless robe. The very intensity of his intuition of the One amid the Many, the strength of his faith in the presence everywhere of God's definite and harmonious purposes, the essential nature of his mind, made his indignation hot and steady. A Spanish poet wrote wisely when he declared that every poet must speak "por la boca de su herida," through the mouth of his wound. The anguish of a thwarted ideal, the righteous anger of seeing God's truth debased, far more than his personal sorrows drove the iron into his soul. The discords of Italy outraged the structural instincts of his being, therefore he spoke as an earnest man would speak in an age to which temperateness was not a virtue.

VI. THE ENERGY OF HIS WILL

Dante's strength of will equaled the clearness of his vision. He was as firm-souled as he was sensitive. To use the terms of his own psychology, the penetration of his mind enkindled powerful emotions, and the ardor of his feelings produced exceptional volitional energy.

Many men in those stormy times were driven into sad and vexatious exile. Some were broken under the woes of their lot; others with practical good sense submitted to the inevitable without fretful murmurs or spiritual struggle; others, in the fires of their discipline, grew in the kindly spiritual graces. But Dante had burning in his soul those fierce elemental fires that transmuted misfortunes into rugged moral strength. He met evil not serenely or patiently, but triumphantly. He did not rise above it, he subdued it, and fed upon it, and was nourished by it. His character became as conspicuous for its massive strength as for its exquisite sensibility. The dreamy student who wrote the "Vita Nuova" became the stern and uncompromising prophet of the "Divina Commedia" because the rigor of his nature equaled the vividness of his imagination. Therefore, instead of the indecision of a Coleridge, we find in him majestic sweetness, pitying strength, tremulous sensitivity fibred like steel. He preserved the charm of Saint Francis while attaining the masculine energy of Hildebrand.

This energy of will was associated with an inordinate egoism. According to a popular legend, he had calmly said, when pressed to go on an important mission: "If I go who stays, and if I stay who goes?" With unabashed assurance he numbers himself with Homer and Virgil and the renowned poets of the classic world, for, as he once wrote in the "Convivio": "The great-minded man ever magnifies himself in his heart,

THE SECRET OF DANTE

and in like manner the pusillanimous holds himself less than he is."[1]

VII. HIS FAITH

With all his qualities of mind and heart and will Dante never could have fought his battles victoriously unless he had been sustained by a most noble faith. What a man firmly believes about the nature of the universe is an all-important consideration. He is strong with the strength, and is moulded by the limitations, of his religious philosophy. On a previous page it has been shown how the theological and scientific systems of his day were precisely fitted to Dante's mind. Comprehensible, definite, ordered, and analyzed, they could be conceived as a whole by an imaginative brain. They also answered satisfactorily most of the questions an eager student in those days would ask. Truth so authoritative, clearly defined, and understandable is powerful to awaken passionate loyalty. To us these medieval systems of thought are uninteresting, but the data of scholastic science, vitalized and visualized by the processes of Dante's mind, had to him a sovereign and commanding splendor capable of sustaining both intellect and heart at their best.

a. *His Conception of God*

Of his youthful experiences he could write: "The life of my heart, that of my inward self, was wont to be a sweet thought which went many times to the feet of God, that is to say, in thought I contemplated the

[1] *Convivio*, I, 11.

Kingdom of the Blessed."[1] In hell he expressed confidence that the Divine Grace would carry him through all difficulties, and he most certainly uttered his permanent conviction in the noble words —

> "There is a light above, which visible
> Makes the Creator unto every creature,
> Who only in beholding Him has peace."[2]

In the heaven of the Fixed Stars he affirms of his Christian faith: "I have it so shining and round that in its stamp nothing is doubtful to me." By nature a mystic, his sense of God was constant and powerful. But what conception of the Deity fascinated his mind and made his life victorious?

To Dante, God was the Supreme Intelligence, creating all, ruling and penetrating all. Being a poet rather than a philosopher, vague generalizations regarding the nature of the Deity were insufficient; he must visualize Him whom he would worship, yet this necessity brings with it all the perils of anthropomorphism. Note how the poet's reason and imagination worked together. Dante was almost a Persian in his love of light. He delighted in it as Homer delighted in the sea, all its manifestations arrested his attention. No nobler symbol could he conceive of the Omnipresent One than that of Living Light. By a strong metaphor that satisfied at once his imagination and reason he affirmed that the Primal Source is "light intellectual full of love, love of true good full of joy, joy that transcends every sweetness."[3] What poet or theologian ever fashioned his thought of the Highest in nobler symbol

[1] *Convivio*, II, 8. [2] *Paradiso*, xxx, 100 ff. [3] *Ibid.*, xxx, 40.

or in words more melodious; giving both a vision of substance satisfying to the most elevated imagination, and an assertion of attributes meeting the needs of the loftiest faith! And the genius of the poet is in nothing more conspicuous than in his ability to permit this Supernal Light to shine through all the pages of his Sublime Canticle. A conception of God as the Eternal Light, light of the mind, light of the heart, light of the conscience, light reflected in nature's glory, held in the thoughts and earnestly contemplated through many years and experiences, would inevitably ennoble and irradiate the believer. For Dante conceived the Primal Light as penetrating as well as transcending the wheel of nature. Pouring forth from the Eternal Fountain, through the burning minds of the nine hierarchies of angels, it floods the universe with energy and splendor. "The glory of Him who moves everything penetrates through the universe, and is resplendent in one part more and in another less."[1] Permeated by the Divine Presence, the universe is fashioned into the form of his thought. His law and purpose are minutely traced from the highest to the lowest. In this divine orderliness "high creatures see the footprints of the Eternal Goodness."

b. *His Conception of Man*

The divine light shines in every man. As fire mounts toward the sun so the divine flame in the human soul by a concrete and perpetual thirst moves toward God. By nature man desires what seems to him good.

[1] *Paradiso*, I, 1 ff.

"And just as a pilgrim who travels by a road on which he never went before thinks that every house which he sees from afar is an inn, and on finding that it is not, fixes his trust on some other, and so from house to house until he comes to the inn, so our soul as soon as ever she enters on the new and hitherto untrodden path of life bends her gaze on the highest good as the goal, and therefore believes that everything she sees which appears to contain some good in itself is that highest good, and because her knowledge is at first imperfect through inexperience and lack of instruction, small goods appear great to her, and therefore her desire is first directed to these."[1] If man wanders into evil it is because he has been deceived by false images of good. In this universe, informed, penetrated and resplendent with the Eternal Goodness, man lives and lives in freedom. Not for a moment does Dante permit in his thought the glory of God to wither with its splendor the free energy of man's will. "The greatest gift which God in his bounty bestowed in creating, and the most conformed to his own goodness, and that which he prizes most, was the freedom of the will."[2] This lifts man out of the order of nature and makes him master of his fate. By virtue of this sovereign endowment he can conquer all the evils and misfortunes of life, changing direst tragedy into comedy. "And free will," he declares, "which, if it endure fatigue in the first battles with the heavens, afterwards, if it be well nurtured, conquers every-

---

[1] *Convivio*, IV, XII; Jackson's translation.
[2] *Paradiso*, v, 19.

thing." Having this awful gift of freedom, man is a responsible being, and Dante holds him strictly to his accountability.

c. *His Conception of Immortality*

His faith in the immortal nature of the soul was as firm as a rock. It could hardly be otherwise with one who saw all life *sub specie æternitatis*. In Florence there were many who called themselves Epicureans and were thoroughgoing materialists, and against them and their doctrine Dante was especially virulent. He gives us his conception of the horror of their condition in the tenth canto of the "Inferno" in which he describes those who maintain this heresy as living in tombs, for he who holds to no life after this is indeed living in his tomb. In the "Convivio" he speaks of the certainty of his faith with great emphasis, and gives his reasons therefor. "But inasmuch as the immortality of the soul has been here touched upon, I will make a digression, discoursing thereof. . . . And by way of preface I say that of all the stupidities that is the most foolish, the basest, and the most pernicious, which believes that after this life there is no other; for if we turn over all the scriptures both of the philosophers and of the other sage writers, all agree in this that within us there is a certain part that endures. And this we see is the earnest contention of Aristotle, in that 'Of the Soul,' this the earnest contention of all the Stoics, this the earnest contention of Tully, especially in that booklet 'Of Old Age'; this we see is the contention of every poet who has spoken according to the faith of the Gentiles; this the contention of every religion, Jews, Saracens, and Tartars, and all others who live according to any law. So that if all of them were deceived there would follow an impossibility which it would be horrible even to handle." [1] He then proceeds to give three principal reasons for his faith. Human nature is the most perfect of all other natures here below. As animals are mortal and cherish no hope of a life hereafter, if man's hope is vain "the flaw in us would be greater than in any other animal," therefore the most perfect animal would be the most imperfect.

Our divination in dreams is then cited. But the strongest reason to his mind is Christ, who hath showed us the way to blessedness, its truth and its light. If our reason sees this doctrine in obscurity it is because in us the mortal mingles with the immortal. He closes the discussion with this strong personal affirmation: "And so I believe, so aver, and so am certain of the passage after this life to another better life where this lady liveth in glory of whom my soul was enamoured."

When we consider the supernal splendor of that conception of a divine universe which Dante held and constantly pondered through many years, and the strength of his conviction that all the events of time are included in the sovereign justice and love of God, and his equally firm conviction in the free and transforming energy of the will, we can see why this sorely tried man could not suffer the deep springs of his nature to be poisoned by disaster. His faith fed his

[1] *Convivio*, II, 9; Temple Classics.

imagination, his intellect and his heart. He did not possess a faith, it possessed him. It rained into his soul vitality and glory.

Such faith, nourishing abundantly the mental and spiritual qualities we have described, put the divine intensity into Dante's face which Tennyson noticed, even as it put the divine and permanent into his poem.

VIII. SUMMARY

For greater clearness of thought it will be well to restate the qualities of nature and inner persuasion which, reacting on the conditions of his life, made Dante the uniquely interesting man he became. The dominant faculty of his mind was his imagination. It was the shaping and glorifying imagination of a great poet, but it was more. It was the spiritual intuition of a seer. This gave him a sense of the Eternal Goodness, and a refuge from all the storms of life. Such a penetrating and visualizing imagination is fruitful in ready pity and tenderest sympathy. By nature he was a lover, but a lover of truth rather than of persons; an idealist more concerned with thought than with individuals. Of tremulous sensibilities his devotion to the loftiest interests aroused in him fiery wrath against the evil in persons or institutions which opposed the Good he so rapturously espoused. His analytical, geometrical mind fitted precisely into the noble catholic system which had for its centre the infinite love of God, and for its circumference a closely articulated scheme of truths and morals. The prevailing creed seemed to chafe him only at one point — God's seeming injustice in condemning to everlasting banishment those who had never heard of Christ.

A nature vivid, masterful, dowered with a spiritual intuition which so easily saw in love the clearest, noblest symbol of the character of the Highest, would inevitably meet personal wrong and intellectual perplexity victoriously. The face of one thus gifted and wounded would be of rugged grandeur, glowing with divine passion. Such endowments and experiences made Francis of Assisi a saint. But in Dante a certain toughness of fibre made him grow stern under the blows of misfortune. His clear and powerful perceptions produced no stigmata, they evoked instead an extraordinary energy of reaction. The anvil was sufficiently massive for the ringing hammer. Through all his embattled life he kept alive the exquisite gentleness of his heart and the glory of his dreams, but he developed a defensive armor. Seer of unity and order, lover of truth, he grappled with his foes and achieved the conquering strength of a spiritual warrior. Had he lived in our day and inherited our weaker sense of human responsibility, our vaster conceptions of the universe, and our juster views of the limitations of human knowledge, his studied indignation would have been less blighting and intolerant. But he could not have written the "Divine Comedy," and he would not have been Dante. Yet his high fantasy would not have failed of the beatific vision and by a different path he would have learned that his "desire and will the Love was turning that moves the Sun and other stars."

CHAPTER IV
DEFECTS OF CHARACTER

It is difficult to judge so positive a nature as Dante's impartially. To those who like him not, his faults magnify themselves out of all proportion, while to those who feel the spell of his power, the splendor of the great qualities of his mind and heart veils his petty defects. The writer confesses that an excuse is associated in his mind with every foible of the poet and that he criticizes only by a conscious effort of the will.

Dante had the faults of his temperament and did not escape the limitations of his time. These blemishes and limitations reveal themselves in his work. "This Dante," says his contemporary Villani, "from his knowledge was somewhat presumptuous, harsh and disdainful; like an ungracious philosopher, he scarcely deigned to converse with laymen." His attitude was proud, censorious and scornful. Without normal, hearty affection, he lacked the genial wholesomeness of a lover of the green earth and of his fellow men. Lover of the finer qualities of womanhood though he was, his habitual reference to womankind was contemptuous. He regarded their intelligence as inferior.[1] So worthless were the women of Florence that he finds a kind word only for Nella, the "little widow" of Forese. Evidence is produced to prove that at one period

[1] *De Vulgari Eloquentia*, I, 1, 6, 7; *Convivio*, IV, XIX, 76 ff. Epistle, x, 10, 224, 225.

of his life he formed guilty liaisons, but some of this testimony is capable of other interpretation, and there are plausible explanations for the rise of the tradition.

The insidious and destructive vice of self-pity was his in a large measure.[1] He was extreme in his medieval intolerance of heresy. As the "shining and dear jewel" of the heaven of Venus he places Folco the troubadour, who as Bishop of Toulouse was a most treacherous and blood-thirsty leader in the extermination of the heretical Albigenses, a "nightingale turned hawk, a shepherd allying himself with the wolves, he made his early sins look white by the blackness of his later virtues, and made religion odious by faithfully serving the church."[2] Yet Dante, knowing this man's excessive cruelty against the heretics, placed him in heaven, doubtless by reason of this very zeal for the faith. A man of broader sympathies would not so have honored a monster of fanaticism.

Fiercely intolerant of individual liberty in religious thinking, Dante was also reactionary in politics. He misread the political movement of his time and championed a theory of empire that was outgrown even in his day. Lowell has spoken of Dante as having the only "open eyes" of his century. But they were open as the eyes of a prisoner looking through slits in a stone wall are open. Much he could not see, for he was a man of theories and formulas; a sophisticated man loaded with an immense apparatus of philosophy and hypotheses. Such never observe broadly or with right perspec-

---

[1] See J. S. Carroll: *Prisoners of Hope*, p. 446.
[2] J. S. Carroll: *In Patria*, p. 152.

DEFECTS OF CHARACTER

tive. Only the free and disinterested mind can see truly. But Dante's mind was from the beginning, even more than that of many of his contemporaries, encased in a system of thought which he never threw off and which lamentably narrowed his vision.

Proud as Lucifer, sensitive in the extreme, volcanic in passional energy, this poet of the justice of God was at times guilty of an untempered speech which seems to spring from personal vindictiveness. Florence, which at times seemed most pleasant and glorious to his memory, at other times he assailed with an energy of wrath as magnificent as it was undiscriminating. Not without joy he found her famous in hell.[1] Of the seventy-nine souls he recognized among the damned, thirty-two were Florentines and forty-three were Tuscans.

Fierce intensity is his characteristic quality and one secret of his fascination. Few readers wish to temper many of the fiery sentences, but the writer confesses that the poet's treatment of Guido Cavalcanti seems ungenerous. Guido was his "first friend," the recognition of the older poet had meant much to the younger, and Dante had expressed his appreciation by the dedication of his first book to him. Then some break occurred, as evidenced by Guido's sonnet reproving Dante for having fallen so low. Even though Dante acted, as he doubtless did, under the highest motives, when as prior he sent his friend into exile from the effects of which he died, this tragic ending should have restrained the poet from any injury to Guido's reputa-

[1] *Inferno*, XXVI, 3.

tion. Yet in a famous passage in the "Purgatorio" he assumes a superiority of genius, and credits himself with greater wisdom, while in hell Guido's father appears ridiculous beside the majestic Farinata.[1] As these verses were written some ten or fifteen years after Guido's death, Dante might have at least omitted to vaunt himself against his friend.

We must remember in extenuation that Dante was endeavoring to write in a spirit of noble and detached veracity. Aristotle's great words were ringing in his ears. He quotes them often. "It will perhaps seem best, and indeed the right course, at least when truth is at stake, to go so far as to sacrifice what is near and dear to us, especially as we are philosophers. For friends and truth are both dear to us, but it is a sacred duty to prefer the truth."[2] He is describing life as he saw it, and puts Cavalcante, as well as Francesca and Latini, in those conditions in which in life they had touched his experience. To be an artist of truth he deliberately stripped himself of personal preferences.

No one will deny that Dante constantly used speech of unwarranted severity and of brutal violence. He could not have been a great lover without being a fierce hater. Wrath is "the second, hotter flame of love." But many of the denunciations which are quoted against him he places in the mouths of spirits whom he met on his journey, and no author is to be

---

[1] *Purgatorio*, XI, 97–99; *Inferno*, X, 60.

[2] *Ethics*, I, 4. Dante refers to this passage in *Convivio*, IV, VIII, Epistle, VIII, 5, and in *De Monarchia*, III, 1.

GUIDO CAVALCANTI

DEFECTS OF CHARACTER

held responsible for the sentiments and language of all his characters. He lived in an age when the end of the world was thought to be imminent, when the freedom of the will was more stressed than now, when toleration was not a virtue and moral courage was rare. Dante was unjust in his attempts at justice, but who would cool a single hot word of his, or take the sting from a single sentence? Far from being a self-centred man, making his likes and dislikes the standards of judgment, he judged men by what were to him absolute standards of right. What weighed upon him were the wrong courses of the world.

But the popular indictment against Dante is that he crowded Hell with so many characters of highest virtue. It seems monstrous to consign Aristotle, Socrates, and Plato even to the mild gloom of Limbo, and the narrow-minded schoolmen to the heaven of the Sun whose glory they outshine.

But there is something to be said in defense of the poet. It must be remembered that he is not always announcing the eternal destiny of the individual. Many of his characters have only symbolic value. Cato was not honored in Purgatory because his merits were greater than those of Aristotle whom Dante so ardently admired, but as a classic symbol of liberty. The "Inferno" is a vision of sin, and the artist is often painting states of the mind. Intense as was his admiration for the poets and philosophers, to have culture and virtue without faith and a full revelation of divine truth was to Dante a sad condition; it was living without hope in constant desire. To his mind those schoolmen actually did live in the Sun of light and hope to which the ancient sages were strangers. He would have said that God, and not he, ordained the supreme minds of Greece and Rome to live in the twilight. Moreover, his material limited him. Who would declare that in Dante's judgment many of the warriors in Mars and the rulers in Jupiter were nearer the throne of God, enjoying a finer ecstasy, than Saint Thomas in the lower heaven of the Sun? Even Dante's genius could not bring Mars closer to the earth than is the Sun!

The damnation of virtuous heathen greatly troubled him and was seldom absent from his mind. In "De Monarchia" he refers to it, and in the "Divine Comedy" repeatedly recurs to the subject. But he was confronted by the clear statements of Scripture and the Church. If it is urged that so great a man should have broken away from the standards of his day, it may be answered that he did most boldly put aside many of its ethical standards, but such a mind as his could find no way of escape from the premises upon which the men of his age reasoned. The training of a thousand years inclined them to unquestioning obedience to the voice of authority. Having accepted an infallible Bible, and an infallible Church, a mind like Dante's was helpless. Yet he did all he could to mitigate the awful dogma. Manfred, who had died excommunicate, and as far as can be known, unrepentant, he placed in Purgatory on an assumed contrition at the moment of death. As Virgil leaves the Earthly Paradise the last words he hears are his own verses sung by the angels, and for him Beatrice utters a prayer.[1]

Dante's final conclusion was that God's justice was too profound for man to fathom and that the judge of all the earth would do right. Had he been a different man and a more independent thinker he might have broken through the limitations of his time, but then he could not have uttered the spirit of the Middle Ages. "The collective thought, the faith, the desire of a nation or a race," says Lowell, "is something organic, and is wiser and stronger than any single person, and will make a great statesman or a great poet out of any man who can entirely surrender himself to it." It was the completeness of surrender to the limitations and grandeur of a mighty epoch which gives Dante his unique significance.

Whatever his blemishes, they were not small or mean in their nature. Neither were they shameful. We do not take a garment and walk backwards lest we look upon his nakedness. Dante is magnificent even in his faults.

[1] Statius and Rhipeus are additional examples. St. Thomas offered him a way of escape in the statement: "If any one who is born in barbaric nations does what lieth in him, God will reveal to him what is necessary to salvation, either by internal inspiration or by a teacher." Dante did not avail himself of this teaching, because, probably, to his mind there was no evidence that to the virtuous heathen there had been granted either a teacher or an internal revelation.

CHAPTER V
THE ARTIST

A BIOGRAPHY does not call for an exhaustive analysis of Dante's artistic genius and method, but the author cannot deny himself a few reflections, which he hopes will not prove unedifying to the reader, on this much discussed subject.

Apparently our poet wrote with ease. When, as in the "Vita Nuova," the purpose came to him to say certain things in verse he does not hint at experiencing any difficulty in saying them. Indeed, he quite explicitly declares that in writing the "Paradiso" his thoughts pressed for utterance. In his first eclogue to Del Virgilio, referring to this canticle then in preparation, he says: "I have, said I, one sheep, thou knowest, well loved; so full of milk she scarce can bear her udders; even now under a mighty rock she chews the late cropped grass; associate with no flock, familiar with no pen; of her own will she ever comes, ne'er must be driven to the milking pail. Her do I think to milk with ready hands." [1] The mood might not be obedient to the will, but, when it served, the words were not born in travail. His sacred poem, indeed, kept him lean for many years, but his labor was over his material, not his expression.

[1] Wicksteed and Gardner: *Dante and Del Virgilio*, p. 157.

I. LOVE OF TECHNIQUE

His genius was quickened in a manner which merits a moment's pause. Artists of the first rank are usually eager for technique. Their genius flows deepest under narrowing restrictions.

> "Yes, when the ways oppose;
> When the hard means rebel,
> Fairer the word outgrows;
> More potent far the spell." [1]

Perfect liberty comes through close obedience to rigid law. Bondage, which is the despair of the pretender to poetry, never fails to inspire the true sons of the Muse.

But Dante invented difficulties to arouse and nourish his genius. The *terza rima* is so arduous a metre that he only has used it successfully. Yet he further limited strictly the number of his cantos, compelled each canticle to symbolize the thirty-three years of the life of Christ, stated definitely the hour of day even amid the glories of Paradise, wove the trivium and the quadrivium into the structure of the "Comedy," refined his verse to the exigencies of the moral and theological systems of the Catholic Church, the philosophy of Aristotle, and the Ptolemaic system of astronomy. It is true that much of this material was so unpoetical that even Dante could at times only smear the honey of the Muse over undoubted prose. As though these difficulties were not enough, he elaborated a system of correspondences, and analogies, mi-

[1] Austin Dobson.

nute, comprehensive, significant, reappearing in every section and forming the structure of the poem.

II. SOURCES OF HIS LITERARY STYLE

From two distinct sources came the strength and witchery of his style. In the school of the troubadours, especially in the spiritual chivalry following Guido Guinicelli, he learned those delicate, courteous, enchanted words which gave incomparable charm to his love songs.

When, after the death of Beatrice, he turned earnestly to the study of Latin, he found in the "stateliest measure ever moulded by the lips of man," the strength of imperial Rome. "By long study and great love" he vaunted that he had achieved a fair Virgilian style which did him honor. Yet the sustained elevation of his speech was due not alone to his mastery of classical Latin, but also to the rare nobility of his own nature. "When there is depravity," says Emerson, "there is a slaughter-house style of thinking."

III. PREDILECTIONS

In the mind of every forcible writer there are certain predilections which determine the current of his thoughts and select and shape his imagery. These predilections result from sensitive spots in the author's nature, or from early and powerful impressions stamped upon the mind. Mental images conceived in some vivid moment of joy or sorrow haunt the chambers of the brain, ghosts of some forgotten experience, which create the metaphors and fashion the vision of the writer. Early experiences, moments of intense feeling, permanently color one's imagination and mark out the channels of future thought. In some luminous and perhaps forgotten hour Homer felt the beauty of the sea and the mystery of the moving air, and ever afterwards their magic recurred in his songs. Virgil was peculiarly affected by the beauty of the trees. The loveliness of flowers touched repeatedly and vigorously the highly strung chords of Keats' nature; their fragrance and charm pervade his poetry, refine and mould his imagery, and at all times most effectively comfort him. Poe found nothing so arresting as the death of a beautiful woman. Writing of Da Vinci, Walter Pater declares, "Two ideas were especially fixed in him as reflexes of things which had touched his brain in childhood beyond the measure of other impressions — the smiling of women and the motion of great waters." A knowledge of these shades of former experiences, which, like invisible helpers of Vulcan, work constantly in the hidden chambers of imagery, forging ideas into shape and beating out the brilliant sparks of fancy, admits us indeed into an author's workshop, where we feel like spies noting forbidden secrets.

Leonardo's prepossession gave us the Mona Lisa. The smile of some girl or woman awoke those ideas and emotions which made the smile to the painter the gateway of mystery and finally led him to paint it as no artist has ever painted it. Not the smile, but the grace of woman, touched Dante's brain in boyhood beyond all other impressions. The trivial incident by which feminine loveliness opened to him the gates of life and of his own salvation he found indelibly written under his memory's first rubric. I have called the quality in women to which Dante was peculiarly susceptible grace rather than beauty, because, as the reader can easily verify, he nowhere in those early pages describes the physical presentment of Beatrice. When he first met her she was most becomingly adorned. To his boyish eyes, she was of "such noble and praiseworthy deportment" that she seemed to him "not the daughter of mortal man, but of God." At the memorable salutation, that which flashed fire into his soul was her "ineffable courtesy." The charm of all the fair ladies who haunt the pages of the "Vita Nuova" is their gentleness and courtesy. This inward grace shining through form and manner led him to think of God as "the Lord of Grace." It is true that in the "Paradiso" it is the eyes and the smile of his beloved that enraptured him, but this is in conformity to the symbolism of wisdom which he had early adopted.

The other object which smote his fancy beyond the measure of all other influences was the light. Light and spiritual grace of woman were the two pervading and ascendant prepossessions of his mind. On the very first page of the "Vita Nuova" he brings them together, and together they glow in celestial splendor in the final pages of the "Divine Comedy." In the first line of his first book he sets the little girl whose grace had awakened his youthful enthusiasm in her proper relation to the heaven of light, and in the second sentence he measures the span of her life against the starry heaven. What experience enkindled his passionate interest in light is unrecorded. Perhaps one night, gazing from his window into the deep sky overarching Florence, the awful beauty and the mystic glory of the stars burned their splendor ineffaceably into his quivering soul, or in some moment of suffering the stars from their serene heights rained down their peace into his fevered heart. Whatever the initial occasion, the wonder of the stars and the loveliness of the light were controlling influences. Eagerly he observed light in all its manifestations, and when he thought of God it could not be under some abstraction such as Reason, or Will, but as Light. The stars comforted his exile and a star shines as the last word of every canticle of the "Comedy." To appreciate keenly what grace and light meant to Dante gives one the clue to his ever-recurrent images and to the sources which quicken his imagination.

IV. MYSTICISM OF BEAUTY

In the chapter on the "Secret of Dante" it was stated that the poet was preëminently a mystic; it is proper here to point out that his mysticism was that of a great artist. If we define mysticism as "an immediate consciousness of personal relations with the Divine," we become aware that, unlike Wordsworth, his mystical sense was not touched to life by the pleasant and sublime aspects of Nature. Nature was indeed the palette from which he took his many colors, but her ordered glories did not stimulate his sense of God or awaken "that serene and blessed mood of harmony, and the deep power of joy" to see into the life of things.

He was too good a Catholic and too convinced a Roman not to find God revealed in history, but it was a deduction of his intellect; he did not see God in the confused life of the men of his day. Rather like Newman he looked into this busy, living world, and saw no reflection of the Creator. It appeared to him "nothing else than the prophet's scroll, full of lamentation, and mourning, and woe." And like Newman he felt the need of an infallible interposition to rescue and guide humanity.

Neither was his the mysticism of a loving and fervent heart. Unlike Saint Francis or Saint Bernard, he had no sweet and precious sense of the presence of Christ during that terrible journey of his. God to him was the Emperor of heaven, and Christ the God-man who had made the supreme atonement, but Dante did not talk with God as friend to friend, or commune with Christ as a dear companion.

His was the mysticism of Shelley maturing into that of Plato. In his "Hymn to Intellectual Beauty," Shelley describes how the awful shadow of the Unseen Power fell upon him, awakening him to ecstasy. For the Italian it was the spiritual beauty of a woman that led his thoughts to the Highest, then after the death of Beatrice the beauty of Truth enamored him. For a time he was but the troubadour singing the glories of Philosophy, then, with the deepening of his life, the aspiration grew within him to compass all truth and see into the heart of things, but it was the ever-brightening beauty of truth that led him upward.

Dante found the way to the Most High not through

THE ARTIST

nature, or through humanity, but through beauty meditated upon and interpreted. The "Divine Comedy" is a greater Hymn to Intellectual Beauty; it is a celebration of the glory of the "Light Intellectual." Dante's mysticism is the poet's passion for beauty ripened into insight of its spiritual meaning. His mystical rapture is not a swoon of delight, it is the vision of Truth.

V. OBSERVATION AND IMAGINATION

Important scientific treatises, profound books on theology, epoch-making histories soon become out of date, but great poetry is always contemporaneous, for the true poets express the truth of things, in forms of beauty, to the melody of words. It is the indissoluble union of truth with beauty that gives to poetry the gift of immortal life. Dante's taste for words and the incomparable melody of his sentences is evident, as is also the unbroken sequence of vivid pictures which his pages leave upon the mind. The truth finds expression in him through a keenness of observation which seized the characteristic detail, and an epic imagination which wove all details into the majesty and strength of a consistent whole.

Flaubert disclosed to his disciple Maupassant the secret of original and accurate description: "Look at a flock of sheep, or a heap of stones in the road. Single out one sheep or one stone. Find out in what respect your sheep or stone differs from all other sheep or stones. And now find one word which expounds that difference, and there you have the secret of style." We know not how Dante trained himself in close observation of nature and man, but he excelled in power of discerning the differentiating characteristic, and then of stating it in the one word or action which would make it live in the memory of the reader. He observed nature and enjoyed it, but light was the only natural phenomenon that long held him.

Observant lover of nature, he looked with even keener eye upon man. He searched for the distinguishing trait, the secret spring of action, the dominant passion; this he stated in a word or revealed in a gesture, or sketched in a line. His supreme principle in composition was to draw out the hidden soul of the object, finding his poetry in the truth of things, and not in the purple and gold of words, rich in poetic association, with which an exuberant fancy might clothe it. His art was to seize and disclose with severe accuracy of words the essential characteristic of an individual. He liberated the latent poetry in a dramatic event; he set no stage lights, nor did he glorify his theme by mists of sentiment. He enforced truth not by exaggeration but by intensity of expression. He spoke in Italics. Shakespeare's "fustian roar" would have been impossible. Imagine him writing such bombastic words as these:

> "Who take the ruffian billows by the top,
>   Curling their monstrous heads, and hanging them
> With deafening clamour in the slippery clouds!"

Yet his was the imagination of an artist and not of a subtle psychologist. If like Browning he had found at the apothecary's a little yellow book, he would not

THE ARTIST

have studied the revealed tragedy from every point of view. With a few strokes he would have limned Pompilia's inmost soul, and drawn her husband's moral deformity in a vivid line, but he would not have followed the gradual transition of decay from stage to stage. He noted effects rather than processes; he visualized emotions instead of analyzing and explaining them.

This ability to fix his eye steadily upon an object, to uncover its innermost quality and to describe what he saw in simple and melodious words might have made Dante a great realist; he was an uncompromising idealist because at the heart of things he found the Eternal. In all his writings we discern

> "the touch that speeds
> Right to the natural heart of things;
> Struck rootage down to where Life feeds
> At the Eternal Springs."

Subtle though his mind was, he was not turned aside or delayed by the finer shadings of right and wrong, but went straight to the core and pronounced judgment on the relation of the thing to the eternal law. Instinctively he sensed the point where the human and the divine met, and upon that relationship he passed stern judgment.

Sir Leslie Stephen affirms that "Tennyson could express what had occurred to everybody in language which could be approached by nobody." Dante has revealed a world whose hellish gloom, fire, and unutterable glory were peculiarly his own. The sea he sailed has ne'er been sailed by any keels except those that follow his wake. The truths which were unfamiliar to nobody became strangely new and powerful to everybody.

If the veracity of reality was in his verses through the freshness and precision of his apprehension of individual objects, majesty was there also through the comprehensive sweep of his imagination. He could carve with the patient skill of the lapidary, but his was also the architectonic energy of the cathedral-builder. When he wrought a minute part he had in mind the design of the whole. The wisdom of an age surpasses the wisdom of any one individual in it. What many generations of men have thought and experienced is greater than the philosophy of even its loftiest genius. One whose mind is capacious enough to surrender itself to the life of an epoch will utter a wisdom beyond his own comprehension and speak in a tone more powerful than he knows. Through Dante the mighty dead of many generations spoke, even as the sovereigns in the heaven of Jupiter uttered one voice through the imperial eagle. His mind grasped the epoch in which he lived as a whole, caught its innermost spirit, comprehended its circumference, and preserved its marvelous beauty. It is in his transcendent ability to make his art equal the vast range of his matter that Dante is so incomparably great. The innumerable details which he wrought so carefully were all rounded into a symmetrical whole. The astonishing quality of the art of the "Comedy" is its marvelous symmetry. His great poem has often aptly been compared to a cathedral, with its confessionals, its crowded sculptures, its mystic lights, its drifting incense, its Rose window "with splendor upon splendor multiplied." A cathedral is certainly greater than the sum of all its parts. It has a majesty, a spirit of adoration, a power to uplift the soul which does not dwell in any single feature. So with the "Divine Comedy." Its intricate, far-reaching, astounding symmetrical unity gives to it a beauty and grandeur of moral power that could not otherwise be expressed. The poetic imagination has achieved no nobler and more delicately structured monument.

VI. ART FOR ART'S SAKE

The phrase so often upon the lips of artists — "art for art's sake" — would have been abhorrent to Dante. He believed that art was a high mode of expressing moral beauty which was too chaste and holy to suffer prostitution. He wrote of love as no other because he carried it upward to its finer issues in spiritual grace; and beauty he moulded with an imperishable touch because of his passionate love of truth. Love, beauty, truth, goodness burned as one light within him. Beauty divorced from truth or righteousness would have been detached from its proper relationship. Unless he has this conviction the ages will accept no man as a supreme artist.

CHAPTER VI
CONCLUSION

THE "Divine Comedy" is one of the supreme poems of the world because Dante was one of the world's greatest men. Such a harvest of thought and experience could not grow on common soil. He ranks with the few central men of history as much by the preeminence of his soul as by the loftiness of his genius. "For Dante," says Carducci, "was above all things a very great poet — a great poet because he was a great man and a great man because he had a great and heroic conscience." But a conscience so heroic can be found only in a nature of massive strength, inflexible, devoted to the noblest ideals and capable of clearest vision. Among

> "The dead, but sceptred sovereigns, who still rule
> Our spirits from their urns," —

none is so unique and none so representative. He stands in splendid isolation in any group of famous men, never mistaken for another. Clear-cut, angular, wrapped in gloom, or transported in divine rapture, he is the only one of his kind.

The preceding pages have been written in vain, if they have not revealed him to be a man of toughest and finest fibre, hating evil as few have hated it, and yet loving as few have loved, governed habitually by no mean motives but passionately attached to the best in literature, the best in life, and the best in the

Universe; eager for poetic excellence and renown, yet more concerned for the good of the world than for his personal fortunes; caring more for his mind than for his body, and more for a balanced ecstasy of spirit than for the riches of the mind; clear and conservative in thought, yet boldly following an audacious imagination in its venture upon uncharted seas; fearless of criticism yet sensitive to fame; loving men, but loving righteousness and truth more; misjudging his times, while seeing with marvelous vision the Eternal Verities; cumbered with useless and false knowledge, yet through it finding the true wisdom; losing the way to pleasure and contentment, and discovering the way to power and God; failing to influence his own city, he has quickened the generations with a fantasy.

As a man and an artist he was singularly great, but not as a thinker. He was big enough intellectually to comprehend the spirit and thought of the Middle Ages, but not independent and original enough to break through its constraining limits. He went to the boundary of the dogmatic system of his day and looked over its narrow rim, but saw nothing save a void beyond. To the permanent thought of the world he added no original insight, and he did little to extend the bounds of human knowledge. But as an artist he was bold and original; his genius swept the whole circle of accepted religious truth from centre to circumference; he seized the heart of the spiritual knowledge of his day and presented it in enduring form and fadeless colors. He discerned that salvation is an ethical process, and in a period of superstition and formalism, he was not betrayed into exalting formal obedience above spiritual regeneration.

He was a bold pioneer in the study of language and had faith enough in his insight to trust his masterpiece and his fame to a despised vernacular which his genius was all-powerful in elevating into the speech of a great people. Departing from all models, he reared a structure of song so unique and glorious that, while he had forerunners, he had no progenitors; admirers and lovers he has had, but no imitators.

To voice completely one of the most significant epochs in history and to usher in another, and in the achievement to shape a character as extraordinary for rugged strength as for exquisite delicacy, is glory enough for one poor mortal.

All the sharp instruments by which greatness is developed and disciplined worked upon him. Poverty kept him close to life's stern realities, exile compelled him to seek a home for his spirit, disappointment was his nourishing bread, and anguish the strong wine that gave him power. Yet his must have been a joy beyond that of most men. If the reading of the "Divine Comedy" gives delight, what must have been the satisfactions of conceiving and writing it! To journey with the mighty dead, to mete out justice according to his thought, to be in the heavens with Beatrice, to experience before his time the blessedness of the redeemed, to look into the face of God! And through it all was the growing conviction that he was an elect man, sure of a place among the world poets.

Moreover, his life was complete beyond that of

most mortals. Keats with the same passion for fame died at twenty-six lamenting that his name was writ in water. Michael Angelo, the servant of the whims of lesser men, left here a statue, there a dome, or a matchless painting. To Dante was given the privilege of gathering his achievements into one miracle of song. The "Divine Comedy" has often been compared to a vast cathedral, but to what master-builder has it been granted to plan and build a cathedral according to his own conception, to carve all its statues, to decorate its ceilings with imperishable color and form, to design the many-hued windows, to erect the high altar and choose the ministering priests, and then to flood the whole with solemn music? What man ever quite so completely found his task and expressed himself in it? Then after his work was done, and before the wonder of the beatific vision had faded from his eyes, or his body was weakened by the infirmities of age, to pass "to that Rome where Christ is Roman!"

His was also a marvelously victorious life. We frequently speak of the problem of life as though it were an enigma to be solved by close reasoning. But it is not. Man is a swimmer in a deep and troubled sea. The practical problem of each one is to meet the next wave triumphantly, and we can do this only as we are sustained by the inner conviction that the onrushing wave can be surmounted, that we are not beating out into a gulf that will finally wash us down, and that there is a good purpose in the buffeting tides and in the Power which cast us into the sea. We must have a glorious faith and a practical courage.

The Florentine poet kept his heart strong by means of a reasoned faith in the greatness and goodness of God. He endured because a Trinal Light looks down upon our tempest here below. "No sublimer spectacle do I know on earth," says Martineau, "than the faculties of a grand and passionate nature . . . falling into stillness before the face of God, and by the awful light of his countenance turned from stormy nobleness into a loving and working power. It is a spectacle which emerges rarely from the battle of the will, spontaneously and often from the repose of faith."

But such high faith may tempt one to ineffectual contemplation. Dante by its inspiration set himself to a great task to which he dedicated all his abilities. Not in imagination only but in fact he followed the dictates of right reason. He obeyed his highest insight; he followed his loftiest ambition, he was governed by his purest love. Love led him to truth, and truth to duty, and duty to immortality. By "yielding his heart to the Purifier, and his will to the Will of the Universe," and then walking steadfastly in the way of love and service he changed the tragedy of his life into a Divine Comedy.

THE END

INDEX

INDEX

Adamo, great-great-great-grandfather of Dante, 62.
Alessandro da Romena, 141.
Alfraganus, 117; 188.
Alighieri, Antonia, 121,122.
Alighieri, Beatrice, 121,122, 203.
Alighieri, Dante, meaning of the name, 63; ancestry, 63; his mother's dream, 65; omens at his birth, 66; his house, 67; early home life, 68; meets Beatrice, 69; self-restraint, 70; studies, 70 ff.; Latini, 71; the Salutation, 72; first sonnet, 73; school of poets in Florence, 76; Dante's use of the circle, 78; deeper sentiment, 79; death of Beatrice, 82; first anniversary, 85; artistic ability, 85; Lady of the Window, 86, 118; his vision, 87; truth of his self-revelation in the Vita Nuova, 90; slow development, 93; cause, 95; character and ability, 96-98; outward life, 98-100; period of discipline, 109; contrast with Milton, 110-113; not a philosopher, 116; eager student, 117; alleged licentiousness, 119; joins Guild of Apothecaries, 124; political activities, 126, 136; debts, 126; the year 1300, 129; elected prior, 133; attends jubilee, 135; Embassy to Rome, 138; decree of exile, 139; wanderings, 141; Henry VII, 143; letters, 144; "Convivio," 148; "De Vulgari Eloquentia," 153; "De Monarchia," 156; politically wrong, 162; mind and character, 163 ff.; critical year, 171 ff.; letters to Cardinals, 189; second decree of exile, 192; at Verona, 195-202; anecdotes, 199; appearance,201; Ravenna, 202 ff.; correspondence with Del Virgilio, 204; with Quirino, 210; letter to Can Grande, 211; "Credo," 212; "Questio," 213; goes to Venice, 215; death, 216; lost cantos, 220; sepulchre, 222; sarcophagus opened, 224; effect of the Catholic system upon, 246; literary style, 247, 258; sense of worth, 247; sense of mission, 249; thirst for fame, 250; growing purity, 251; secret of Dante, 253-274; his wrath, 262-265, 278; defects, 275-282; artist, 293; conclusion, 294.
Alighieri, Francesco, half-brother of Dante, 64, 126.
Alighieri, Jacopo, Dante's son, 121, 122, 127, 220 ff.
Alighieri, Leonardo, great-grandson of Dante, 67, 122.
Alighieri, Pietro, Dante's son, 121, 127, 203, 220.
Alighieri, Tana, half-sister of Dante, 64.
Angelo, Michael, offered to prepare a sepulchre for Dante, 225; contrasted with Dante, 297.
Angiolieri, Cecco, 75.
Aquinas, St. Thomas, ability, 4; Dante's knowledge of, 188; on damnation of heathen, 281.
Arezzo, 141, 142.
Aristotle, quoted by Dante, 157; his master, 188; on truth, 278.
Arnold, Matthew, on Beatrice, 107.

INDEX

Athanasius, quoted, 165.
Augustine, quoted, 240.
Avellana, Fonte, Dante's refuge, 182, 191.

Beatrice, Dante's daughter, *see* Alighieri.
Beatrice, *see* Portinari.
Bella, Giano della, 41, 123.
Benevento, battle of, 24.
Benvenuto, quoted, 119, 121.
Bernard of Clairvaux, quoted, 8, 66.
Biagi e Passerini, 128 n.
Bible, 117.
Blacks and Whites, origin of conflict, 131; Whites send embassy to Rome, 138; exiled, 139; symbolized by the leopard, 175.
Boccaccio, Vita di Dante quoted, 65, 70, 119; description of Beatrice, 101; sources of information of Beatrice, 102; Dante's marriage, 121; Dante's influence, 127, 138; account of finding seven cantos of "Inferno," 178; Dante's power of attention, 185; invitation to Ravenna, 202; taught rhetoric, 204; reverence for Can Grande, 211; Dante's death, 218; the lost cantos, 220.
Boëthius, influence on Dante, 114, 115, 117, 187.
Bologna, students, 5; Dante in, 143; offered laurel crown at, 204.
Boniface VIII, career, 25; on the Florentines, 53; interest in Florence, 132, 134; Jubilee, 135; debate with Florence, 137; relations with Dante, 138.
Boston, among famous cities, 56.
Browning, Robert, quoted, 5, 85 n.; contrasted with Dante, 94, 95, 290.
Bruni, Lionardo, quoted, 66, 70, 85, 98, 122, 127, 141, 142.

Byron, Lord, contrasted with Dante, 94; Goethe's remark, 254.

Cacciaguida, great-great-grandfather of Dante, 61.
Campagni, Dino, quoted, 138, 139.
Canatro, Bernardus de, epitaph on Dante, 222.
Can Grande, *see* Scala.
Carducci, on Dante, 294.
Carlyle, Thomas, on French Revolution, 242; not a guide, 263.
Carroll, J. S., quoted, 276.
Cavalcanti, Guido, his house, 67; his character and genius, 74; friendship with Dante, 76; reproves Dante, 120; exile and death, 134; Dante's ungenerous treatment of, 277.
Charles of Anjou, 24.
Charles the Great, head of the church, 11; his political theory, 11, 12.
Charles of Valois, 137–139; the lion, 175.
Church, union with state, 11; result for Germany and Italy, 12–16; victory over state, 25.
Cicero, studied by Dante, 114; influence on Dante, 116.
Cino da Pistoia, friend of Dante, 75, 84; style, 153.
Cipolla, quoted, 195.
Cities, of Germany and Italy, 16; effect on talent, 17; rise of free cities, 16–22; famous cities of the world, 55–57.
Clement V, 144, 147, 189.
Coleridge, S. T., contrasted with Dante, 94.
"Commedia," meaning of, 229; a self-conscious effort, 230; a political document, 230–233; religious significance, 233; permanent element, 237; effect on the mind, 238; Dante's growing

INDEX 303

power while writing, 244 ff.; like a cathedral, 292, 297.
Constantine the Great, head of the church, 11.
"Convivio" described, 148 ff.; its revelation of Dante, 165.
Corsi, D. M., Cardinal, restores Dante's tomb, 223.
"Credo," account of, 212.

Damnation of heathen, 246, 279.
Dante Alighieri, see Alighieri, Dante.
Dante da Maiano, 76.
Dante Society, Cambridge, Mass., report 1891 quoted, 127, 128, 134, 137, 142, 143 (1892), 192 (1892).
Del Lungo, quoted, 101 n., 104, 106, 140, 141.
De Quincey, Thomas, quoted, 238.
"Divina Commedia," see Commedia.
Dobson, Austin, quoted, 283.
Donati, Corso, 130, 134, 139.
Donati, Forese, 119.
Donati, Gemma, Dante's wife, 86, 121.

Edward I, on representation, 48.
Emerson, on genius, vii; on difference of wit, 259; "Slaughterhouse thinking," 284.
Empire, Holy Roman, see Holy Roman Empire.
England, 15, 16.

Fagginola, Uguccione della, Dante with, 192, 195.
Farinata degli Uberti, 35, 36.
Fiamazzo, A., 128.
Fitzgerald, on Dante's bust, 253.
Flaubert, on accurate description, 289.
Fletcher, J. B., as permanent element in Comedy, 240.

Florence, history of, 27-57; early days, 27-28; conflict between feudal and industrial classes, 29; primo popolo, 32; the Guelf Party, 37; its Guilds, 38; Ordinances of Justice, 41, 123; instability, 43; poets in, 74; in 1300, 129; Dante's desire to be crowned in, 207.
Forli, Dante in, 143.
Francesca da Rimini, episode retouched, 209.
Fraticelli, P., quoted, 124, 128, 179 n.
Frederick Barbarossa, 15, 19.
Frederick II, 4, 15, 24.
Frescobaldi, Dino, 75.

Gardner, E. G., quoted, 55; translator with Wicksteed of Dante and Del Virgilio, 208, 209, 282; Dante's mysticism, 255.
Gentucca, 191.
Germany, its place in the Holy Roman Empire, 12; effect of union with Italy, 15-16; powerful cities, 16; a belated state, 16.
Ghibelline and Guelf, origin of names, 22; political ideals, 23; introduced in Florence, 31; victory of Guelfs, 36; relation to Blacks and Whites, 132.
Gianni, Lapo, 75.
Giardino, Piero, account of the lost cantos, 221.
Gibbon, quoted, 115.
Gladstone, Morley on, 240.
Godenzo, 141.
Goethe, quoted, 17; contrasted with Dante, 94, 253; on Byron, 254.
Gonzaga, L. V., Cardinal, erects present mausoleum, 223.
Gorgonza, 141.
Grandgent, C. H., author's indebtedness to, xii.
Guelf Party, 37, 48.

304 INDEX

Guilds of Florence, 38; difference in temper, 47.
Guinicelli, Guido, 74, 187.

Henry, Aurelia, translation of "De Monarchia," 157 n.; 167 n.
Henry VII of Luxemburg, his character, 143; in Italy, 145; death, 146; relation to "De Monarchia," 158, 159; the Veltro, 178 n.
Hildebrand, his ideal, 13, 14.
Holy Roman Empire, its theory, 12; its conflict with the Church, 11–16; result for Germany and Italy, 15.
Homer, 1, 71, 117, 187, 268; lover of the sea, 285.
Horace, 117, 187.

Ilario, Frate, his letter, 179.
Imagination, Dante's, 257 ff., 273.
"Inferno," meaning of opening allegory, 173 ff.; written amidst confusion, 184; new power displayed, 186; essential meaning, 234, 240, 242; Florentines damned in, 277.
Innocent III, 4, 14.
Investiture, right of, 14.
Italian Cardinals, letter to, 189.
Italy, union with Germany, 15–16; rich in famous cities, 16; effect of, 17–22.

Jackson, W. W., translation of "Convivio" quoted, 218, 270.
Jacopo, Dante's son, *see* Alighieri.
Johnson, Henry, his translation quoted, 115, 243.
Juvenal, 188.

Keats, John, contrasted with Dante, 93, 96, 297; love of flowers, 285.
Kuhns, Oscar, author's indebtedness to, xii.

Latham, C. S., translator of Dante's letters, 194 n.
Latini, Brunetto, 71, 187.
"Letters," Dante's letter to Italian cardinals, 189; Florentine Friend, 192.
Lombardi, Pietro, restores Dante's tomb, 223.
Lowell, J. R., Dante's mysticism, 254; collective thought of a race, 281.
Lucan, 117, 187.
Lucca, Dante in, 143, 191; Dante's fondness for camps, 183, 191.
Lucia, her identity, 66.
Lunigiana, Dante in, 143.

Machiavelli, on causes of Florentine instability, 44, 49; virtue of Florence, 54.
Malaspini, tribute to, 143; host of Dante, 178.
Martello, Carlo, visits Florence, 125.
Martineau, J., quoted, 298.
Mezzano, Minghino da, epitaph on Dante, 223.
Mill, J. S., on Victor Hugo, 263.
Milton, John, contrasted with Dante, 94, 110–113, 183.
"Monarchia De," described, 156 ff.; reveals Dante's character, 166.
Moncetti, editor of the "Questio," 213.
Montesquieu, on separation of judicial power, 51.
Moore, Edward, 101 n., 117 n., 120, 124, 158; on Dante's learning, 188; defends the "Questio," 214.
Morley, John, on Gladstone, 240; on Victor Hugo, 263; on Carlyle, 263.
Mussato, Albertino, opinion of Can Grande, 199.
Mysticism, Dante's, 254 ff., 287.

INDEX

305

Newman, J. H., likeness to Dante, 288.
Norton, C. E., quoted, 143-148; translations used, xii; his interest in Dante, 239.

Orlando, Guido, 75.
Orosius, Paulus, 188.
Ovid, 117, 187.
Oxford, students in, 5.

Papacy, conflict with Empire, 11-16; at Avignon, 147; the wolf, 175.
"Paradiso," date of, 206; Dante's mood while writing, 206; dedicated to Can Grande, 211; unrevised, 217; lost cantos, 220; its meaning, 236, 242; rare beauty, 238.
Paris, students, 5; Dante in, 143.
Parodi, quoted, 178 n.
Passerini, L., 128 n.
Pater, Walter, Florentine preoccupied with death, 256; on Da Vinci, 285.
Petrarch, 142, 199.
Pietra, odes to, 119.
Pietro, Dante's son, *see* Alighieri.
Plato, on lovers of wisdom, 181.
Poe, E. A., 285.
Poggi, Andrea, Dante's nephew, 64; known to Boccaccio, 178, 195.
Poggi, Leon, 64.
Polenta, Guido da, Dante's host, 203, 207, 216, 218.
Portinari, Beatrice, first meeting with Dante, 69; salutation, 72; denied recognition, 77; her mockery, 78; apotheosis, 80-83, 87; death, 82; her identity, 101-108; often a stage figure, 231; Dante does not portray her, 257, 265; symbol of divine truth, 261.
Portinari, Folco, his home, 67; his will, 102; events of life, 104.

Ptolemy, 117.
"Purgatorio," its meaning, 235, 242.

"Questio de Aqua et Terra," 213 ff.
Quirino, Giovanni, tribute to Dante, 209; Dante's reply, 210; letter to Can Grande, 211.

Ragg, "Dante and his Italy," quoted, 139.
Ravenna, description of, 203; influence on the Comedy, 208.
Rossetti, D. G., quoted, 73-84, 96, 120.
Ruskin, John, on Can Grande, 196.

Sacramental nature of the world, Dante's faith in, 256.
Saintsbury, G., 156.
Santi, Antonio, 224.
Savonarola, Michele, anecdote by, 200.
Scala, Can Grande della, his princely hospitality, 195; Dante's feeling for, 197, 211; Mussato's opinion of, 199; treatment of Dante, 199-201; Dante's letter to, 211.
Scartazzini, G. A., 128 n.
Selfe, R., translation of Villani acknowledged in footnotes.
Seneca, 188.
Shadwell, C. L., on the "Questio," 214.
Shakespeare, William, contrasted with Dante, 95, 97, 239; his "W. H.," 108; needed pressure, 183; indifferent to his works, 230; "fustian roar," 290.
Shelley, P. B., love for Amelia Viviani, 92; contrasted with Dante, 94, 96, 288.
Sismondi, quoted, 197.
Sixth Century, spiritual vitality, 4.

INDEX

Smith, J. R., his translation of Boccaccio acknowledged, 65 n.
Sophocles, quoted, 255.
Staley, E., "Guilds of Florence," quoted, 40, 54.

Tennyson, Lord, quoted, 7; contrasted with Dante, 94, 95, 127 n., 291; on the divine intensity, 253.
Thayer, W. R., quoted on influence of Dante, 239.
Thirteenth Century, creative power, 3; illustrious names, 4; its achievements, 5; its ideals, 6; sacramental conception of nature, 7; intolerant, 8; authority, 8; contrasted with the twentieth century, 9; brighter side, 10; passion for learning, 10; Church and State, 11–16.
Toynbee, Paget, quoted, 62, 63, 66 n., 101 n., 117, 122, 143, 179, 191, 197, 198, 201, 214.
Tyndall, John, on the Mystery, 241.

Uguccione della Fagginola, *see* Fagginola.

Venice, Dante's embassy to, 215.
Verona, Dante in, 142; congenial to Dante, 183; Ghibelline stronghold, 195; anecdote, 202; disputation at, 213.
Villani, Filippo, quoted, 216.
Villani, Giovanni, quoted, 31, 36, 100, 121, 125, 129, 131, 133, 275; resolves to write chronicle, 135, 151.
Villari, quoted, 50, 71.
Vinci, da, Walter Pater on, 285.
Virgil, 117, 187; verses sung by the angels, 281; lover of trees, 285.
Virgilio, Giovanni del, Dante's correspondence with, 204; writes inscription for Dante's tomb, 208.
"Vita Nuova," its narrative, 68–88; date, 88; credibility, 90.
"Vulgari Eloquentia De," described, 153 ff.; illegitimate form of verse, 180.

White, A. C., translation of the "Questio," 215 n.
Wicksteed, P. H., translation by, acknowledged in footnotes; on the "Questio," 214; Dante and del Virgilio, 208, 209, 282.
Witte, Karl, essays on Dante, 67 n.

The Riverside Press
CAMBRIDGE . MASSACHUSETTS
U . S . A

Reprint Publishing

For People Who Go For Originals.

This book is a facsimile reprint of the original edition. The term refers to the facsimile with an original in size and design exactly matching simulation as photographic or scanned reproduction.

Facsimile editions offer us the chance to join in the library of historical, cultural and scientific history of mankind, and to rediscover.

The books of the facsimile edition may have marks, notations and other marginalia and pages with errors contained in the original volume. These traces of the past refers to the historical journey that has covered the book.

ISBN 978-3-95940-132-6

Facsimile reprint of the original edition
Copyright © 2015 Reprint Publishing
All rights reserved.

www.reprintpublishing.com

www.ingramcontent.com/pod-product-compliance
Lightning Source LLC
Chambersburg PA
CBHW050551170426
43201CB00011B/1652